AF552462

READING GANDHI

READING GANDHI

Ravi Ranjan

ANMOL PUBLICATIONS PVT. LTD.
NEW DELHI-110 002 (INDIA)

ANMOL PUBLICATIONS PVT. LTD.

Regd. Office: 4360/4, Ansari Road, Daryaganj,
New Delhi-110002 (India)
Tel.: 23278000, 23261597, 23286875, 23255577
Fax: 91-11-23280289
Email: anmolpub@gmail.com
Visit us at: www.anmolpublications.com

Branch Office: No. 1015, Ist Main Road, BSK IIIrd Stage
IIIrd Phase, IIIrd Block, Bangalore-560 085 (India)
Tel.: 080-41723429 • Fax: 080-26723604
Email: anmolpublicationsbangalore@gmail.com

Reading Gandhi

First Edition, 2010

ISBN 978-81-261-4550-8

PRINTED IN INDIA

Printed at Mehra Offset Press, Delhi.

Contents

Preface

Reading Gandhi is intended to be a study in the interpretation of Gandhian philosophy. It examines the nature and relevance of political thought, approaches to interpretation, particularly textual and contextual approaches, followed by an indepth study of the significance of Hind Swaraj, Concept of Satyagraha, Sarvodaya, Swadeshi, Nonviolence, Status of Women, Gandhi's Philosophy, Trusteeship and Dandi March.

Mahatma Gandhi motivated the Indians and the world at large by an astounding amount of written and spoken words. The book left behind by Gandhiji for posterity is at once enlightening, enriching but mind-boggling. Gandhiji has asked us to understand the spirit of his writing and not merely find the meanings. For, every term Gandhiji uses, has different connotations in different contexts. Gandhian thought processes promote a heightened historical, political, spiritual and of course an academic interest through a simple and direct language.

This book seeks to provide a new insight to the readers for understanding Gandhian thought and its relevance in the contemporary world. Special care has been taken to cater to the need of the newly introduced paper Reading Gandhi.

—Editor

1

Introduction

In January 1948, before three pistol shots put an end to his life, Gandhi had been on the political stage for more than fifty years. He had inspired two generations of India, patriots, shaken an empire and sparked off a revolution which was to change the face of Africa and Asia. To millions of his own people, he was the Mahatma-the great soul-whose sacred glimpse was a reward in itself. By the end of 1947 he had lived down much of the suspicion, ridicule and opposition which he had to face, when he first raised the banner of revolt against racial exclusiveness and imperial domination. His ideas, once dismissed as quaint and utopian, had begun to strike answering chords in some of the finest minds in the world. "Generations to come, it may be", Einstein had said of Gandhi in July 1944, "will scarcely believe that such one as this ever in flesh and blood walked upon earth."

Though his life had been continual unfolding of an endless drama, Gandhi himself seemed the least dramatic of men. It would be difficult to imagine a man with fewer trappings of political eminence or with less of the popular image of a heroic figure. With his loin cloth, steel-rimmed glasses, rough sandals, a toothless smile and a voice which rarely rose above a whisper, he had a disarming humility. He used a stone instead of soap for his bath, wrote his letters on little bits of paper with little stumps of pencils which he could hardly hold between his fingers, shaved with a crude country razor and ate with a wooden spoon from a prisoner's bowl. He was, if one were to use the famous words of the Buddha, a man who had "by rousing himself, by earnestness, by restraint and control, made for himself an island which no flood could overwhelm."

Gandhi's, deepest strivings were spiritual, but he did not-as had been the custom in his country-retire to a cave in the Himalayas to seek his salvation. He carried his cave within him. He did not know, he said, any religion apart from human activity; the spiritual law did not work in a vacuum, but expressed itself through the ordinary activities of life. This aspiration to relate the spirit-not the forms-of religion to the problems of everyday life runs like a thread through Gandhi's career; his uneventful childhood, the slow unfolding and the near-failure of his youth, reluctant plunge into the politics of Natal, the long, unequal struggle in South Africa, and the vicissitudes of the Indian struggle for freedom, which under his leadership was to culminate in a triumph not untinged with tragedy.

Childhood

Mohandas Gandhi was born on October 2,1869, at Porbandar, on the western coast of India. His grandfather Uttamchand Gandhi and father Karamchand Gandhi occupied the high office of the diwan (Chief Minister) of Porbandar. To be Diwan of one of the princely states was on sinecure. Porbandar was one of some three hundred 'native' states in western India which were ruled by princes whom the accident of birth and the support of the British kept on the throne.

To steer one's course safely between wayward Indian princes, the overbearing British 'Political Agent' of the suzerain power and the long-suffering subjects required a high degree of patience, diplomatic skill and commonsense. Both Uttamchand and Karamchand were good administrators. But they were also upright and honourable men. Loyal to their masters, they did not flinch from offering unpalatable advice. They paid the price for the courage of their convictions. Uttamchand Gandhi had his hose besieged and shelled by the ruler's troops and had to flee the State; his son Karamchand also preferred to leave Porbandar, rather than compromise with his principles.

Karamchand Gandhi was, in the words of his son, "a lover of his clan, truthful, brave, generous." The strongest formative influence on young Mohandas, however, was that of his mother Putlibai. She was a capable woman who made herself felt in court circles through her friendship with the ladies of the palace, but her chief interest was in the home. When there was sickness in the family, she wore herself out in days and nights of nursing. She had little of the weaknesses, common to women of her age and class, for finery or jewellery. Her life was an endless chain of fasts and vows through which her frame seemed to be borne only by the strength of her faith.

The children clung to her as she divided her day between the home and the temple. Her fasts and vows puzzled and fascinated them. She was not versed in the scriptures; indeed except for a smattering of Gujarati, she was practically unlettered. But her abounding lover, her endless austcritics and her iron will, left a permanent impression upon Mohandas, her youngest son. The image of woman he imbibed from his mother was one of love and sacrifice.

Something of her maternal love he came to possess himself, and as he grew, it flowed out in an ever-increasing measure, bursting the bonds of family and community, until it embraced the whole of humanity. To his mother, he owed not only a passion for nursing which later made him wash leper's sores in his Ashram, but also an inspiration for his techniques of appealing to the heart through self-suffering-a technique which wives and mothers have practised from time immemorial.

Young Mohandas' school career was undistinguished. He did not shine in the classroom or in the playground. Quiet, shy and retiring, he was tongue-tied in company. He did not mind being rated as a mediocre student, but he was exceedingly jealous of his reputation. He was proud of the fact that he had never told a lie to his teachers or classmates; the slightest aspersion on his character drew his tears. Like most growing children he passed through a rebellious phase, but contrary to the impression fostered by his autobiography, Gandhi's adolescence was no stormier than that of many of his contemporaries. Adventures into the forbidden land of meat-eating and smoking and petty pilfering were, and are not uncommon among boys of his age. What was extraordinary was the way his adventures ended. In every case when he had gone astray, he posed for himself a problem for which he sought a solution by framing a proposition in moral algebra. 'Never again' was his promise to himself after each escapade. And he kept the promise.

Off to England

Mohan passed the matriculation examination of Bombay University in 1887. His father's death a year earlier had strained the means of the family. Being the only boy in the family who had persevered in his studies, its hopes rested on him and he was sent to Bhavnagar, the nearest town with a college. Unfortunately for Mohan the teaching was in English. He was unable to follow the lectures and despaired of making any progress. Meanwhile, Mavji Dave, a friend of the family, suggested that Mohan should go to English to qualify at the bar. Mohan jumped at the idea of going abroad. His elder brother had no doubt that the proposal was attractive but wondered how they could afford it. His mother was reluctant to let her youngest boy sail to an alien land to face unknown temptations and dangers. The Modh Bania caste to which the Gandhis belonged, threatened to excommunicate the whole family if its injunction against foreign travel was infringed. All these hurdles were, however, successfully overcome by Mohan's determination to go abroad, and in September 1888, at the age of 18, he sailed for England.

From the rural surroundings of Rajkot to the cosmopolitan atmosphere of a steamship was a tremendous change for Mohan. Adaptation to Western food, dress and etiquette was a painful process. Both on board the ship and in London in the first few weeks, Mohan could not help feeling that he was making a fool of himself. He had promised his mother before leaving India that he would not "touch wine, woman or meat". The vegetarian vow became a continual source of embarrassment to him. His friends feared that his food fads would ruin his health, and make of him, socially, a square peg. To disarm his critics and to prove that, vegetarianism apart, he was not impervious to the new environment, he decided to put on a thick veneer of 'English culture'. Having made up his mind to become an 'English Gentleman', he spared neither time nor money. Whatever the cost, the veneer had to be the best in the market. New suits were ordered from the most fashionable tailors in London; the watch was adorned with a double gold chain from India; under expert tuition, lessons began in elocution, dancing and music.

Gandhi could not, however, throw himself into this experiment with complete self-abandon. The habit of introspection had never deserted him. English dancing and music did nit come easy to him. He began to see that drapers and dance halls could turn him into an English gentleman, but only an English gentleman about town. After a brief three months' excursion, the introvert returned to his shell. There was a rebound from extreme extravagance to meticulous economy. He began to keep an account of every farthing he spent. He changed his rooms, cooked his own breakfast and, to save bus fares, walked eight to ten miles daily. He was able to pare down his expenses to £2 a month. He began to feel keenly the obligations to his family and was glad that he had reduced the calls on his brother for funds. Simplicity harmonized his inward and outward life; the dandyism of the first three months had been only a defensive armour against those who considered him a misfit in English society.

Vegetarianism, which had been a source of embarrassment to him, soon became an asset. He came across a book entitled Plea for Vegetarianism by Henry S. Salt, whose arguments went home. A meatless diet had been hitherto a matter of sentiment to him; henceforth, it was one of reasoned conviction. Vegetarianism was no longer an inconvenient obligation to his parents; it became a mission, the starting point of a discipline of body and mind which was to transform his life. With the zeal of a new convert, Gandhi devoured books on developed an interest in cooking, outgrew the taste for condiments, and came to the sensible conclusion that the seat of taste is not in the tongue but in the mind. The control of the palate was one of the first steps in that discipline which was to culminate many years later in total sublimation.

The immediate effect of vegetarianism was to give a new poise to young Gandhi, and to draw him out of his shell. He made his first venture into journalism by contributing nine articles to the Vegetarian. These articles, largely descriptive, and had occasional flashes of humour. That he should have sent these articles for publication at all is a notable achievement, if we recall that back home in Bhavnagar College he had been unable to follow lectures in English. He became a member of the Executive committee of the London Vegetarian Society. In Bays water where he stayed for a short time, he formed a vegetarian club. He came into contact with at least one eminent vegetarian, Sir Edwin Arnold, the author of the Light of Asia and The song Celestial, the two books which moved him deeply. He was stirred by the life if the Buddha and the message of the Gita. In the vegetarian restaurants and boarding houses of London he came across not only food faddists but also a few devout men of religion. He owed his introduction to the Bible to one such contact.

The New Testament, particularly the Sermon on the Mount went straight to his heart. The verses, "But I say unto you that ye resist not evil; but whosoever shall thee at the law and take away thy coat, let him have thy cloak also" reminded him of the lines of the Gujarati poet, Shamal Bhatt, which he used to hum as a child:

- For a bowl of water give a goodly meal;
- For a kindly greeting bow thou down with zeal;
- For a single penny pay thou back with gold;
- If the life be rescued, life do not withhold.
- Thus the words and actions of the wise regard;
- Every little service tenfold they reward.
- But the truly noble know all men as one,
- And return with gladness good for evil done.

The teachings of the Bible, the Buddha and Bhatt fused in his mind. The idea of returning love for hatred, and good for evil, captivated him; he did not yet comprehend it full, but it continued to ferment in his impressionable mind.

In 1891 Gandhi passed the law examination successfully, but was assailed by doubts and anxieties. He had read the law, but could he practise it? He found it hard enough to speak to strangers in a small party. How would he be able to cross swords with his rivals in the courtroom? He had hard of legal luminaries like Sir Pherozeshah Mehta of Bombay and could well imagine the sorry figure he would cut in comparison. It was thus "with just a little leaven of hope mixed with despair" that he sailed for India.

A great shock lay in store for him when he landed at Bombay. His mother had died while he was in England. It was only natural that he should have been anxious to justify the hopes of his family which had invested so much on his foreign education. His elder brother frankly expected rich dividends in the form of "wealth, and name and fame". The barrister's degree, however, was not an open sesame to the top of the bar. Gandhi noticed that the homebred Vakils of Rajkot knew more of Indian law and charged lower fees than England sure ridicule; Gandhi, therefore, accepted the advice of friends to go to Bombay to study India law and to secure what briefs he could.

His experience in Bombay was no happier than in Rajkot. After waiting unconscionably, he got his first brief for the modest fee of thirty rupees. As he rose to cross-examine a witness, he was unable to collect his thoughts, collapsed into his chair and refunded the fee to his client. This was a disgraceful debut, which filled the young barrister with black despair as to his future in a profession he had entered at such a heavy cost.

The straits to which he had been reduced may be surmised from the fact that he applied and was turned down for a part time job as a teacher in a Bombay high school with the modest salary of seventy rupees (£5 1/2) a month. It was with some relief that he discovered that he had a flair for drafting memorials and petitions. He wound up his little establishment in Bombay and returned to Rajkot where petition-writing brought him an income of three hundred rupees a month. He might have settled down as a barrister scribe if he had not incurred the displeasure of the British Political Agent in Rajkot in whose court most of his work lay. So, when an offer of a job came to him from South Africa, he gladly accepted it. The contract was for a year in connection with a civil suit; the remuneration was £105, a first-class return fare and actual expenses. The fee was modest and it was not quite clear whether he was engaged as counsel or as a clerk, but he was in no position to pick and choose. He could hardly have imagined the new vistas of maturity and public service which the South African adventure was to open to him.

In 1891 Gandhi passed the law examination successfully, but was assailed by doubts and anxieties. He had read the law, but could he practise it? He found it hard enough to speak to strangers in a small party. How would he be able to cross swords with his rivals in the courtroom? He had hard of legal luminaries like Sir Pherozeshah Mehta of Bombay and could well imagine the sorry figure he would cut in comparison. It was thus "with just a little leaven of hope mixed with despair" that he sailed for India. A great shock lay in store for him when he landed at Bombay. His mother had died while he was in England. It was only natural that he should have been anxious to justify the hopes of his family which had invested so much on his foreign education. His elder brother frankly expected rich dividends in the form of "wealth, and name and fame". The barrister's degree, however, was not an open sesame to the top of the bar. Gandhi noticed that the homebred Vakils of Rajkot knew more of Indian law and charged lower fees than England sure ridicule; Gandhi, therefore, accepted the advice of friends to go to Bombay to study India law and to secure what briefs he could.

His experience in Bombay was no happier than in Rajkot. After waiting unconscionably, he got his first brief for the modest fee of thirty rupees. As he rose to cross-examine a witness, he was unable to collect his thoughts, collapsed into his chair and refunded the fee to his client. This was a disgraceful debut, which filled the young barrister with black despair as to his future in a profession he had entered at such a heavy cost.

The straits to which he had been reduced may be surmised from the fact that he applied and was turned down for a part time job as a teacher in a Bombay high school with the modest salary of seventy rupees (£5 1/2) a month. It was with some relief that he discovered that he had a flair for drafting memorials and petitions. He wound up his little establishment in Bombay and returned to Rajkot where petition-writing brought him an income of three hundred rupees a month. He might have settled down as a barrister scribe if he had not incurred the displeasure of the British Political Agent in Rajkot in whose court most of his work lay. So, when an offer of a job came to him from South Africa, he gladly accepted it. The contract was for a year in connection with a civil suit; the remuneration was £105, a first-class return fare and actual expenses. The fee was modest and it was not quite clear whether he was engaged as counsel or as a clerk, but he was in no position to pick and choose. He could hardly have imagined the new vistas of maturity and public service which the South African adventure was to open to him.

In the 'Dark Continent'

Gandhi landed at Durban in May 1893. His employer Dada Abdulla, one of the wealthiest Indian merchants in Natal, took him to see the Durban court. When the European magistrate ordered Gandhi to take off his turban, he refused, left the courtroom and wrote a letter of protest in the local press in which he was mentioned "as an unwelcome visitor". The experience in Durban, however, was nothing compared with what befell him in the course of his journey from Durban to Pretoria. When his train reached Maritzburg late in the evening, he was ordered to leave the first class compartment and shift to the van compartment. He refused, but was unceremoniously turned out of the carriage. It was a bitterly cold night as he crept into the unlit waiting-room of Maritzburg station and brooded over what had happened. His client had given him no warning of the humiliating conditions under which Indians lived in South Africa. Should he not call off the contract and return to India? Should he accept these affronts as part of the bargain? So far Gandhi had not been conspicuous for assertiveness; on the contrary he had been pathologically shy and retiring. But something happened to him in that windswept waiting-room of Maritzburg railway station as he smarted under the insult inflicted on him. The iron entered his soul. In retrospect, this incident seemed to him as one of the most creative experiences of his life. From that hour, he refused to accept injustice as a part of the natural-or unnatural-order in South Africa. He would reason, he would plead; he would appeal to the better judgment and the latent humanity of the ruling race; he would resist, but he would never be a willing victim of racial arrogance. It was not so much a question of redeeming his own self-respect as that of his community, his country, even of humanity.

The helpless resignation of the mass of Indian settlers, the fact that they were illiterate, had few rights and did not know how to assert the rights they had. All this had the miraculous effect of dissipating young Gandhi's own diffidence. The feeling of inferiority which had dogged him as a student in England and as a budding lawyer in India vanished. In Bombay he had been unable to face a small cause court but one of the first things he did on arrival at Pretoria was to convene a meeting of the Indian residents "to present to them a picture of their condition in Transvaal".

During the next twelve months, Gandhi was busy with the civil suit which had brought him to Pretoria. In June 1894, he returned to Durban to sail for India. At the farewell party which his grateful client Dada Abdulla gave him at Sydenham, a pleasant suburb of Durban, Gandhi happened to glance through the pages of the Natal Mercury, and learnt that a bill was being introduced into the Natal Legislature to disfranchise India settlers. Gandhi's host and other Indian merchants present at the party were unable to throw any light on this measure. They knew enough English to be able to converse with their white customers, but few of them could read newspapers, much less follow the proceedings of the Natal Legislature. They had come to Natal for trade, and politics did not interest them. They had not yet realized that politics could affect their trade. "This is the first nail into our coffin", was Gandhi's comment. The Indian merchants pleaded with him to stay on in Natal to take up the fight on their behalf. Gandhi agreed to defer his stay for a month.

Gandhi lost no time in settling down to work; the farewell party converted itself into a political committee to plan Indian opposition to the bill. A sound instinct seems to have guided the young barrister in organizing his first political campaign. He infused a spirit of solidarity into the heterogeneous elements composing the Indian community, and brought home the implications of the disfranchising measures not only to his own people, but to the saner section of the European public opinion and the Natal Government Most important of all, he gave the widest publicity to his campaign to quicken the conscience of the peoples and Governments of India and Great Britain; through petitions to the legislatures, statements in newspapers, letters to prominent persons in Natal, Britain and India, and through public meeting, Gandhi stressed the justice of the Indians, case. All this created a great stir but the disfranchising bill was nevertheless passed by the Natal Legislature. On the insistence of his Indian friends in Durban, Gandhi agreed to prolong his stay in Natal, and was enrolled as an advocate to the Supreme Court. Since he retaining fees to produce a minimum 300 a year which he reckoned enough to pay his way in Durban.

The Young Politician

The first experience of political agitation into which Gandhi had been pitch forked cured him of what once had seemed an incorrigible self-consciousness. Not that he had a sudden attack of egotism; he was conscious of his limitations, and in a letter dated July 5, 1894 to Dadabhai Naoroji, the eminent leader of the Indian National Congress, wrote: "A word for myself and I have done. I am inexperienced and young and, therefore, quite liable to make mistakes. The responsibility undertaken is quite out of proportion to my ability. So, you will see that I have not taken the matter up, which is beyond my ability, in order to enrich myself at the expense of the Indians. I am the only available person who can handle the question." The concept of inferiority is a relative one; in a community looking to him for leadership, Gandhi forgot his own limitations. As the only available person, he undertook a task from which elsewhere he would have shrunk.

Gandhi had come to South Africa in 1893 for a year. He could hardly have imagined that he would have to stay on for the best part of two decades. The struggle of the Indian immigrants for elementary civic rights was to be long and hard The disfranchising of the Indians which had been the immediate cause of Gandhi's intervention in the politics of Natal was only a symptom of the racial malaise that had begun to afflict the Dark Continent. "The Asiatics", wrote Lord Milner, "are strangers forcing themselves upon a community reluctant to receive them." In fact, the Indian emigration to South Africa in the eighteen-sixties started at the instance of the European settlers who were in possession of vast virgin lands ideal for tea, coffee and sugar plantations, but lacked manpower. The Negro could not be compelled to work after the abolition of slavery. Recruiting agents of the European planters toured some of the poorest and most congested districts of India and painted rosy prospects of work in Natal. Free passage, board and lodging; a wage of ten shillings a month for the first year rising by one shilling every year; and the right to a free return passage to India after five years' 'indenture' (or alternatively, the option to settle in the land of their adoption) drew thousands of poor and illiterate Indians to distant Natal.

The European planters and merchants did not relish the idea of Indian Labourers settling down as free citizens at the end of the five year' 'indenture'. A tax of £3 was therefore levied on every member of the family of an ex-indentured labourer even though he was merely exercising his right to settle in Natal in terms of the agreement which had governed his emigration from India. It was a crippling tax for the poor wretches whose wages ranged between ten and twelve shillings month. The Indian merchant who had followed the Indian labourer to Natal had disabilities of his own. No one could trade without a licence, which a European could have for the asking and Indian only after much effort and expense, if at all. And since an educational test in a European language was made a sine quanon for an immigrant from India, except of course the semi-slave indentured labourers who continued to be imported.

The legal disabilities on Indians were bad enough, but the daily humiliations they suffered were worse. They were commonly described as "Asian dirt to be heartily curse, chokeful of vice, that live upon rice and the black vermin". They were not allowed to walk on footpaths. First and second class tickets were not issued to them. If a white passenger objected, they could be unceremoniously bundled out of a railway compartment; they had sometimes to travel on footboards of trains. European hotels would not admit them.

Gandhi realized that what the India urgently needed was a permanent organization to look after their interests. Out of deference to Dadabhai Naoroji, Who had presided over the Indian National Congress in 1893, he called the new organization Natal Indian Congress. He was not conversant with the constitution and functions of the Indian National Congress. This ignorance proved an asset, as he fashioned the Natal Congress in his own way to suit the needs of the Natal Indians, as a live body functioning throughout the year and dedicated not only to politics but to the moral and social uplift of its members. Though it served a community which had very little political experience, it was not a one-man show. An indefatigable secretary though he was, Gandhi enlisted popular interest and enthusiasm at every step. He made the enrolment of members and the collection of subscriptions into something more than a routine. He employed a gently but irresistible technique for exerting moral pressure on halfhearted supporters. Once in a small village, he sat through the night and refused to take his dinner until at dawn his host, an Indian merchant, agreed to raise his subscription for the Natal Indian Congress from three to six pounds.

In these early years of his politics apprenticeship, Gandhi formulated his own code of conduct for a politician. He did not accept the popular view that in politics one must fight for one's; arty, right or wrong. He avoided exaggeration and discouraged it in his colleagues. The Natal Indian Congress was not merely an instrument for the defence of political and economic rights for the Indian minority, but also a lever for its internal reform and unity. He did not spare his own people and roundly criticized them for their shortcomings. He was not only the stoutest champion of the Natal Indians, but also their severest critic.

Under his leadership, the Indian community in Natal endeavoured to secure the repeal of discriminatory laws and vexatious regulations and stave off further oppressive measures. Gandhi was in touch with Naoroji and other members of the British committee of the Indian National Congress in London. He sought their advice and support in representing the South African Indian Indian's case to the Secretary of State for India, and British Colonial Secretary. He was an indefatigable correspondent, bombarding his friends, opponents, newspaper editors and men in authority in three continents, with telegrams, letters and memoranda on the grievances of the India in South Africa. It is a measure of Gandhi's success as a publicist that the Indian National Congress Recorded its protest against the disabilities imposed upon the Indian settlers in South Africa, and the London Times devoted several leading articles to this problem. In 1896 he paid a brief visit to India to canvass public support for the cause he had made his own. On return to Natal from this trip on January 10,1897, he was nearly lynched in the streets Durban by a mob of Europeans who had been infuriated by Press reports of Gandhi's advocacy of the Indian cause in his native land.

On the outbreak of the Boer War in 1899, Gandhi organized an Indian Ambulance Corps of 1100 men. Vere Stent, the editor of the Pretoria News, has left a fascinating pen-portrait of Gandhi in the battlefield: "After a night's work which had shattered men with much bigger frames, I came across Gandhi in the early morning sitting by the roadside-eating a regulation biscuit. Every man in (General) Buller's force was dull and depressed, and damnation was heartily invoked on everything. But Gandhi was stoic in his bearing, cheerful and confident in his conversation and had a kindly eye." It must be recognised that Gandhi's ideas on nonviolence had not yet fully matured. His argument at this time was that Indian settlers in British colonies, while demanding all the privileges of citizenship must also accept all its obligations, which included participation in the defence of the country of adoption. Gandhi's gesture in raising an ambulance corps on behalf of a minority which was denied elementary rights was a fine one, but it was wasted. The end of the Boer War brought no relief to the Indians. Their grievances remained unredressed. Indeed, new chains were forged for them in the former Boer Colonies.

Satyagraha Struggle in South Africa

It was the passage of the Asiatic Registration Act in Transvaal in 1907 which convinced Gandhi that the method of protest, petition and prayer which he had sedulously pursued for nearly fourteen years had failed. It was at this juncture that he evolved a new technique, which came to be known as Passive Resistance; but as it ruled out both verbal and physical violence, it differed in important respects from the campaign waged on behalf of the suffragettes in England. The principles and techniques of Gandhi's movement were to evolve gradually in the ensuing months ant years; its author was a man for whom theory was the handmaid of action. It is not possible here to give a detailed account of the Satyagraha struggle which Gandhi led in South Africa for seven years. It required great courage, patience and organizing ability to persuade the small Indian community to pit itself against the government. Gandhi had to reckon with the immense political and economic power wielded by the dominant European community, the stubbornness of the local government in South Africa, the reluctance of the British Colonial Office to antagonize the Union Government in Pretoria, the apathy of the Government of India and the limited resources of the small India minority fighting for its survival on an alien soil. Gandhi himself worked under terrific pressure. In January 1908, he was arrested for breach of the registration law and clapped into prison. The following month he was released after an understanding seemed to have been reached with the government. A few days later, he was beaten up and severely injured by a compatriot, who accused him of betraying the Indian cause. The truce with the Transvaal Government did not last long. The Satyagraha campaign had to be renewed. There were acts of defiance by the Indians and punitive measures by the authorities. Gandhi set up a small colony-Tolstoy Farm-at an 1100 acre site, 21 miles from Johannesburg where his colleagues in the Satyagraha struggle and their families could support a frugal and hard existence-which was in fact harder than life in jail-by-running a cooperative farm. "We had all become labourers," Gandhi recalled later, "put on labourer's dress, but in the European style, *viz.*, Workman's trousers and shirts which were imitated from prisoner's uniform". Those who went to Johannesburg on private errands had to walk. Gandhi himself, though past forty and living only on fruits, did not think much of walking forty miles a day; he once did 55 miles without feeling any the worse for it. All residents of Tolstoy Farm including children had their quota of manual labour. Those who had known this austere discipline could have little fear of goal.

In 1912, Gokhale, one of the most eminent Indian politicians of the day, paid a visit to South Africa and discussed the problems of the Indian community with General Smuts and other members of the South African Government. He returned to India with the impression that the Asiatic Registration Act and the hated £3 tax on the ex-indentured labourers would be abolished. When this did not happen, and an additional provocation was given by Supreme Court Judgment invalidating marriages of non-Christians in South Africa, Gandhi launched what turned out to be the final phase of his struggle in South Africa.

A party of eleven Indian women, including Gandhi's wife Kasturba, courted imprisonment by crossing from Natal into Transvaal without a permit. The Indian labourers in the coal mines at New Castle went on a sympathetic strike. The mine-owners retaliated by cutting off water and electric connection to the areas where the labourers lived. Gandhi had no option but to take charge of the miners and their families, 2037 men, 127 women and 57 children. He decided to walk them from New Castle to Tolstoy Farm, but was arrested on the way. In Volksrust jail he was make to dig stones and sweep the compound. Later he was transferred to Pretoria jail and lodged in a dark cell ten feet long and seven feet wine, which was lit up at night only to check up on the prisoner. He was denied a bench, refused permission to walk in the cell and subjected to numberless pinpricks. Summoned for evidence in a case, he was marched to the court with handcuffs on his hands and manacles on his feet. Meanwhile, the Indian labourers had been put into special trains, and taken back to New Castle mines where they were forced to go underground by mounted military police.

The 'blood and iron' policy of the South African Government stirred India deeply. Gokhale sent two earnest Christian young men, C.F. Andrews and Pearson, to assist Gandhi. Lord Hardinge, the viceroy of India, courageously denounced the high-handed policies of the South African Government. Negotiations began between Gandhi and the South African Government under pressure from Delhi and London. Eventually an agreement was reached. Some of the major points on which the Satyagraha struggle had been waged were conceded to the Indians. The tax on the ex-indentured labourers was abolished; marriages performed according to Indian rites were legalized, and a domicile certificate bearing the holder's thumb-imprint was too a sufficient evidence of the right to enter South Africa.

In 1939, a quarter of a century after the conclusion of the Satyagraha campaign, General Smuts, Gandhi's chief antagonist in South Africa, recalled: "Gandhi himself received-what no doubt he desired-a short period of rest and quiet in goal. For him everything went according to plan. For me-the defender of law and order-there was the usual trying situation, the odium of carrying out a law which had no strong public support, and finally the discomfiture when the law had to be repealed. For him it was a successful coup." In goal Gandhi had prepared a pair of sandals for General Smuts, who wrote that there was no hatred and personal ill-feeling, and when the fight was over, "there was the atmosphere in which decent peace would be concluded.

The Making of Mahatma

In 1914 Gandhi left South Africa. He had gone there as a junior counsel of a commercial firm for £105 a year; he had stayed on to command, and then voluntarily to give up a peak practice of £5000 a year. In Bombay as a young lawyer he had a nervous breakdown while cross-examining witnesses in a petty civil suit;

in the South Africa, he had founded a new political organization with the sure touch of a seasoned politician. The hostility of the European politicians and officials and the helplessness of the Indian merchants and labourers had put him on his mettle.

No glittering rewards for him; the perils ranged from professional pinpricks to lynching. Nevertheless, it was a piece of good fortune that he began his professional and political career in South Africa. Dwarfed as he had felt by the great lawyers and leader of India, it is unlikely that he would have developed much initiative in his homeland. When he founded the Natal Indian Congress at the age of twenty-five, he was writing on a tabula rasa: he could try out ideas which in an established political organization would have been laughed out court.

What had truth and vows to do with politics? It was a question which often recurred in Indian politics, and if Gandhi was not confounded by it, it was because, far back in South Africa, he had observed and confirmed the connection. For a man who was no doctrinaire, and whose theory often lagged behind practice, it was a decided advantage that the scene of his early activities should have been one where he was unfettered by political precedents or professionals. Natal and Transvaal were no bigger than some of the smallest provinces of India. The struggle for Indian independence was conducted Gandhi on much larger scale and on much bigger issues, but there were not a few occasions when he derived inspiration from his experience in South Africa. Not only his politics, but his personality took shape in South Africa. The most formative years of his life had been spent there. His interest in moral and religious questions dated back to his early childhood. But it was only in South Africa that he had an opportunity of studying them systematically. His Quaker friends in Pretoria failed to convert him to Christianity, but they whetted his innate appetite for religious studies. He delved deep into Christianity and other religions, including his own. In his first year in South Africa he read 'quite eighty books', most of them on religion. One of these was Tolstoy's Kingdom of God is Within You. Tolstoy became his favourite author and in the coming years he read the Gospels in Brief, What to do? The Slavery of Our Times, How Shall We Escape? Letters to a Hindu and The First Step. Tolstoy's bold idealism and fearless candour gripped him, his Christian anarchism dissipated the spell of institutional religion. Tolstoy's emphasis on the necessity of an accord between moral principles and daily life confirmed his own strivings for self-improvement.

Few men read so little to so much profit as Gandhi did. A book was for Gandhi not a mere diversion for the hour, it was embodied experience, which had to be accepted or rejected. Ruskin's Unto The Last drove him with compelling urgency from the capital of Natal to the wilderness of Zululand to practise a life of voluntary poverty, and literally to live by the sweat of his brow. It was in Tolstoy's books that we may seek one of the strongest influences on Gandhi. He was, of course, not given to indiscriminate imitation. But in Tolstoy he found a writer whose views elaborated his own inchoate beliefs. It was not only on the organized or covert violence of the modern state and the right of the citizen to civil disobedience that Gandhi found support in Tolstoy.

There were innumerable subjects, ranging from modern civilization and industrialism to sex and schools, on which he tended to agree with Tolstoy's analysis. There was an exchange of letters between the two which gives an impression of gratitude and reverence by the young Indian on the threshold of his career, and of delightful surprise by the aged Tolstoy. "And so your activity in Transvaal," wrote Tolstoy to Gandhi, "as it seems to us, at the end of the world, is the most essential work, the most important of all the work now being done in the world, and in which not only the nations of the Christian, but of all the world will undoubtedly take part." While books on Christianity and Islam were easily available in South Africa, Gandhi had to send for books on Hinduism from India. He corresponded with his friend Raychandbhai, whose influence in favour of Hinduism was decisive at a time when Gandhi's Quaker friends believed him to be on the way to baptism. The study of comparative religion, the browsing on theological works, the conversations and correspondence with the learned, brought Gandhi to the conclusion that true religion was more a matter of the heart than of the intellect, and that genuine beliefs were those which were literally lived.

Gandhi's style of life was also transformed during these years. From the Gita which he described as his "spiritual dictionary", he had imbibed the ideal of "non-possession" which set him on the road to voluntary poverty, and of "selfless action " which equipped him with an extraordinary stamina for his public life. He trained himself as a dispenser in a charitable hospital in order to be able to attend on the 'indentured' labourers, the poorest Indians in South Africa. At Phoenix near Durban, and at Tolstoy Farm near Johannesburg, he set up little colonies, where he and those who shared his ideals, could find a haven from the heat and dust of towns, and men's greed and hatred, A pen-portrait of Gandhi as he was in his late thirties has been left by his first biographer Rev. Joseph J. Doke of Johannesburg: "A small, lithe, spare figure stood before me, and a refined earnest face looked into mine.

The skin was dark, the eyes dark, but the smile which lighted up the face, and that direct fearless glance simply took one's heart by storm. I judged him to be some thirty-eight years of age, which proved correct. He spoke English perfectly and was evidently a man of culture. There was a quite assured strength about him, a greatness of heart, a transparent honesty that attracted me at once to the Indian leader. Our Indian friend lives on a higher plane than most men do. His actions, like the actions of Mary of Bethany, are often counted eccentric, and not infrequently misunderstood. Those who do not know him think there is some unworthy motive behind, some Oriental 'slimness' to account for such profound unworldliness. But those who know him well are ashamed of themselves in his presence. Money, I think has no charm for him. His compatriots...wonder at him, grow angry at his strange unselfishness, and love him with the love of pride and trust. He is one of those outstanding characters with whom to walk is a liberal education...whom to know is to love."

Return to India

A hero's welcome awaited Gandhi when he landed on January 9, 1915, at the Apollo Bunder in Bombay. Three days later he was honoured by the people of Bombay at a magnificent reception in the palatial house of a Bombay magnate Jehangir Petit. The Government of India joined with the people of India in showering honours on Gandhi. He received a "Kaiser-I-Hind" gold medal in the King's birthday honours list of 1915. His association with Gokhale was guarantee enough of his being a safe politician. Of course, he had led an extra-constitutional movement in South Africa, defied laws and filled goals, but the cause for which he had fought appeared as much humanitarian as political, dear to all Indian as and all Englishmen whose sense of humanity had not been blunted by racial arrogance or political expediency. Lord Hardinge's open support of the Satyagraha movement had in any case removed the stigma of rebellion from South Africa's Indian movement.

Gandhi was in no hurry to plunge into politics. His political mentor on the Indian scene was Gokhale. One of the first things Gokhale did was to extract a promise from Gandhi that he would not express himself upon public questions for a year, which was to be a "year of probation". Gokhale was very keen that Gandhi should join the Servants of India Society in Poona. Gandhi was only too willing to fall in with the wishes of Gokhale, but several members of the Society feared that there was too great a gap between the ideals and methods of the Society and those of Gandhi. While the question of his admission as a 'Servant of India' was being debated, Gandhi visited his home towns of Porbandar and Rajkot and went on to Santiniketan in West Bengal, the cosmopolitan University of the Poet Rabindranath Tagore.

The trip to Santiniketan ended abruptly with a telegram from Poona that Gokhale was dead. Gandhi was stunned. He mourned Gokhale by going barefoot for a year, and out of respect for the memory of his mentor, made another effort to seek admission to the Servants of India Society. Finding a sharp division of opinion in the Society on this point, he withdrew his application for admission. During 1915-the year of probation-Gandhi eschewed politics severely. In his speeches and writings he confined himself to the reform of the individual and the society and avoided the issues which dominated Indian politics. His restraint was partly due to self-imposed silence and partly to the fact that he was still studying conditions in India and making up his mind.

Gandhism

Talking about "Gandhism" Gandhi had said "There is no such thing as 'Gandhism', and I do not want to leave any sect after me. I do not claim to have originated any new principle or doctrine. I have simply tried in my own way to apply the eternal truths to our daily life and problems.". He said "The opinions I have formed and the conclusions I have arrived at are not final. I may change them tomorrow." "I have nothing new to teach the world. Truth and nonviolence are as old as the hills." He added

Eminent scholar, Professor Ramjee Singh has called Mahatma Gandhi as the Bodhisattva of the twentieth century.

Satyagraha: Satyagraha is formed by two Sanskrit words Satya (truth) and Agraha (holding firmly to). The term was popularized during the Indian Independence Movement, and is used in many Indian languages including Hindi.

Satya

The pivotal and defining element of Gandhism is satya, a Sanskrit word usually translated into English as truth, whose literal meaning is 'what actually is' (deriving from the root verb *as* meaning 'to be'). The principle of Satya as espoused by Gandhi needed that Truth must pervade all considerations of politics, ego, society and convention. Gandhi did not consider himself to be a pacifist, socialist or on any definable spectrum of politics. He professed to adhere to the pure, existing facts of life to make his decisions. Gandhi's commitments to nonviolence, human freedom, equality and justice arose from his personal examination.

Truth is interpreted subjectively. Gandhism does not demand that its adherents agree to Gandhi's own principles to the letter, but in spirit. If one honestly believes that violence is sometimes necessary, it is *truthful* to believe in it. When Gandhi returned to India in the middle of World War I, he said he would have supported the British in the war. It would have been wrong, according to Gandhi, to demand equal rights for Indians in the Empire, and not contribute to its defence. On the other hand, by the time of the advance of the Japanese in World War II, Gandhi had given up notions of fighting alongside the British and argued for nonviolence instead. Gandhiji the father of nation was a propounder of Ahimsa.

Gandhi developed a way of life by his constant "experimenting with truth" — a phrase that formed the subtitle to his autobiography. He was prepared to learn through trial and error, often admitting to mistakes and changing his behaviour accordingly. This was particularly notable when Gandhi stopped all nationwide civil resistance in 1922 after the Chauri Chaura incident. He would forsake political independence for truth — believing that Indians should not become murderers and commit the very evils they were accusing the British of perpetrating in India.

Gandhism is more about the spirit of Gandhi's journey to discover the truth, than what he finally considered to be the truth. It is the foundation of Gandhi's teachings, and the spirit of his whole life to examine and understand for oneself, and not take anybody or any ideology for granted.

Gandhi said: "The Truth is far more powerful than any weapon of mass destruction."

Gandhi's philosophy encompassed ontology and its association with truth. For Gandhi, "to be" did not mean to exist within the realm of time, as it has in the past with the Greek philosophers. But rather, "to exist" meant to exist within the realm of truth, or to use the term Gandhi did, satya. Gandhi summarized his beliefs first when he said "God is Truth", which his experimenting later prompted him to change to "Truth is God". The first statement seemed insufficient to Gandhi, as the mistake could be made that Gandhi was using truth as a description of God, as opposed to God as an aspect of satya. Satya (truth) in Gandhi's philosophy is God. It shares all the characteristics of the Hindu concept of God, or Brahman, and is believed by Gandhians to live within each person as their conscience while at the same time guiding the universe.

Brahmacharya and Ahimsa

The concept of nonviolence (ahimsa) and nonresistance has a long history in Indian religious thought and has had many revivals in Hindu, Buddhist, Jain and Christian contexts. Gandhi explains his philosophy and way of life in his autobiography, *The Story of My Experiments with Truth*. He was quoted saying:

"What difference does it make to the dead, the orphans, and the homeless, whether the mad destruction is wrought under the name of totalitarianism or the holy name of liberty and democracy?"

"An eye for an eye makes the whole world blind".

"It has always been easier to destroy than to create".

"There are many causes that I am prepared to die for but no causes that I am prepared to kill for".

At the age of 36, Gandhi adopted the vow of brahmacharya, or celibacy. He committed himself to the control of the senses, thoughts and actions. Celibacy was important to Gandhi for not only purifying himself of any lust and sexual urges, but also to purify his love for his wife as genuine and not an outlet for any turmoil or aggression within his mind.

Ahimsa, or nonviolence, was another key tenet of Gandhi's beliefs. He held that total nonviolence would rid a person of anger, obsession and destructive impulses. While his vegetarianism was inspired by his rearing in the Hindu-Jain culture of Gujarat, it was also an extension of ahimsa.

On July 6, 1940, Gandhi published an article in *Harijan* which applied these philosophies to the question of British involvement in World War II. Homer Jack notes in his reprint of this article, "To Every Briton" (*The Gandhi Reader*) that, "to Gandhi, all war was wrong, and suddenly it 'came to him like a flash' to appeal to the British to adopt the method of nonviolence." In this article, Gandhi stated,

I appeal to every Briton, wherever he may be now, to accept the method of nonviolence instead of that of war, for the adjustment of relations between nations and other matters [...] I do not want Briton to be defeated, nor do I want her to be victorious in a trial of brute strength [...] I venture to present you with a nobler and braver way worthier of the bravest soldier. I want you to fight Nazism without arms, or, if I am to maintain military terminology, with nonviolent arms. I would like you to lay down the arms you have as being useless for saving you or humanity. You will invite Herr Hitler and Signor Mussolini to take what they want of the countries you call your possessions. Let them take possession of your beautiful island, with your many beautiful buildings. You will give all these but neither your souls, nor your minds. If these gentlemen choose to occupy your homes, you will vacate them. If they do not give you free passage out, you will allow yourself, man, woman, and child, to be slaughtered, but you will refuse to owe allegiance to them [...] my nonviolence demands universal love, and you are not a small part of it. It is that love which has prompted my appeal to you.

Economics

Gandhi espoused an economic theory of self-sufficiency and simple living. He envisioned a more agrarian India upon independence that would focus on meeting the material needs of its citizenry prior to generating wealth and industrializing.

Khadi

Gandhi also adopted the clothing style of most Indians in the early 20th century. His adoption of Khadi, or homespun cloth, was intended to help eradicate the evils of poverty, social and economic discrimination. It was also aimed as a challenge to the contrast that he saw between most Indians, who were poor and traditional, and the richer classes of educated, liberal-minded Indians who had adopted Western mannerisms, clothing and practices.

The clothing policy was designed to protest against the violence of British economic policies in India. Millions of poor Indian workers had been left unemployed and entrenched in poverty, owing to the industrialization of cotton processing in Britain. Gandhi promoted Khadi as a direct boycott of the Lancashire cotton industry, linking British imperialism to Indian poverty. He focused on persuading all members of the Indian National Congress to spend some time each day hand-spinning on the charkha (spinning wheel). In addition to its point as an economic campaign, the drive for hand-spinning was an attempt to connect the privileged Indian Brahmans and lawyers of Congress to connect with the mass of Indian peasantry.

Many prominent figures of the Indian independence movement, including Motilal Nehru, were persuaded by Gandhi to renounce their smart London-made clothes in favour of Khadi.

Fasting

To Gandhi, fasting was an important method of exerting mental control over base desires. In his autobiography, Gandhi analyzes the need to fast to eradicate his desire for delicious, spicy food. He believed that abstention would diminish his sensual faculties, bringing the body increasingly under the mind's absolute control. Gandhi was opposed to the partaking of meat, alcohol, stimulants, salt and most spices, and also eliminated different types of cooking from the food he ate. Fasting would also put the body through unusual hardship, which Gandhi believed would cleanse the spirit by stimulating the courage to withstand all impulses and pain. Gandhi undertook a "Fast Unto Death" on three notable occasions:

- when he wanted to stop all revolutionary activities after the Chauri Chaura incident of 1922;
- when he feared that the 1934 communal award giving separate electorates to Untouchable Hindus would politically divide the Hindu people;
- and in 1947, when he wanted to stop the bloodshed between Hindus and Muslims in Bengal and Delhi.

In all three cases, Gandhi was able to abandon his fast before death. There was some controversy over the 1934 fast, which brought him into conflict with the Untouchable leader B.R. Ambedkar. In the end, Gandhi and Ambedkar both made some concessions to negotiate the Poona Pact, which abandoned the call for separate electorates in turn for voluntary representation and a commitment to abolish untouchability. Gandhi also used the fasts as a penance, blaming himself for inciting Chauri Chaura and the divisive communal politics of both 1934 and 1947, especially the Partition of India. Gandhi sought to purify his soul and expiate his sins, in what he saw as his role in allowing terrible tragedies to happen. It took a heavy toll on his physical health and often brought him close to death.

Religion

Hindu Universalism denotes the ideology that all religions are true and therefore worthy of toleration and respect. It was articulated by Gandhi: "After long study and experience, I have come to the conclusion that all religions are true; all religions have some error in them; all religions are almost as dear to me as my own Hinduism, in as much as all human beings should be as dear to one as one's own close relatives. My own veneration for other faiths is the same as that for my own faith; therefore no thought of conversion is possible."

Gandhi believed that at the core of every religion was truth (satya), nonviolence (ahimsa) and the Golden Rule. He was deeply influenced by the Christian teaching of "turning the other cheek", once stating that if Christianity practised the Sermon on the Mount, he would indeed be a Christian. Gandhi felt that one should be aware of worshipping the symbols and idols of the religion and not its teachings, such as worshipping the crucifix whilst ignoring its significance as a symbol for self-sacrifice.

Although Gandhi was raised as a Hindu he was critical of most religions, including Hinduism. He wrote in his autobiography: *"Thus if I could not accept Christianity either as a perfect, or the greatest religion, neither was I then convinced of Hinduism being such. Hindu defects were pressingly visible to me. If untouchability could be a part of Hinduism, it could but be a rotten part or an excrescence. I could not understand the raison d'etre of a multitude of sects and castes. What was the meaning of saying that the Vedas were the inspired Word of God? If they were inspired, why not also the Bible and the Koran? As Christian friends were endeavouring to convert me, so were Muslim friends. Abdullah Sheth had kept on inducing me to study Islam, and of course he had always something to say regarding its beauty".*

He then went on to say: *"As soon as we lose the moral basis, we cease to be religious. There is no such thing as religion overriding morality. Man, for instance, cannot be untruthful, cruel or incontinent and claim to have God on his side".* Gandhi was critical of the hypocrisy in organised religion, rather than the principles on which they were based. He also said the following about Hinduism:

"Hinduism as I know it entirely satisfies my soul, fills my whole being... When doubts haunt me, when disappointments stare me in the face, and when I see not one ray of light on the horizon, I turn to the Bhagavad Gita, and find a verse to comfort me; and I immediately begin to smile in the midst of overwhelming sorrow. My life has been full of tragedies and if they have not left any visible and indelible effect on me, I owe it to the teachings of the Bhagavad Gita".

The concept of Islamic jihad can also be taken to mean a nonviolent struggle or satyagraha, in the way Gandhi practiced it. On Islam he said:

"The sayings of Muhammad are a treasure of wisdom, not only for Muslims but for all of mankind". Later in his life when he was asked whether he was a Hindu, he replied:

"Yes I am. I am also a Christian, a Muslim, a Buddhist and a Jew". Gandhi's religious views are reflected in the hymns his group often sang:

- Vaishnav jan to Call them Vishnava, those who understand the sufferings of others...
- Raghupati Raghava Raja Ram Call him Rama or God or Allah...

Nehru's India

Gandhi was assassinated in 1948, but his teachings and philosophy would play a major role in India's economic and social development and foreign relations for decades to come.

Sarvodaya is a term meaning 'universal uplift' or 'progress of all'. It was coined by Gandhi in 1908 as a title for his translation of John Ruskin's *Unto This Last.* Later, nonviolence leader Vinoba Bhave used the term to refer to the struggle of post-independence Gandhians to ensure that self-determination and equality reached the masses and the downtrodden. Sarvodaya workers associated with Vinoba, including Jaya Prakash Narayan and Dada Dharmadhikari, undertook various projects aimed at encouraging popular self-organisation during the 1950s and 1960s. Many groups descended from these networks continue to function locally in India today.

While the problem of the desperate poverty of tens of millions of landless farmers across the country had to be addressed, Gandhi did not believe that class warfare was inevitable, as Lenin, Mao Zedong and Stalin did. Bhave and other Gandhi disciples organized the Bhoodan campaign encouraging landlords across the country to award land to their farmers. They were encouraged to acknowledge the desperate poverty and mistreatment of these farmers, to accept them as fellow Indians and their brethren. This peaceful land distribution program was frowned upon by supporters of free-market economics, the Communists and socialists alike, but did enjoy good successes.

The Prime Minister of India, Jawaharlal Nehru, was often considered Gandhi's successor, although he was not religious and often disagreed with Gandhi. He was, however, deeply influenced by Gandhi personally as well as politically, and used his premiership to pursue ideological policies based on Gandhi's principles. Nehru's foreign policy was staunch anti-colonialism and neutrality in the Cold War. Nehru backed the independence movement in Tanzania and other African nations, as well as the American Civil Rights Movement led by Martin Luther King Jr. and the anti-apartheid struggle of Nelson Mandela and the African National Congress in South Africa. Nehru refused to align with either the United States or the Soviet Union, and helped found the Non-Aligned Movement.

Nehru also pushed through major legislation that granted legal rights and freedoms to Indian women, and outlawed untouchability and many different kinds of social discrimination, in the face of strong opposition from orthodox Hindus.

Not all of Nehru's policies were Gandhian. Nehru refused to condemn the USSR's 1956-57 invasion of Hungary to put down an anti-communist, popular revolt. Some of his economic policies were criticised for removing the right of property and freedoms from the landowing peasants of Gujarat for whom Gandhi had fought for in the early 1920s. Nehru's socialism sometimes conflicted with Gandhism.

Nehru's biggest failure is often considered to be the 1962 Sino-Indian War, though his policy is said to have been inspired by Gandhian pacifism. In this instance, it led to the defeat of the Indian Army against a surprise Chinese invasion. Nehru had neglected the defence budget and disallowed the Army to prepare, which caught the soldiers in India's north eastern frontier off-guard with lack of supplies and reinforcements.

Freedom

Gandhi's deep commitment and disciplined belief in nonviolent civil disobedience as a way to oppose tyranny, oppression and injustice has inspired many subsequent political figures, including Martin Luther King Jr. of the United States, Julius Nyerere of Tanzania, Nelson Mandela and Steve Biko of South Africa.

Gandhi's early life work in South Africa between the years 1910 and 1915, for the rights of Indian residents oppressed by the racist, white minority South African regime inspired the later work of the African National Congress. From the 1950s, the ANC organized nonviolent civil disobedience akin to the campaign advanced by the Indian National Congress under the inspiration of Gandhi between the 1920s and 1940s. ANC activists braved the sticks and bullets of the police, water-hoses, tear gas and dogs to protest against tyranny, racism and oppression in South Africa. Many, especially Mandela, languished for decades in jail, while the world outside was divided in its effort to remove apartheid. Steve Biko, perhaps the most vocal adherent to nonviolent civil resistance, was allegedly murdered in 1977 by agents of the regime.

When the first universal, free elections were held in South Africa in 1994, the ANC was elected and Mandela became President. Mandela made a special visit to India and publicly honoured Gandhi as the man who inspired the freedom struggle of black South Africans. Statues of Gandhi have been erected in Natal, Pretoria and Johannesburg.

Martin Luther King Jr., a young Christian minister and leader of the American Civil Rights Movement seeking the liberation of African Americans from racial segregation in the American South, and also from economic and social injustice and political disenfranchisement, travelled to India in 1962 to meet Jawaharlal Nehru. The two discussed Gandhi's teachings, and the methodology of organizing peaceful resistance. The graphic imagery of black protesters being hounded by police, beaten and brutalized, evoked admiration for King and the protesters across America and the world, and precipitated the 1964 Civil Rights Act.

The nonviolent Solidarity movement of Lech Wa³êsa of Poland overthrew a Soviet-backed communist government after two decades of peaceful resistance and strikes in 1989, beginning the downfall of the Soviet Communist empire. Myanmar's Aung San Suu Kyi remains under house arrest, and her National League for Democracy suppressed in their nonviolent quest for democracy and freedom in military-controlled Myanmar. This struggle was inaugurated when the military dismissed the results of the 1991 democratic elections and imposed military rule.

"Without Truth, Nothing"

Mohandas Gandhi's early life was a series of personal struggles to decipher the truth about life's important issues and discover the true way of living. He admitted in his autobiography to beating his young wife, and indulging in carnal pleasures out of lust, jealousy and possessiveness, not genuine love. He had eaten meat, smoked a cigarette, and almost visited a prostitute. It was only after much personal turmoil and repeated failures that Gandhi developed his philosophy.

Gandhi disliked having a cult following, and was averse to being addressed as *Mahatma,* claiming that he was not a perfect human being. In 1942, while he had already condemned Adolf Hitler, Benito Mussolini and the Japanese militarists, Gandhi took on an offensive in civil resistance, called the Quit India Movement, which was even more dangerous and definitive owing to its direct call for Indian independence. Gandhi did not see the British as defenders of freedom giving their continuance of imperialist domination in India. He did not feel a need to take sides with world powers.

Gandhism is brutal adherence to truth. If it means condemning the practice of untouchability in Hindu society, it means condemning the victimization of Muslim women and coerced conversions to Islam and Christianity in the same breath. Gandhism has no respect for power. No institution or individual is infallible, save God. Gandhi believed that all humans are susceptible to sinful actions and behaviour, and the worst of dictators were essentially the same despite the difference in their lives, beliefs and actions. Despite this, he held firmly that humans had no right to punish each other. He believed punishment to be the responsibility of God.

Gandhians Today

Despite Gandhi's adherence to Hindu cultural and religious values, Gandhism is broad over everything save the truth, which is definite and inviolable. There have been Muslim Gandhians, such as Khan Abdul Ghaffar Khan, known as the "Frontier Gandhi"; Christian Gandhians, such as Horace Alexander; Jewish Gandhians, such as Herman Kallenbach; and atheist Gandhians, such as Jawaharlal Nehru.

To become a Gandhian, one must set upon the same personal journey to seek truth and build one's life around it. It is not necessary to arrive at the same conclusions as Gandhi. But undergoing personal challenges, travails and the testing of one's spirit, resolve and fundamental values is a definitive element.

Criticism and Controversy

Gandhi's rigid ahimsa implies pacifism, and is thus a source of criticism from across the political spectrum.

Concept of Partition

As a rule, Gandhi was opposed to the concept of partition as it contradicted his vision of religious unity. Of the partition of India to create Pakistan, he wrote in *Harijan* on 6 October 1946: [The demand for Pakistan] as put forth by the Moslem League is un-Islamic and I have not hesitated to call it sinful. Islam stands for unity and the brotherhood of mankind, not for disrupting the oneness of the human family. Therefore, those who want to divide India into possibly warring groups are enemies alike of India and Islam. They may cut me into pieces but they cannot make me subscribe to something which I consider to be wrong [...] we must not cease to aspire, in spite of [the] wild talk, to befriend all Moslems and hold them fast as prisoners of our love.

However, as Homer Jack notes of Gandhi's long correspondence with Jinnah on the topic of Pakistan: "Although Gandhi was personally opposed to the partition of India, he proposed an agreement [...] which provided that the Congress and the Moslem League would cooperate to attain independence under a provisional government, after which the question of partition would be decided by a plebiscite in the districts having a Moslem majority."

These dual positions on the topic of the partition of India opened Gandhi up to criticism from both Hindus and Muslims. Muhammad Ali Jinnah and contemporary Pakistanis condemned Gandhi for undermining Muslim political rights. Vinayak Damodar Savarkar and his allies condemned Gandhi, accusing him of politically appeasing Muslims while turning a blind eye to their atrocities against Hindus, and for allowing the creation of Pakistan (despite having publicly declared that "before partitioning India, my body will have to be cut into two pieces"). In contemporary times, Marxist academicians like Ayesha Jalal blame Gandhi and the Congress for being unwilling to share power with Muslims and thus hastening partition. Hindus such as Pravin Togadia and Narendra Modi have also criticized Gandhi's leadership and actions on this topic. Gandhi also came under some political fire for his criticism of those who attempted to achieve independence through more violent means. His refusal to protest against the hanging of Bhagat Singh, Sukhdev, Udham Singh and Rajguru were sources of condemnation among some parties. Economists, such as Jagdish Bhagwati, have criticized Gandhi's ideas of swadeshi.

Of this criticism, Gandhi stated, "There was a time when people listened to me because I showed them how to give fight to the British without arms when they had no arms [...] but today I am told that my nonviolence can be of no avail against the [Hindu-Moslem riots] and, therefore, people should arm themselves for self-defense."

Gandhi also expressed his dislike for partition during the late 1930s in response to the topic of the partition of Palestine to create Israel. He stated in *Harijan* on 26 October 1938: Several letters have been received by me asking me to declare my views about the Arab-Jew question in Palestine and persecution of the Jews in Germany. It is not without hesitation that I venture to offer my views on this very difficult question. My sympathies are all with the Jews. I have known them intimately in South Africa. Some of them became lifelong companions. Through these friends I came to learn much of their age-long persecution. They have been the untouchables of Christianity [...] But my sympathy does not blind me to the requirements of justice. The cry for the national home for the Jews does not make much appeal to me. The sanction for it is sought in the Bible and the tenacity with which the Jews have hankered after return to Palestine. Why should they not, like other peoples of the earth, make that country their home where they are born and where they earn their livelihood? Palestine belongs to the Arabs in the same sense that England belongs to the English or France to the French. It is wrong and inhuman to impose the Jews on the Arabs. What is going on in Palestine today cannot be justified by any moral code of conduct.

He continued this argument in a number of articles reprinted in Homer Jack's *The Gandhi Reader: A Sourcebook of His Life and Writings.* In the first, "Zionism and Anti-Semitism," written in 1938, Gandhi commented upon the 1930s persecution of the Jews in Germany within the context of Satyagraha. He offered nonviolence as a method of combating the difficulties Jews faced in Germany, stating,

> If I were a Jew and were born in Germany and earned my livelihood there, I would claim Germany as my home even as the tallest Gentile German might, and challenge him to shoot me or cast me in the dungeon; I would refuse to be expelled or to submit to discriminating treatment. And for doing this I should not wait for the fellow Jews to join me in civil resistance, but would have confidence that in the end the rest were bound to follow my example. If one Jew or all the Jews were to accept the prescription here offered, he or they cannot be worse off than now. And suffering voluntarily undergone will bring them an inner strength and joy [...] the calculated violence of Hitler may even result in a general massacre of the Jews by way of his first answer to the declaration of such hostilities. But if the Jewish mind could be prepared for voluntary suffering, even the massacre I have imagined could be turned into a day of thanksgiving and joy that Jehovah had wrought deliverance of the race even at the hands of the tyrant. For to the God-fearing, death has no terror.

Gandhi was highly criticized for these statements and responded in the article "Questions on the Jews" with "Friends have sent me two newspaper cuttings criticizing my appeal to the Jews. The two critics suggest that in presenting nonviolence to the Jews as a remedy against the wrong done to them, I have suggested nothing new....what I have pleaded for is renunciation of violence of the heart and consequent active exercise of the force generated by the great renunciation. He responded to the criticisms in "Reply to Jewish Friends" and "Jews and Palestine." by arguing that "What I have pleaded for is renunciation of violence of the heart and consequent active exercise of the force generated by the great renunciation."

2

Hind Swaraj

"Civilisation is not an incurable disease, but it should never be forgotten that the English people are at present afflicted by it."

Talk about turning things on their head!

My reading of Gandhi's Hind Swaraj or Indian Home Rule was an incredibly inspiring and invigorating experience. Swaraj means freedom and in this little text of Gandhi's he speaks to why the freedom-and self-rule-that Indians were longing for, was not true freedom. Indeed they wanted India to be free of the English, but not of the mechanisms of governance and or the aim of society of the English. "you want the tiger's nature, but not the tiger."

And through a simple constructed conversation between Gandhi and a young questioner who is pro-independence, but also pro-western civilisation, Gandhi proceeds to share his insightful and at times startling view of what true freedom is and what it takes to gain it, and how true freedom and western civilisation are at odds with each other-and in my reading of it, I would say, even for the westerner. So while it is writen in the context of Indian independence, it is relevant to all, and it is as relevant today as it was when it was written 93 years ago.

Civilisation

Despite the challenges faced by our civilisation and especially our focus on material progress, we continue toiling away within the systems we have developed, believing that if we just work a little harder, things will work out for the best. In a candid and clear way Gandhi lends us one perspective on why it is the essence of our civilisation and values that is wrong, and that it will only continue devouring and destroying communities, lives and the earth. His view on the English back then was that they wished to convert the whole world into a vast market for their goods, and that was all. Everything else was done with that aim. And looking around us now much later it seems that they-and other trading nations-have done just that. "There is no end to the victims destroyed in the fire of civilization. Its deadly effect is that people come under its scorching flames believing it to be all good."

He criticised key professions and roles in the western societal structure including law and medicine. And his insights into the harm they can bring is quite compelling: When someone brings a case to court, most of the time both parties will be more or less at fault. A court of law judges one 100%, and the lawyers job is to side with his or her client. Thus any real quest for truth and for resolving the dispute in a way that may also heal the division between the two parties, is put aside in the interest of winning. It is a win-loose system, in which the winner too loses much, as ill-will and encouragement to fighting is promoted.

Doctor and modern medicine... help us ignore the symptoms. Take for example overeating, head aches, etc.. If I have indulged in a vice, which leads me to feeling ill, and the doctor cures me (gives me tables for indigestion, pills to combat the headache etc.), chances are I will repeat the vice, and not learn the relationship between unhealthy living and health problems. "Had the doctor not intervened, nature would have done its work, and I would have acquired mastery over myself, would have been freed from vica and would have become happy."

Today we spend billions of dollars, marks or pounds annually on lifestyle related diseases, that might never have come so far if prevention and a focus on healthy living had been placed above cure, which is the primary job of our doctors. "Civilisation" says Gandhi "is that mode of conduct which points out to man the path of duty. Performance of duty and observance of morality are convertible terms. To obtain morality is to attain mastery over our mind and our passions. So doing, we know ourselves. The gujarati equivalent for civilisation means 'good conduct.'"

In our societies it seems that civilisation is geared entirely towards dominion over nature, her resources, and the creation of ever more complicated and mind-blowing tools. In the traditional

India they saw that happiness was largely a mental condition, and that was their aim.

"If we become free, India is free. And in this thought you have a definition of Swaraj [freedom/home rule]. It is Swaraj when we learn to rule ourselves. It is, therefore, in the palm of our hands. Do not consider this Swaraj to be like a dream. There is no idea of sitting still. The Swaraj that I wish to picture is such that, after we have once realised it, we shall endeavour to the end of our life time to persuade others to do likewise. But such Swaraj has to be experienced, by each one for himself. One drowning man will never save another. Slaves ourselves, it would be mere pretension to think of freeing others."

And it was developing this understanding of freedom, that led to his remarkable ideas (and subsequent results) of opposing the British by Soul-force. As he said, "We simply want to find out what is right and act accordingly." And in that it became unthinkable to kill and to nurture hatred against the British. But it also became unthinkable to follow laws or demands by the British that went against his conscience and understanding of truth and goodness. And so he suggested that people simply choose no longer to be governed by the British. "If man will only realise that it is unmanly to obey laws that are unjust, no man's tyranny will enslave him. This is the key to self-rule or home-rule"

And to the British his message was, "You can govern us only so long as we remain the governed; we shall no longer have any dealings with you." "The force implied in this may be described as love force, soul-force, or more popularly, but less accurately, passive resistance. When I refuse to do a thing that is repugnant to my conscience, I use soul force. This force is indestructible. The force of arms is powerless when matched against the force of love or the soul."

His words have inspired and challenged me. I have quickened my own path to personal freedom through a deepening of the practice of meditation. However, I have wondered what Gandhi's commitment to truth, love and to living with total integrity might mean for me, and the way I live my life today, where I am aware that I am an active co-participant in a global system of capitalism which I no longer believe in, and which I believe has negative and destructive consequences for people and nature across the world. What does it mean to choose no longer to be governed by, or be active participants to such a system?

Swaraj in One Year

Much laughter has been indulged in at my expense for having told the Congress audience at Calcutta that if there was sufficient response to my programme of noncooperation Swaraj would be attained in one year. Some have ignored my condition and laughed because of the impossibility of getting Swaraj anyhow within one year. Others have spelt the 'if' in capitals and suggested that if 'ifs' were permissible in argument, any absurdity could be proved to be a possibility. My proposition however is based on a mathematical calculation. And I venture to say that true Swaraj is a practical impossibility without due fulfilment of my conditions. Swaraj means a state such that we can maintain our separate existence without the presence of the English. If it is to be a partnership, it must be partnership at will. There can be no Swaraj without our feeling and being the equals of Englishmen. Today we feel that we are dependent upon them for our internal and external security, for an armed peace between the Hindus and the Mussulmans, for our education and for the supply of daily wants, nay, even for the settlement of our religious squabbles. The Rajahs are dependent upon the British for their powers and the millionaires for their millions. The British know our helplessness and Sir Thomas Holland cracks jokes quite legitimately at the expense of non-co-operationists. To get Swaraj then is to get rid of our helplessness. The problem is no doubt stupendous even as it is for the fabled lion who having been brought up in the company of goats found it impossible to feel that he was a lion. As Tolstoy used to put it, mankind often laboured under hypnotism. Under its spell continuously we feel the feeling of helplessness. The British themselves cannot be expected to help us out of it. On the contrary, they din into our ears that we shall be fit to govern ourselves only by slow educative processes. The "Times" suggested that if we boycott the councils we shall lose the opportunity of a training in Swaraj. I have no doubt that there are many who believe what the "Times" says. It even resorts to a falsehood. It audaciously says that Lord Milner's Mission listened to the Egyptians only when they were ready to lift the boycott of the Egyptian Council. For me the only training in Swaraj we need is the ability to defend ourselves against the whole world and to live our natural life in perfect freedom even though it may be full of defects. Good Government is no substitute for self-Government. The Afghans have a bad Government but it is self-Government. I envy them. The Japanese learnt the art through a sea of blood. And if we today had the power to drive out the English by superior brute force, we would be counted their superiors, and in spite of our inexperience in debating at the Council table or in holding executive offices, we would be held fit to govern ourselves. For brute force is the only test the west has hitherto recognised. The Germans were defeated not because they were necessarily in the wrong, but because the allied Powers were found to possess greater brute strength. In the end therefore India must either learn the art of war which the British will not teach her or, she must follow her own way of discipline and self-sacrifice through noncooperation. It is as amazing as it is humiliating that less than one hundred-thousand white men should be able to rule three hundred and fifteen million Indians. They do so somewhat undoubtedly by force, but more by securing our cooperation in a thousand ways and making us more and more helpless and dependent on them as time goes forward. Let us not mistake reformed councils, more lawcourts and even governorships for real freedom or power. They are but subtler methods of emasculation. The British cannot rule us by mere force. And so they resort to all means, honourable and dishonourable, in order to retain their hold on India. They want India's billions and they want India's man power for their imperialistic greed. If we refuse to supply them with men and money, we achieve our goal, namely, Swaraj, equality, manliness.

The cup of our humiliation was filled during the closing scenes in the Viceregal Council. Mr. Shustri could not move his resolution on the Punjab. The Indian victims of Jullianwala received Rs. 1,250, the English victims of mob-frenzy received lakhs. The officials who were guilty of crimes against those whose servants they were, were reprimanded. And the councillors were satisfied. If India were powerful, India would not have stood this addition of insult, to her injury. I do not blame the British. If we were weak in numbers as they are, we too would perhaps have resorted to the same methods as they are now employing. Terrorism and deception are weapons not of the strong but of the weak. The British are weak in numbers we are weak in spite of our numbers. The result is that each is dragging the other down. It is common experience that Englishmen lose in character after residence in India and that Indians lose in courage and manliness by contact with Englishmen. This process of weakening is good neither for us, two nations, nor for the world.

But if we Indians take care of ourselves the English and the rest of the world would take care of themselves. Our contributions to the world's progress must therefore consist in setting our own house in order.

Training in arms for the present is out of the question. I go a step further and believe that India has a better mission for the world. It is within her to show that she can achieve her destiny by pure self-sacrifice, i.e., self-purification. This can be done only by noncooperation. And noncooperation is possible only when those who commenced to cooperate being the process of withdrawal. If we can but free ourselves from the threefold *maya* of Government-controlled schools, Government law-courts and legislative councils, and truly control our own education regulate our disputes and be indifferent to their legislation, we are ready to govern ourselves and we are only then ready to ask the government servants, whether civil or military, to resign, and the taxpayers to suspend payment of taxes.

And is it such an impracticable proposition to expect parents to withdraw their children from schools and colleges and establish their own institutions or to ask lawyers to suspend their practice and devote their whole time attention to national service against payment where necessary, of their maintenance, or to ask candidates for councils not to enter councils and lend their passive or active assistance to the legislative machinery through which all control is exercised. The movement of noncooperation is nothing but an attempt to isolate the brute force of the British from all the trappings under which it is hidden and to show that brute force by itself cannot for one single moment hold India.

But I frankly confess that, until the three conditions mentioned by me are fulfilled, there is no Swaraj. We may not go on taking our college degrees, taking thousands of rupees monthly from clients for cases which can be finished in five minutes and taking the keenest delight in wasting national time on the council floor and still expect to gain national self-respect. The last though not the least important part of the Maya still remains to be considered. That is Swadeshi. Had we not abandoned Swadeshi, we need not have been in the present fallen state. If we would get rid of the economic slavery, we must manufacture our own cloth and at the present moment only by hand-spinning and hand weaving.

All this means discipline, self-denial, self-sacrifice, organising ability, confidence and courage. If we show this in one year among the classes that today count, and make public opinion, we certainly gain Swaraj within one year. If I am told that even we who lead have not these qualities in us, there certainly will never be Swaraj for India, but then we shall have no right to blame the English for what they are doing. Our salvation and its time are solely dependent upon us.

British Rule—An Evil

The *Interpreter* is however more to the point in asking, "Does Mr. Gandhi hold without hesitation or reserve that British rule in India is altogether an evil and that the people of India are to be taught so to regard it? He must hold it to be so evil that the wrongs it does outweigh the benefit it confers, for only so is noncooperation to be justified at the bar of conscience or of Christ." My answer is emphatically in the affirmative. So long as I believed that the sum total of the energy of the British Empire was good, I clung to it despite what I used to regard as temporary aberrations. I am not sorry for having done so. But having my eyes opened, it would be sin for me to associate myself with the Empire unless it purges itself of its evil character. I write this with sorrow and I should be pleased if I discovered that I was in error and that my present attitude was a reaction. The continuous financial drain, the emasculation of the Punjab and the betrayal of the Muslim sentiment constitute, in my humble opinion, a threefold robbery of India. 'The blessings of *pax Britanica*' I reckon, therefore, to be a curse. We would have at least remained like the other nations brave men and women, instead of feeling as we do so utterly helpless, if we had no British Rule imposing on us an armed peace. 'The blessing' of roads and railways is a return no self-respecting nation would accept for its degradation. 'The blessing' of education is proving one of the greatest obstacles in our progress towards freedom.

A Movement of Purification

The fact is that noncooperation by reason of its nonviolence has become a religious and purifying movement. It is daily bringing strength to the nation, showing it its weak spots and the remedy for removing them. It is a movement of self-reliance. It is the mightiest force for revolutionising opinion and stimulating thought. It is a movement of self-imposed suffering and therefore possesses automatic checks against extravagance or impatience. The capacity of the nation for suffering regulates its advance towards freedom. It isolates the force of evil by refraining from participation in it, in any shape or form.

Swaraj My Ideal

The following is a fairly full report of Mr. Gandhi's important speech at Calcutta on the 13th December 1920:—

The very fact, that so many of you cannot understand Hindi which is bound to be the National medium of expression throughout Hindustan in gatherings of Indians belonging to different parts of the land, shows the depth of the degradation to which we have sunk, and points to the supreme necessity of the noncooperation movement which is intended to lift us out of that condition. This Government has been instrumental in degrading this great nation in various ways, and it is impossible to be free from it without cooperation amongst ourselves which is in turn impossible without a national medium of expression.

But I am not here to day to plead for the medium. I am to plead for the acceptance by the country of the programme of nonviolent, progressive noncooperation. Now all the words that I have used here are absolutely necessary and the two adjectives 'progressive' and 'nonviolent' are integral part of a whole. With me nonviolence is part of my religion, a matter of creed. But with the great number of Mussalmans nonviolence is a policy, with thousand, if not millions of Hindus, it is equally a matter of policy. But whether it is a creed or a policy, it is utterly impossible for you to finish the programme for the enfranchisement of the millions of India, without recognising the necessity and the value of nonviolence. Violence may for a moment avail to secure a certain measure of success but it could not in the long run achieve any appreciable result. On the other hand all violence would prove destructive to the honour and self-respect of the nation. The blue books issued by the Government of India show that inasmuch as we have used violence, military expenditure has gone up, not proportionately but in geometrical progression. The bonds of our slavery have been forged all the stronger for our having offered violence. And the whole history of British rule in India is a demonstration of the fact that we have never been able to offer successful violence. Whilst therefore I say that rather than have the yoke of a Government that has so emasculated us, I would welcome violence. I would urge with all the emphasis that I can command that India will never be able to regain her own by methods of violence.

Lord Ronaldshay who has done me the honour of reading my booklet on Home Rule has warned my countrymen against engaging themselves in a struggle for a Swaraj such as is described in that booklet. Now though I do not want to withdraw a single word of it, I would say to you on this occasion that I do not ask India to follow out today the methods prescribed in my booklet. If they could do that they would have Home Rule not in a year but in a day, and India by realising that ideal wants to acquire an ascendancy over the rest of the world. But it must remain a day dream more or less for the time being. What I am doing today is that I am giving the country a pardonable programme not the abolition of law courts, posts, telegraphs and of railways but for the attainment of Parliamentary Swarja. I am telling you to do that so long as we do not isolate ourselves from this Government, we are co-operating with it through schools, law courts and councils, through service civil and military and payment of taxes and foreign trade.

The moment this fact is realised and noncooperation is effected, this Government must totter to pieces. If I know that the masses were prepared for the whole programme at once, I would not delay in putting it at once to work. It is not possible at the present moment, to prevent the masses from bursting out into wrath against those who come to execute the law, it is not possible, that the military would lay down their arms without the slightest violence. If that were possible today, I would propose all the stages of noncooperation to be worked simultaneously. But we have not secured that control over the masses, we have uselessly frittered away precious years of the nation's life in mastering a language which we need least for winning our liberty; we have frittered away all those years in learning liberty from Milton and Shakespeare, in deriving inspiration from the pages of Mill, whilst liberty could be learnt at our doors. We have thus succeeded in isolating ourselves from the masses: we have been westernised. We have failed these 35 years to utilise our education in order to permeate the masses. We have sat upon the pedestal and from there delivered harangues to them in a language they do not understand and we see today that we are unable to conduct large gatherings in a disciplined manner. And discipline is the essence of success. Here is therefore one reason why I have introduced the word 'progressive' in the noncooperation Resolution. Without any impertinence I may say that I understand the mass mind better than any one amongst the educated Indians. I contend that the masses are not ready for suspension of payment of taxes. They have not yet learnt sufficient self-control. If I was sure of nonviolence on their part I would ask them to suspend payment today and not waste a single moment of the nations time. With me the liberty of India has become a passion. Liberty of Islam is as dear to me. I would not therefore delay a moment if I found that the whole of the programme could be enforced at once.

It grieves me to miss the faces of dear and revered leaders in this assembly. We miss here the trumpet voice of Surendranath Banorji, who has rendered inestimable service to the country. And though we stand as poles asunder today, though we may have sharp differences with him, we must express them with becoming restraint. I do not ask you to give up a single iota of principle. I urge nonviolence in language and in deed. If nonviolence is essential in our dealings with Government, it is more essential in our dealings with our leaders. And it grieves me deeply to hear of recent instances of violence reported to have been used in East Bongal against our own people. I was pained to hear that the ears of a man who had voted at the recent elections had been cut, and night soil had been thrown into the bed of a man who had stood as a candidate. Noncooperation is never going to succeed in this way. It will not succeed unless we create an atmosphere of perfect freedom, unless we prize our opponents liberty as much as our own. The liberty of faith, conscience, thought and action which we claim for ourselves must be conceded equally to others. Non cooperation is a process of purification and we must continually try to touch the hearts of those who differ from us, their minds, and their emotions, but never their bodies. Discipline and restraint are the cardinal principles of our conduct and I warn you against any sort of tyrannical social ostracism. I was deeply grieved therefore to hear of the insult offered to a dead body in Delhi and feel that if it was the action of non-co-operators they have disgraced themselves and their creed. I repeat we cannot deliver our land through violence.

It was not a joke when I said on the congress platform that Swaraj could be established in one year if there was sufficient response from the nation. Three months of this year are gone. If we are true to our salt, true to our nation, true to the songs we sing, if we are true to the Bhagwad Gita and the Koran, we would finish the programme in the remaining nine months and deliver Islam the Punjab and India.

I have proposed a limited programme workable within one year, having a special regard to the educated classes. We seem to be labouring under the illusion that we cannot possibly live without Councils, law courts and schools provided by the Government. The moment we are disillusioned we have Swaraj. It is demoralising both for Government and the governed that a hundred thousand pilgrims should dictate terms to a nation composed of three hundred millions. And how is it they can thus dictate terms. It is because we have been divided and they have ruled. I have never forgotten Humes' frank confession that the British Government was sustained by the policy of "Divide and Rule." Therefore it is that I have laid stress upon Hindu Muslim Unity as one of the important essentials for the success of Noncooperation. But, it should be no lip unity, nor bunia unity it should be a unity broad based on a recognition of the heart. If we want to save Hinduism, I say for Gods sake, do not seek to bargain with the Mussalmans. I have been going about with Maulana Shaukat Ali all these months, but I have not so much as whispered anything about the protection of the cow. My alliance with the Ali Brothers is one of honour. I feel that I am on my honour, the whole of Hinduism is on its honour, and if it will not be found wanting, it will do its duty towards the Mussalmans of India. Any bargaining would be degrading to us. Light brings light not darkness, and nobility done with a noble purpose will be twice rewarded. It will be God alone who can protect the cow. Ask me not today—'what about the cow,' ask me after Islam is vindicated through India. Ask the Rajas what they do to entertain their English guests. Do they not provide beef and champagne for their guests. Persuade them first to stop cow killing and then think of bargaining with Mussalmans. And how are we Hindus behaving ourselves towards the cow and her progeny! Do we treat her as our religion requires us? Not till we have set our own house in order and saved the cow from the Englishmen have we the right to plead on her behalf with the Mussalmans. And the best way of saving the cow from them is to give them unconditional help in their hour of trouble.

Similarly what do we owe the Punjab? The whole of India was made to crawl on her belly in as much as a single Punjabi was made to crawl in that dirty lane in Amritsar, the whole womanhood of India was unveiled in as much as the innocent woman of Manianwalla were unveiled by an insolent office; and Indian childhood was dishonoured in that, that school children of tender age were made to walk four times a day to stated places within the martial area in the Punjab and to salute the Union Jack, through the effect of which order two children, seven years old died of sunstroke having been made to wait in the noonday sun. In my opinion it is a sin to attend the schools and colleges conducted under the aegis of this Government so long as it has not purged itself of these crimes by proper repentance. We may not with any sense of self-respect plead before the courts of the Government when we remember that it was through the Punjab Courts that innocent men were sentenced to be imprisoned and hanged. We become participators in the crime of the Government by voluntarily helping it or being helped by it.

The women of India have intuitively understood the spiritual nature of the struggle. Thousands have attended to listen to the message of nonviolent noncooperation and have given me their precious ornaments for the purpose of advancing the cause of Swaraj. Is it any wonder if I believe the possibility of gaining Swaraj within a year after all these wonderful demonstrations? I would be guilty of want of faith in God if I under-rated the significance of the response from the women of India. I hope that the students will do their duty. The country certainly expects the lawyers who have hitherto led public agitation to recognise the new awakening.

I have used strong language but I have done so with the greatest deliberation, I am not actuated by any feeling of revenge. I do not consider Englishmen as my enemy. I recognise the worth of many. I enjoy the privilege of having many English friends, but I am a determined enemy of the English rule as is conducted at present and if the power—tapasya—of one man could destroy it, I would certainly destroy it, if it could not be mended. An Empire that stands for injustice and breach of faith does not deserve to stand if its custodians will not repent and noncooperation has been devised in order to enable the nation to compel justice.

I hope that Bengal will take her proper place in this movement of self-purification. Bengal began Swadeshi and national education when the rest of India was sleeping. I hope that Bengal will come to the front in this movement for gaining Swaraj and gaining justice for the Khilafat and the Punjab through purification and self-sacrifice.

On the Wrong Track

Lord Ronaldshay has been doing me the favour of reading my booklet on Indian Home Rule which is a translation of Hind Swaraj. His Lordship told his audience that if Swaraj meant what I had described it to be in the booklet, the Bengalis would have none of it. I am sorry that Swaraj of the Congress resolution does not mean the Swaraj depicted in the booklet; Swaraj according to the Congress means Swaraj that the people of India want, not what the British Government may condescend to give. In so far as I can see, Swaraj will be a Parliament chosen by the people with the fullest power over the finance, the police, the military, the navy, the courts, and the educational institutions.

I am free to confess that the Swaraj I expect to gain within one year, if India responds will be such Swaraj as will make practically impossible the repetition of the Khilafat and the Punjab wrongs, and will enable the nation to do good or evil as it chooses, and not he 'good' at the dictation of an irresponsible, insolent, and godless bureaucracy. Under that Swaraj the nation will have the power to impose a heavy protective tariff on such foreign goods as are capable of being manufactured in India, as also the power to refuse to send a single soldier outside India for the purpose of enslaving the surrounding or remote nationalities. The Swaraj that I dream of will be a possibility only, when the nation is free to make its choice both of good and evil. I adhere to all I have said in that booklet and I would certainly recommend it to the reader. Government over self is the truest Swaraj, it is synonymous with *moksha* or salvation, and I have seen nothing to alter the view that doctors, lawyers, and railways are no help, and are often a hindrance, to the one thing worth striving after. But I know that association, a satanic activity, such as the Government is engaged in, makes even an effort for such freedom a practical impossibility. I cannot tender allegiance to God and Satan at the same time.

Concept of Swaraj

Swaraj can mean generally self-governance or "home-rule" (*swa*-"self", *raj*-"rule") but the word usually refers to Mahatma Gandhi's concept for Indian independence from foreign domination. Swaraj lays stress on governance not by a hierarchical government, but self governance through individuals and community building. The focus is on political decentralization. Since this is against the political and social systems followed by Britain, Gandhi's concept of Swaraj laid stress on India discarding British political, economic, bureaucratic, legal, military, and educational institutions.

Although Gandhi's aim of totally implementing the concepts of Swaraj in India was not achieved, the voluntary work organizations which he founded for this purpose did serve as precursors and role models for peoples movements, voluntary organisations and some of the non-governmental organisations that were subsequently launched in various parts of India. The Bhoodan movement which presaged land reform legislation activity throughout India, ultimately leading to India discarding the Zamindari system, was also inspired by the ideas of Swaraj.

Key Concepts

Swaraj is a kind of Individualist Anarchism. It warrants a stateless society as according to Gandhi the overall impact of the state on the people is harmful. He called the state a "soulless machine" which, ultimately, does the greatest harm to mankind. The raison d'etre of the state is that it is an instrument of serving the people. But Gandhi feared that in the name of moulding the state into a suitable instrument of serving people, the state would abrogate the rights of the citizens and arrogate to itself the role of grand protector and demand abject acquiescence from them. This would create a paradoxical situation where the citizens would be alienated from the state and at the same time enslaved to it which according to Gandhi was demoralising and dangerous. If Gandhi's close acquaintance with the working of the state apparatus in South Africa and in India strengthened his suspicion of a centralized, monolithic state, his intimate association with the Congress and its leaders confirmed his fears about the corrupting influence of political power and his skepticism about the efficacy of the party systems of power politics (due to which he resigned from the Congress on more than one occasion only to be persuaded back each time) and his study of the British parliamentary systems convinced him that representative democracy was incapable of meting out justice to people. So he thought it necessary to evolve a mechanism to achieve the twin objectives of empowering the people and 'empowering' the state. It was for this that he developed the two pronged strategy of resistance (to the state) and reconstruction (through voluntary and participatory social action).

Although the word Swaraj means self-rule, Gandhi gave it the content of an integral revolution that encompasses all spheres of life. "At the individual level Swaraj is vitally connected with the capacity for dispassionate self-assessment, ceaseless self-purification and growing self-reliance". Politically swaraj is self-government and not good government (for Gandhi, good government is no substitute for self government) and it means a continuous effort to be independent of government control, whether it is foreign government or whether it is national. In other words, it is sovereignty of the people based on pure moral authority. Economically, Swaraj means full economic freedom for the toiling millions. And in its fullest sense, Swaraj is much more than freedom from all restraints, it is self-rule, self-restraint and could be equated with *moksha* or salvation.

Adopting Swaraj means implementing a system whereby the state machinery is virtually nil, and the real power directly resides in the hands of people. Gandhi said, "Power resides in the people, they can use it at any time." This philosophy rests inside an individual who has to learn to be master of his own self and spreads upwards to the level of his community which must be dependent only on itself. Gandhi said, "In such a state (where swaraj is achieved) everyone is his own ruler. He rules himself in such a manner that he is never a hindrance to his neighbour"; and also "It is Swaraj when we learn to rule ourselves."

Gandhi explained his vision in 1946: "Independence begins at the bottom... A society must be build in which every village has to be self sustained and capable of managing its own affairs... It will be trained and prepared to perish in the attempt to defend itself against any onslaught from without... This does not exclude dependence on and willing help from neighbours or from the world. It will be a free and voluntary play of mutual forces... In this structure composed of innumerable villages, there will be ever widening, never ascending circles. Life will not be a pyramid with the apex sustained by the bottom. But it will be an oceanic circle whose center will be the individual. Therefore the outermost circumference will not wield power to crush the inner circle but will give strength to all within and derive its own strength from it."

Gandhi was undaunted by the task of implementing such a utopian vision in India. He believed that by transforming enough individuals and communities society at large would change. He said, "It may be taunted with the retort that this is all Utopian and, therefore not worth a single thought... Let India live for the true picture, though never realizable in its completeness. We must have a proper picture of what we want before we can have something approaching it."

Efforts for Implementation

In 1917, Gandhi asked Indians nationwide to sign a petition demanding Swaraj. This petition was supported by, among others, Sardar Vallabhbhai Patel, Vinayak Damodar Savarkar, Maulana

Abul Kalam Azad and Ram Manohar Lohia. Critics include Muhammad Ali Jinnah (who said that only a constitutional struggle could lead to independence; see Proposed Indian Round Table Conference 1922) and Rabindranath Tagore.

In 1919, the Navajivan Trust, a publishing house, was founded by Gandhi to educate through publications common Indians about the principles of Swaraj, in their native tongue. The trust is still in existence today and according to its initial promises is totally self reliant having accepted absolutely no donation or grant throughout its existence.

Since achieving Swaraj could not be possible without the elimination of all forms of domination, Gandhi decided to undertake a number of constructive activities aimed at reducing the dependence of Indians from the British and simultaneously also making them self-reliant. Therefore, he founded many voluntary organisations throughout his life to carry out such social welfare programs.

The All India Spinners Association, the All India Village Industries Association, the Harijan Sewak Sangh and the Leprosy Foundation were some of the organizations he formed. The thrust of all these activities was social and not political. Gandhi also decided to popularise the spinning wheel in India to make hand-spun cloth out of Khadi. The intention was to reduce India's dependence on foreign made cloth. This movement called *The Khadi Movement* later gained fame by the term *Swadeshi*. Gandhi himself spun and weaved cloth from spinning wheels and handlooms in his *ashram*. The spinning wheel or the *Charkha* became a symbol of the Indian freedom struggle, and was incorporated into many flags.

At the Indian National Congress annual session in September 1920, delegates supported Swaraj, and in the same year they agreed with Khilafat leaders to work and fight together for both causes. This can be regarded as the official launching of the Swaraj movement by the Congress. However, the Congress idea of Swaraj was significantly different from that of Gandhi. The Gandhian idea of Swaraj outlined in his book *Hind Swaraj* was not acceptable to many Congress leaders. Jawaharlal Nehru later dismissed it as "completely unreal" and declared that neither he nor the Congress had ever considered the picture presented in it. The Congress treated Swaraj more as a politically inclined goal demanding complete political independence from the British.

After Gandhi

After Gandhi's assassination Vinoba Bhave formed the Sarva Seva Sangh at the national level and Sarvodya Mandals at the regional level to the carry on integrated village service-with the end purpose of achieving the goal of Swaraj. Two major nonviolent movements for socio-economic and political revolution in India: the Bhoodan movement led by Vinoba Bhave and the Total Revolution movement led by Jayaprakash Narayan were actually held under the aegis of the ideas of Swaraj. These movements had some success, but due to the socialist tendencies of Nehruvian India were not able to unleash the kind of revolution that was aimed at.

Gandhi's model of Swaraj was almost entirely discarded by the Indian government. He had wanted a system of a classless, stateless direct democracy. In what is known as his *Last Will and Testament* Gandhi suggested the disbanding of the Congress as a political forum. He said, "Its task is done. The next task is to move into villages and revitalize life there to build a new socioeconomic structure from the bottom upwards." He wanted the Congress party to change into a constructive work organisation-Lok Sewak Sangh was the name he proposed-to conscientise and mobilise the people to work and struggle for Swaraj. However none of these objectives were achieved when India became independent. India, although a federation, got a strong central government. Representative democracy, rather than direct democracy was adopted. The Congress Party was not disbanded. Rather it went on to become one of the frontrunners in running the government of India.

Additionally, modern India has kept in place many aspects of British (and Western) influence, including widespread use of the English language, Common-law, industrialization, liberal democracy, military organisation, and bureaucracy.

What is Swaraj?

The concept of swaraj, or self-rule, was developed during the Indian freedom struggle. In his book Hind Swaraj (1909), Gandhi sought to clarify that the meaning behind swaraj was much more than simply "wanting [systems of] English rule without the Englishman; the tiger's nature but not the tiger." The crux of his argument centered on the belief that the socio-spiritual underpinnings of British political, economic, bureaucratic, legal, military, and educational institutions were inherently unjust, exploitative and alienating. As Pinto explicates, "The principal theme of Hind Swaraj is the moral inadequacy of western civilization, especially its industrialism, as the model for free India." Gandhi was particularly critical of the deeply embedded principles of 'might is right' and 'survival of the fittest'.

On another level, the call for swaraj represents a genuine attempt to regain control of the 'self'-our self-respect, self-responsibility, and capacities for self-realization-from institutions of dehumanization. As Gandhi states, "It is swaraj when we learn to rule ourselves." The real goal of the freedom struggle was not only to secure political azadi (independence) from Britain, but rather to gain true swaraj (liberation and self-rule).

Gandhi wanted all those who believed in swaraj: (1) to reject and wholly uproot the British raj (rule) from within themselves and their communities; and, (2) to regenerate new reference points, systems, and structures that enable individual and collective self-development. This regeneration was to grow from the strengths, perspectives, wisdom and experiences of people living in village India, rather than from cities in Britain, America, and even in India for that matter. Understanding the real 'Self', and its relation to communities and society, is critical to the project of attaining swaraj.

How is this relevant for us today? We feel that South Asia (along with the rest of the world) is experiencing a tremendous crisis, one overwhelming in its scale and pace of growth. While it is easy to get caught up in the symptoms of this crisis (the brutal violence, the enormous inequities, the extinction of cultures and languages, the degradation of the environment), it is equally, if not more, important to understand its roots. We must creatively analyse the content and the consequences of our current economic, political, social, and educational systems, without reverting to a romanticized past of so-called untouched or pristine traditions. From these critical reflections, we must generate new spaces, systems, and processes-based on moral and holistic visions of human potential and human progress-which can lead us out of the global self-destruction which engulfs us. Throughout it all, we must consider and negotiate our own roles, while asking ourselves how we are either working for solutions or contributing to making the crisis worse. Thus, today, we recognize Gandhi's concept of swaraj integral to three parallel action-reflection agendas for the 21st century:

Decolonization of the Mind

Though the British were nonviolently compelled to physically withdrew from India in 1947, they left behind: Lord Macauley's governing class "of persons, Indian in blood and colour, but British in taste, in opinions, morals and in intellect"; several structures (political, economic, bureaucratic, legal, military and educational) which extended great privileges and powers to this elite class while devaluing peoples with other knowledge and cultural systems; and, a huge subclass of peoples impotently dependent on this elite class, their structures, knowledge systems, and 'modern' notions of progress. In sum, the British left behind a debilitating deficit framework in which Indians either saw (and continue to see) themselves as falsely inferior or chauvinistically superior to their former masters. In both cases, the reference points were in relation to catching up or surpassing the masters at their own game.

Deeply inspired by principled and radical critiques of the modern urban-industrial-military paradigm and the consequent alienation of human beings raised by thinkers and activists such as, Leo Tolstoy, John Ruskin, David Thoreau, and Ralph Waldo Emerson, Gandhi firmly believed that only when Indians dispelled their illusions about the 'progress' of modern Western civilization and the superiority of its role models could they move towards real liberation. Thus, on one level, Hind Swaraj can be seen to represent a post-modern critique of development. It calls for profoundly questioning and challenging the legitimacy of modern science/technology, the nation-state, the global economy, and factory-schooling – oppressive systems and structures of power which serve to define our existence. Ashis Nandy describes the starting point for a generative (rather than nihilistic) process of decolonization, "Criticism is the main thing [to building another kind of world]. It forces us to admit that no worldview, no ideology, no transformative principle automatically becomes morally acceptable just because, at this point of time, no one has produced a viable or convincing alternative to it. That keeps intact our moral sensitivities and forces us to search harder for new alternatives." We must regain our faith that there are other options for living.

However, this criticism must go beyond simply an institutional analysis if it wishes to be truly generative. Makarand Paranjape argues that decolonization must be "more centered on the Self than on the Other. By decolonizing myself, I mean developing myself and my society fully, realizing our potential, enlarging our capacities – rather than displacing, overthrowing or defeating the Other." *Swaraj* means engaging in processes of self-understanding and self-reflection to rebuild a self-confidence that is free from arrogance, hatred or egoism. We must acknowledge that we are both 'oppressed' and 'oppressors' and seek to understand what roles we play as oppressors and in supporting institutions of oppression. We must also re-evaluate our own wants and needs and seek to understand how these are manipulated and controlled by others.

Decolonization of the Mind

Though the British were nonviolently compelled to physically withdrew from India in 1947, they left behind: Lord Macauley's governing class "of persons, Indian in blood and colour, but British in taste, in opinions, morals and in intellect"; several structures (political, economic, bureaucratic, legal, military and educational) which extended great privileges and powers to this elite class while devaluing peoples with other knowledge and cultural systems; and, a huge subclass of peoples impotently dependent on this elite class, their structures, knowledge systems, and 'modern' notions of progress. In sum, the British left behind a debilitating deficit framework in which Indians either saw (and continue to see) themselves as falsely inferior or chauvinistically superior to their former masters. In both cases, the reference points were in relation to catching up or surpassing the masters at their own game. Deeply inspired by principled and radical critiques of the modern urban-industrial-military paradigm and the consequent alienation of human beings raised by thinkers and activists such as, Leo Tolstoy, John Ruskin, David Thoreau, and Ralph Waldo Emerson, Gandhi firmly believed that only when Indians dispelled their illusions about the 'progress' of modern Western civilization and the superiority of its role models could they move towards real liberation. Thus, on one level, Hind Swaraj can be seen to represent a post-modern critique of development. It calls for profoundly questioning and challenging the legitimacy of modern science/technology, the nation-state, the global economy, and factory-schooling – oppressive systems and structures of power which serve to define our existence. Ashis Nandy describes the starting point for a generative (rather than nihilistic) process of decolonization, "Criticism is the main thing [to building another kind of world]. It forces us to admit that no worldview, no ideology, no transformative principle automatically becomes morally acceptable just because, at this point of time, no one has produced a viable or convincing alternative to it. That keeps intact our moral sensitivities and forces us to search harder for new alternatives." We must regain our faith that there are other options for living.

However, this criticism must go beyond simply an institutional analysis if it wishes to be truly generative. Makarand Paranjape argues that decolonization must be "more centered on the Self than on the Other. By decolonizing myself, I mean developing myself and my society fully, realizing our potential, enlarging our capacities – rather than displacing, overthrowing or defeating the Other." *Swaraj* means engaging in processes of self-understanding and self-reflection to rebuild a self-confidence that is free from arrogance, hatred or egoism. We must acknowledge that we are both 'oppressed' and 'oppressors' and seek to understand what roles we play as oppressors and in supporting institutions of oppression. We must also re-evaluate our own wants and needs and seek to understand how these are manipulated and controlled by others.

Creative Regeneration

Gandhi's notion of Swaraj was, however, much more than simply a reactionary attempt towards decolonization in which the reference points for action and reflection were framed solely in relation to colonialism. The genius of Gandhi lies in taking us beyond post-modernist critiques of deconstructing the existing system and also beyond bivalent solutions, which force us to choose only between tradition vs. modernity. Swaraj is essentially a constructivist agenda and is linked to creating a new path for humanity. With this in mind, Gandhi links his Constructive Work Programme for village regeneration as a critical process in achieving purna (complete) swaraj. In this vision of development, action and reflection are necessarily deeply intertwined.

Swaraj is relevant to us today, in that, it represents a deep recognition that people themselves must continuously strive to create a different set of reference points, institutions, structures and processes-which are consistent with the diverse cultures, values, philosophies, wisdom traditions, and needs of the subcontinent as well as with the principles of the natural world-to inspire and guide their own development. Such development must be geared towards supporting the struggle to liberate our individual and collective potentialities and to discover what it means to be fully human. It must be linked to and guided by larger principles of justice, love and hope.

Critical to the concept of swaraj is a pluralistic and organic outlook on development: there is not, nor can there ever be, just one model for the entire world. Swaraj also requires that we regain our faith in the capacity of human beings and restore agency/locus of power back to individual and local communities (and stop seeing human beings as 'victims' or 'beneficiaries' or 'targets'). The process of swaraj seeks to create a reflective and participatory context for people to ask who we have been, who we are, and who we want to become, without the interference and intervention from externally-driven, prescriptive and homogenizing models of development. Underlying, catalyzing and providing continuous feedback to this process must be new opportunities and systems for conscious learning, un-learning, and re-learning which unleash the creativity, sensitivity and intrinsic motivation of people.

Interpreting Gandhi's Hind Swaraj

GANDHI's *Hind Swaraj* (HS) is surely a foundational text for any understanding of the man and his mission. In dialogue with the text in its context, with the author and among ourselves, we hope to locate the text within it's own horizon of meaning and then interrogate it from within our own contemporary. For Gandhi's text is "a proclamation of ideological independence" [Dalton 1993:61] he never compromised, his "confession of the faith" [Nanda 1974:66] he never abandoned, "a rather incendiary manifesto" [Erikson 1969:217] to enkindle his revolution. No wonder it was banned by the colonial government in 1910 for fear of sedition.

Gandhi's Critique of the Modern West

For Gandhi civilisation was by definition a moral enterprise: "Civilisation is that mode of conduct which points out to man the path of duty" (HS, Ch 13). Hence it is the very basic ethos of this modern west that Gandhi sets himself against. For he finds two unacceptable and unethical principles at its very core: 'might is right' and the 'survival of the fittest'. The first legitimated the politics of power as expounded earlier by Machiaveli; the second idealised the economics of self-interest as proposed by Adam Smith. In the west "with rare exceptions, alternatives to western civilisation are always sought within its own basic thought system" [Saran 1980:681].

The three recurrent themes in *Hind Swaraj* which we will discuss here are: colonial imperialism, industrial capitalism, and rationalist materialism.

Colonial imperialism: Gandhi categorically insisted that "the English have not taken India; we have given it to them. They are not in India because of their strength: but because we keep them" (HS, Ch 7). He was one of the earliest to realise that colonialism was something to be overcome in our own consciousness first [Nandy 1983:63]. Unless this 'Intimate Enemy' was exorcised and exiled, unless we addressed this 'Loss and Recovery of Self Under Colonialism' (ibid), we would always be a people enslaved by one power or another, whether foreign or native. Certainly, Gandhi would not want to exchange an external colonialism for an internal one, a white sahib for a brown one, or compensate the loss of 'Hindustan' with 'Englistan' (HS, Ch 4).

British India colonialism was first justified by a supposedly Christianising mission, but very soon this was articulated in terms of a civilising one. In rejecting this modern civilisation, Gandhi is subverting the legitimacy of the colonial enterprise at its core. For there could be no colonialism without a civilising mission [Nandy 1983:11] since it could hardly be sustained in India by brute force.

Industrial capitalism: Gandhi sees capitalism as the dynamic behind colonial imperialism. Lenin too had said as much, and like Marx, Gandhi's rejection of capitalism is based on a profound repugnance to a system where profit is allowed to degrade labour, where the machines are valued more than humans, where automation is preferred to humanism.

It was this that moved Gandhi to his somewhat hyperbolic claim: "Machinery is the chief symbol of modern civilisation; it represents a great sin" (HS, Ch 19). However, by 1919 his views on machinery do begin to change right up to 1947, as he gradually comes to concede some positive aspects like time and labour saving, even as he warns against the negative ones of concentrating wealth and displacing workers [Parel 1997:164-70]. He was acutely sensitive to how machinery can dehumanise and technology alienate, and he extends his critique to the professions of medicine and law (HS, Chs 11, 12). The poor hardly benefit from these professional services, though they are often their victims. He backs up his criticism of these professions in *Hind Swaraj* with a later suggestion for their nationalisation (CW, 68:97).

Rationalist materialism: Technology is but the expression of science, which in modern civilisation becomes an uncompromising rationalism. For Gandhi this is but a dangerously truncated humanism. His incisive remark is much to the point: "Just as dirt is matter misplaced, reason misplaced is lunacy! I plead not for the suppression of Reason, but for a due recognition of that in us which sanctifies reason itself' (CW, 6:106). Certainly, Gandhi is right in insisting on the unreasonableness of not setting any limits to reason.

More recently a post-modern world has emphasised the aggressive and destructive march of this 'age of reason'. However, Gandhi would test his faith with his reason, but he would not allow his reason to destroy his faith. What makes such technological rationalism even more destructive in Gandhi's view, is its flawed materialism. That is, the negation of the spiritual, the transcendent, or in other words, the denial of a religious worldview.

For Gandhi truth, was much more than could be grasped by science or reason. For him there was a reality beyond that perceived by the senses. It is this transcendent reality that gave meaning and value to our present one. In this Gandhi is very much in the mainstream of Hindu tradition. Indeed, most religious traditions would be similarly sensitive to such a transcendent world, even when it is not perceived as wholly other-worldly. In a more secular world today we may not be sympathetic to such a worldview. And yet a materialism that is deterministic leaves no scope for human freedom and hope. Gandhi emphasises this reaching out to a beyond, that gives this freedom and hope its dynamism and a reach beyond its grasp.

Relevance of Gandhi's Critique Today

Gandhi's critique of modern civilisation does overlook many of its strengths; its scientific and critical spirit of inquiry; its human control over the natural world; its organisational capacity. Such achievement would imply a certain 'spiritual dimension' that Gandhi seems to have missed [Parekh 1997:35]. However, the focus of his criticism is modern civilisation of a specific period; his condemnation of colonialism focuses on its imperialistic inspiration; his rejection of industrialism derives mostly from its capitalist context; his apprehensions about rationality regard its truncation by materialism. However, once the real limitations of Gandhi's critique are acknowledged, then we can better contextualise and interpret his relevance for us today, whether this be with regard to politics in our neo-colonial world, or technologies in our post-industrial times, or culture in our post-modern age. These will now be some of the issues on which we must allow Gandhi to interrogate us. For "the kinds of questions Gandhi asked nearly eight decades ago are the ones which now face both the underdeveloped and the post-industrial societies caught up in a deep upsurge of confusion and disillusionment" [Sethi 1979:3].

Neo-colonialism: Gandhi's rejection of the supposedly civilising mission of colonialism brings into question the whole legitimacy of colonial rule, at a fundamental ethical level. He would have

India unlearn much that she has from the modern west. For if Indians "would but revert to their own glorious civilisation, either the English would adopt the latter and become Indianised or find their occupation in India gone" (HS, Preface to English edition). Thus, he opens up a host of ethical issues between the coloniser and the colonised, the dominant and the dominated, the oppressor and oppressed. The post-colonial era brought such issues into sharper focus across the world. Now with globalisation leading to a unipolar world, such concerns with empowerment and disempowerment, dependency and interdependency, have gained, not lost their urgency. Moreover, closer home this widening divide bears down on us more decisively than ever before.

Our new economic policy increasingly represents a whole new vision of society, that takes for granted the internal colonialism we are experiencing today, as for instance between Bharat and India, the bahujan and the twice-born jatis, the avarna and the savarna castes, the toiling masses and the privileged classes, the oppressed people and the oppressor groups, the minority traditions and the majority one. Thus, our post-colonial world can only be described as a neo-colonial one, internationally divided into developed and developing nations, as also intra-nationally between privileged and underprivileged citizens. Moreover, these divisions are mutually reinforced, not just economically and politically but culturally and socially as well. Moreover, the west is still the centre of our world for we have not the self-respect, the self-reliance, the self-sufficiency to centre ourselves and so we condemn ourselves to remain on the periphery of someone else's centre. For the colonial masters had stripped our collective identity of any intrinsic dignity by denigrating us as a cowardly and passive people. Gandhi sought to reverse the damage to our collective psyche by his "redefinition of courage and effective resistance in terms of, or through nonviolence" [Roy 1986:185]. The issue then of our identity as a nation and a people still remains to be resolved. Such identities are only viable in a genuinely multicultural world. Gandhi's urging in this regard is certainly relevant today in our own society where the propagation of a cultural nationalism is growing every day. Yet "nothing could be more anti-Indian than attempts to make an ideology of Indianness and to fight, instead of incorporating or bypassing non-Indianness" [Nandy 1980:112].

Post-industrialism: With the new technologies there was much hope for a new freedom from degrading and monotonous work. However, what seems to have come in to replace this degrading monotony is not a new dignity of labour but rather a compulsive consumerist society, which is but dehumanising in newer ways. This should hardly surprise us since the ethic underlying post-industrialism is the same as that which underpinned industrial capitalism, namely, the profit motive and the market mechanism.

Gandhi's critique was precisely a condemnation of these. If we find his ideas of trusteeship a little naive and impractical, we still have no alternative answer to humanising a system that seems to have betrayed what possibilities it might have had of bringing freedom and dignity to the toiling masses. Moreover, technology has its own intrinsic dynamism, that instrumentalises our world and inevitably leads to a disenchantment that bring us to the 'iron cage', as Weber warned long ago. Our environmental crises are surely a manifestation of this loss of innocence, even to the point when we want newer technologies to repair the damage already done by the older ones. Gandhi was precisely rejecting such a naive "nineteenth century optimism which sought for the positive sciences the liberation of humanity" [Nandy 1986:102]. But such anti-modernism then was ahead of its time!

Post-modernism: The excessive and aggressive rationalism of the age of reason, now seems to have turned on itself with the post-modem revolt. But this has thrown up its own irrationalities. It seems to have lost the liberating project that was implicit in modernity. For the kind of relativising and subjectivising of ethics that post-modernism has led to, undermines the claims of any justice. For there can hardly be any mutually accepted legitimacy to arbitrate conflicting claims, when consensus irrevocably breaks down. So, might becomes right, and the power its own legitimation.

Gandhi's trenchant critique of modernity was focused on modernist rationalism, but it was equally opposed to a post-modern rejection of rationality. What Gandhi was pleading for is a richer concept of rationality and a meta-theory of rationalism [Parekh 1995:165-66]. He wanted to contain excessive rationality within reasonable bounds without an irrational revolt against reason itself, but he would emphatically reject any forced choice between totalising rationalism and relativising subjectivism.

Gandhi's Affirmation of Indian Culture

Gandhi's *Hind Swaraj* presents us with an idealised version of Indian culture that is completely counterpunctal to the 'modern west'. Here we pick out three seminal themes: swaraj, swadeshi and satya.

Swaraj: Gandhi radically re-interprets 'swaraj' and gives it a dual meaning. The original Gujarati text uses 'swaraj' in both senses. Gandhi's English translation makes the duality explicit: swaraj as 'self-rule' and as 'self-government'. The first as self-control, rule over oneself, was the foundation for the second, self-government. In this second sense, local self~government was what Gandhi really had in mind. Gandhi very decidedly gives priority to self-rule over self-government, and to both over political independence, swatantrata.

Essential to both meanings swaraj, was a sense of self-respect that is precisely Gandhi's answer to colonial rule. For Gandhi freedom in its most fundamental sense had to mean freedom for self-realisation. But it had to be a freedom for all, for the toiling masses, and the privileged classes, and most importantly for the least and last Indian. In this sense, sarvodaya was precisely the patriotism that Gandhi espoused. It focused on people's welfare not on national pride: "By patriotism I mean the welfare of the whole people, and, if I could secure it at the hands of the English, I should bow down my head to them" (HS. Ch 15). So he could write: "my patriotism is for me a stage on my journey to the land of freedom and peace" *(Young India,* April 13, 1924, p 112). And yet swaraj was not something given by the leaders, Indian or British, it was something that had to be taken by the people for themselves.

Clearly, the foundation of swaraj in both its senses had to be threefold: self-respect, self-realisation and self-reliance. This is what Gandhi tried to symbolise with the chakra and Khadi, both much misunderstood symbols today. For Gandhi Khadi "is the symbol of the unity of Indian humanity, of its economic freedom and equality and therefore ultimately in the poetic expression of Jawaharlal Nehru, the livery of India's freedom" (CW75:146-66). Today the chakra and Khadi have not retained this powerful multivalent symbolism.

Yet the ethic that Gandhi was trying to introduce and inscribe into Indian political life was that "real swaraj will not be the acquisition of authority by a few but the acquisition of the capacity of all to resist authority when it is abused" [Prabhu 1961:4-5]. For Gandhi "Civilisation is that mode of conduct which points out to man the path duty" (HS, Ch 13). The basis then of his swaraj could not be just rights, it had to be duties as well. For Gandhi real rights are legitimated by duties they flow from, for both are founded on satya and dharma. The modern theory of rights reverses this priority and founds rights on the dignity and freedom of the individual. But comprehensive morality can never be adequately articulated or correctly grasped in terms of rights alone.

Swadeshi: Swadeshi is the means for Gandhi's quest for swaraj. Fundamentally it meant 'localism'. This was not an isolated localism of the "deserted village", that Goldsmith romanticed, or the degradation of caste oppression that Ambedkar revolted against, but rather the local neighbourhood community, the village as the node in a network of oceanic circles that over-lapped and spread out in its ever widening embrace. It is this commitment of the individual to his 'desh' that was Gandhi's Indian alternative to western nationalism [Parekh 1995:56-57].

Gandhi perceived that power in India was inevitably monopolised by the urban elite, at the expense of village folk, and was trying to reverse this dependency to make the state serve the weaker sections. His was an egalitarian, not just a romantic, inspiration. Mao attempted as much in China. But the village Gandhi idealised was not just a geographic place, or a statistic, or a social class. It was an event, a dream, a happening, a culture. As he used "the term 'village' implied not an entity, but a set of values" [Sethi 1979:23]. It brought together his three basic themes of swaraj: self-respect, self-realisation and self-reliance.

In privileging the rural over the urban, Gandhi was arguing for a minimal state, since he saw the state essentially as an instrument of violence. It was only in the communal cauldron at the time of partition, that he began to see the need of state power to contain and end the violence. And yet our experience of the post-colonial state in this hod of dialogue that would bring two disagreeing parties not just into mutual agreement, but into the realisation of a deeper truth together. The dichotomy between the oppressor and the oppressed is transcended in this 'heightened mutuality', but even beyond this "satyagraha ruptures the tricotomy among the oppressor, oppressed and emancipator" [Pantham 1986:179], for it seeks to involve all three in this quest of greater self-realisation of the truth. From the satyagrahi as the initiator, this required a demanding discipline.

But satyagraha was also a politic strategy. In *Hind Swaraj* Gandhi defines 'passive resistance' as he called it then as "a method of securing rights by person suffering"(HS, Ch 17). Clearly, "Gandhi's satyagraha then was an ingenious combination of reason, morality and politics; it appealed to the opponent's head, heart and interests" [Parekh 1995:156].

This was a "vernacular model of action [Parekh 1995:211] that the people understood. But it was Gandhi who first used it so effectively to moblise them and to appeal to their oppressors. In fact he was the first leader to bring nonviolence to centre stage in the struggle for freedom with the British. He was well aware that adopting "methods of violence to drive out the English" would be a "suicidal policy"(HS, Ch 15). And his *Hind Swaraj* was precisely intended to stymie such a soul-destroying venture.

Gandhi's re-interpretation: Gandhi locates himself as an insider to mainstream Hinduism, the 'sanathan dharma'. Hence, the radicality of his re-interpretation goes unnoticed. Gandhi does not reject, he simply affirms what he considers to be authentic, and allows the inauthentic to be sloughed off. For "Gandhi's Hinduism was ultimately reduced to a few fundamental beliefs: the supreme reality of God, the ultimate unity of all life and the value of love (ahimsa) as a means of realising God" [Nanda 1985:6]. His profound redefinition of Hinduism gave it a radically novel orientation. In sum, "Gandhi's Hinduism had a secularised content but a spiritual form and was at once both secular and non-secular" [Parekh1995:109]. Thus one of the most remarkable and yet unremarked re-interpretations of Hinduism that Gandhi effected was that of the Gita, a text intended to persuade a reluctant warrior on the legitimacy and even the necessity of joining the battle. Gandhi reworks its 'nishkamakarma' to become the basis of his ahimsa and satyagraha!

We have only to contrast Gandhi's Hinduism with V D Savarkar's hindutva to see how starkly contrapunctal they are!

Hence, in spite of its pretensions to be nationalist and modern, its militant chauvinism and authoritarian fundamentalism make hindutva the very antithesis of Gandhi's Hinduism. Hindutva is in fact but a contemporary synthesis of brahmanism! This is why in the end the Mahatma is vehemently opposed by the traditional Hindu elite, who felt threatened by the challenge he posed.

But precisely because he presents himself as a Hindu in his interpretation of Indian culture, he was seen as too inclusive by traditional Hindus, and at the same time as not ecumenical enough by contemporary non-Hindus. Hence his appeals for Hindu-Muslim unity were rejected, by the Muslims as being too Hindu, and questioned by the Hindus for not being Hindu enough.

Gandhi's failure to bridge the religious divide between Hindu and Muslim, was matched in many ways by his failure to bridge the caste divide between dalits and others. He never quite understood Jinnah, or his appeal to Muslim nationalism. One could say the same in regard to Ambedkar and dalits, who have never forgotten or forgiven Gandhi for the imposition of the Pune Pact. We can only wonder now whether separate electorates for dalits then would have made reservations for them unnecessary now. What we do know is that the caste divide has only deepened with increasing conflict and indeed the same can be said about the religious divide and religious conflict in this country.

Yet for Gandhi the unity of humankind was premised on the oneness of the cosmos, which was a philosophical principle that was ontologically prior to diversity. Once the legitimacy of religious diversity is rooted in the fundamental Jaina principle of 'anekantavada', the many sidedness of truth, then religious tolerance is a necessary consequence — not a negative tolerance of distance and coexistence, but rather one of communication and enrichment [Heredia 1997].

In cultural matters, Gandhi wanted all cultures to be enriched by each other without losing their identity. But such cultural assimilation, was opposed by political revivalists and religious nationalists. Yet for Gandhi open and understanding dialogue must precede, not follow, a free and adaptive assimilation. Thus, an enriched diversity would then contribute to a more invigourated pluralism and an enhanced unity. This was precisely Gandhi's understanding of Indian culture and civilisation, and he had, indeed, grasped its fundamental strength and the secret of its survival.

Our World Today

We must now situate ourselves with regard to the critical issues of our world today to enter into dialogue with him. Here we have chosen three such issues as being the most fruitful for this encounter: the collapse of socialism and the crisis of capitalism, gobalisation in an interdependent world, and the unresolved violence of our atomic age.

Post-socialism: In our present world, the socialist ideal is being discredited as a god that failed, when it is rather the once socialist states that have collapsed. Moreover, today the crisis of capitalism is everyday more apparent, with the collapse of the much acclaimed Asian tigers as the new model for the cornucopia of development and progress; and the growing unemployment in the west cannot but presage further crises there as well. With liberalisation and privatisation as accepted policy in our country today, the Bharat verses India divide, that Gandhi had intuited long ago, is, if anything, rapidly and disastrously growing. Only now the elite of Bharat seems to have been co-opted by the privileged of India, even as the refugees of India have been forced into an urbanised Bharat. Much has been made about the disagreements between Gandhi and Nehru. But in the exchange of letters in 1945 [Parel 1997:149-56], it is quite clear that the axis of their reconciliation was precisely around this quest for equality. Their paths may have been different but Nehru's socialism and Gandhi's swaraj were both oriented to this quest for equity and equality across all the divides, of caste, class, region, etc.

Gandhi was quite radical in urging equality, even more so than the communists. He would have equal wages and bread labour for all. In his 'Constructive Programme' (CW, 75:146-66), Gandhi's concept of equality is not grounded in impersonal and competitive individualism, as it seems to be in the west, but in cooperative and compassionate nonviolence, on 'fraternity' not just 'liberty'. In the beginning, he saw no contradiction between such fraternal equality and the idealised hierarchy of varna. But in his later years he reversed himself to urge that "classless society is the ideal, not merely to be at aimed at but to be worked for" (*Harijan*, February 17, 1946, p 9). By now he was promoting inter-caste marriages and hoping "there would be only one caste known by the beautiful name Bhangi, that is to say the reformer or remover of all dirt" (*Harijan*, July 7, 1946, p 212).

But if Gandhi's quest for equality is something that our complex world cannot accommodate, we seem to have given up not just this ideal of equality, but even the quest for equity in the distribution of the rewards and burdens of our society. And yet today Gandhi's proletarian 'levelling down' certainly seems to be much more viable that Tagore's elitist 'levelling up'. In such a scenario the relevance of Gandhi's idea of sarvodaya as the goal of swaraj is something we need to re-examine. Certainly, a decentralised participative democratic and humane society, is a more attractive, and one may dare say, a more vialable ideal today, than the kind of consumerism and inequitous divisions that the new economic policy in our country seems to welcome.

Indeed, the principle of subsidiarity seems to be the only viable solution to national governments that are too large to address local problems, while being too small to cope with global ones. Today the 73rd and 74th amendment to the Constitution once again affirm panchayati raj and tribal self-rule. We are coming back to a devolution of powers that Gandhi had urged in his ideal of swaraj and had tried to have written in to our Constitution. Hopefully this will be a presage of more to come.

Globalisation: Globalisation and the alienating homogeneity that it must inevitably promote, is the very opposite of the localism and the celebration of diversity that Gandhi's swadeshi was meant to encourage. However, Gandhi's principle of swadeshi, "simply means that the most effective organisation of social, economic and political functions must follow the natural contours of the neighbourhood," thus affirming "the primacy of the immediate community" [Roy 1985:114]. Gandhi's "goodness politics" as it has been called [Saran 1980:691], could only really operate on such a scale. For "Gandhi decentralisation means the creation of parallel politics in which the people's power is institutionalised to counter the centralising and alienating forces of the modern state... Thus the Gandhian decentralised polity has a built-in process of the withering away of the state" [Sethi 1986:229].

But before this is dismissed as too naive or impractical for our sophisticated and complicated world, we might pause to think of the kind of politics our centralised states have in fact spawned. The very hegemonic homogeneity it promotes succeeds less at obliterating difference than at alienating minorities and enkindling their resentment. On the contrary, to take a lesson from ecology, micro-variability is needed for macro-stability in political and economic systems as well.

Gandhi's swadeshi could never mean ethnocentrism. Unlike some Hindu and Muslim 'nationalists' Gandhi never used 'nationalism' for narrow sectarian purposes. He mobilised his people as 'Indians' not as Hindus or Muslims. His nationalism was anti-imperialistic not chauvinistic, a struggle for political justice and cultural dignity [Nandy 1994:3]. He was a patriot who wanted "Indian nationalism to be nonviolent, anti-militaristic and therefore a variant of universalism" [Nandy 1995:14]. He was only too aware of the number of 'nationalities' that could be moblised in India, once the genie was out of the bottle!

An ecological understanding is now propelling us to a new and deep realisation of our interdependence. We have only one earth, we must learn to share and care. We are but a contingent part of the cosmos, debtors born, whose proper response to life must be the 'yagna', service-offering of our lives for others [Parekh 1995:88]. Thus, with regard to the economy and polity, Gandhi would have the village as his world; but with regard to culture and religion, it was the world that was his village! Surely, here we have a viable example of thinking globally and acting locally. Indeed, our global ecological crisis has begun to press on us anew the relevance of Gandhi's paradoxical ideas. For the institutional individualism that seemed to be the very foundation of the democratic quest in the west seems quite inadequate to the ecological crises of today. For it privileges individual rights over the common good. But even enlightened self-interest has no answer to the 'tragedy of the commons' accept an external coercion.

However, for Gandhi, "individuality" must be "oriented to self-realisation through self-knowledge... in a network of interdependence and harmony informed by ahimsa" [Roy 1986a:84]. Nor was this to be an interdependence of dominant-subservient relationships so prevalent in our local communities and global societies. His swadeshi envisaged a more personalised and communitarian society on a human scale, yet extending to include both the biotic and even the cosmic community. This was the logical extension of the Jaina doctrine of 'syadvada', that everything is related to everything in the universe in 'a great chain of being'.

However, the Gandhian ideal was a community modelled on the joint family and on varna as a non-competitive division of labour. Later in his life his own promotion of inter-caste marriages testifies to a change in his views. Yet even as we critique such Gandhian ideas, we must discover in dialogue what value and relevance they have for us today. For ultimately Gandhi insists on both: that the community is not a mere means for the self-interest of the individual and that the individual in not a mere resource for the concerns of the community. And this would go for the community of communities, that our global community must be.

Violence: There can be no negating the liberation that modernity has brought in our post-modern world to vast masses of people. But for all its much vaulted 'rationality' some would rather say because of it, modernity has failed to cope with this endemic irrationality of violence. If Gandhi's ahimsa seems impractical, what are the alternative we have trapped ourselves in? If Gandhi was right that "to arm India on a large scale is to Europeanise it," (HS, Ch 15) then what would nuclear arms do? Americanise us? And this is an initiative being pushed by our cultural nationalists! But then in a globalized world it is surely only the elite that will get to strut and fret upon this global stage, while the masses of our people are a passive and manipulated audience to this theatre of the macabre.

The whole effort of the modern world in dealing with violence has the 'Sermon on the Mount' and reads one into the other. In fact, if he has Christianised Hinduism he has certainly also presented us with a Hinduised Christian spirituality.

Precisely as a re-interpretation from within, Gandhi can so much to more effectively and authentically integrate into his synthesis elements from without. Thus he reconciles meaningful faith and reasonable modernity. In the best traditions of this land he combined both faith and reason, for each is implicated in each other. Gandhi would constantly critique faith to ascertain whether it was meaningful and reasonable in terms of basic human value commitments. And so too he would demand of reason the same fidelity to these values as well.

However, the ascetic dimension of Gandhi's integration at times loses the aesthetic one. A criticism of Gandhi's ashrams was that it grew only vegetables not flowers [Parekh 1995:209]. Growing vegetables represented more than the Gandhian pre-occupation with vegetarianism and bread-labour. But in rightly emphasising the need for renunciation, certainly a message that our consumerist and self-indulgent world needs more than ever today, the Gandhian ashram seemed to miss out on the need for celebration, which our tired and alienated, dis-spirited and pessimistic world needs almost as much.

A re-interpretation of Gandhi would precisely allow such a celebration. While Gandhi's understanding of 'moksha' as service is a seminal breakthrough, even this can be enriched by affirming, not negating the other dimensions of life. It is only thus that we will be able to bring some wholeness to, in Iris Murdoch's unforgettable phrase, the "broken totality," of our modern world.

Conclusion: Partners in Dialogue

Gandhi's life was a continuing series of controversies and contestations with those in power on behalf of the powerless. He never lacked opponents, among the British and even the Indian elites, and often found himself isolated and alone particularly at the end of his life, which was far from being one long triumphant procession. Yet one of the great contributions of Gandhi was precisely his centring of the periphery: in politics with 'anthyodaya'; in religion by de-brahamising Hinduism, de-institutionalising practice and personalising belief; in education by his proposal for 'nai talim' or basic education as it came to be called; in the economy by symbolically urging khadhi. Not all of these efforts were successful or perhaps even practical, but they did make a contribution which is still valid today. And all Gandhi's original ideas can be found seeded already in his *Hind Swaraj*.

Today we need a new developmental model, and increasingly people are beginning to see that. It has to begin by "Putting the

Last First" [Chambers 1983], to come back to the last Indian that Gandhi would have as the talisman of our social planning. No one can claim that Gandhi's reformist appeal has fulfilled the 'revolution of raising expectations' of our masses. This only underscores the need for a more fine-tuned analysis and a wider dialogue in our society for constructive change given the limits of reformism and the constraints on revolution. If we are looking for a new synthesis for a counter-culture, we must take Gandhi as a dialogue partner in this project but first we must redefine and re-interpret him. Such an encounter will help us to re-examine and reconstruct ourselves as well.

Gandhi has been severely criticised as impractical, as someone who took out an impossible overdraft on human moral resources. But this is to claim that human beings are not capable of a metanoia, a radical change of heart, that can open up new perspectives, not just for individuals and groups, but for entire societies and whole cultures as well. We need organic intellectuals and transformative activists who can articulate and precipitate such a social movement. The cascading crises that our society and our world is experiencing, only underlines more emphatically the need to find new ways of redefining ourselves and understanding our problems, before we can begin to respond to the situation.

3

Gandhi and Satyagraha

Introduction

With satyagraha, Mahatma Gandhi ushered in a new era of civilian resistance on the political scenario of the world. The word was coined to aptly define the mode of nonviolent resistance that the Indians at South Africa were building against the oppressive British colonialists. The word has been variedly interpreted, but literally it is a combination of two words, signifying truth and force. By connotation, it means an unshaken faith in truth, unwavering even in the face of adversity. Satyagraha for Gandhi was the only legitimate way to earn one's political rights, as it was based on the ideals of truth and nonviolence. Satyagraha was the key aspect of all revolutions of the Indian National Movement in the Gandhian era of Indian history for more twenty long years, and its legacy was carried on long after him as Martin Luther King used it in his battle against racism. Satyagraha has not been free of criticism, but its methodologies have gained wide acceptance around the world as a more potent tool of resistance than armed violence.

Origins of Satyagraha: Term and Influences

Gandhi was in need of a term to connote the revolution against the British imperialists that he organized in South Africa. 'Passive resistance', his first perfunctory choice, was not only a foreign term that Gandhi had strong reservations about, but the connotations of the term was also inadequate to highlight the aspect of truth and moral courage that Gandhi associated with nonviolent political resistance. Moreover, it put political ends at the forefront, dissociated from deeper ideological values. Gandhi needed an Indian name that could encompass all these aspects of the revolution within it. A competition was thrown open in the local newspaper, 'Indian Opinion', and 'sadagraha' was elected as the best entry. Gandhi took the term, but changed it to 'satyagraha' highlighting the aspect of 'truth' in it. 'Satyagraha' was based on the principles of nonviolence, which was the founding principle of Gandhi's political ideology, that was based on as much as theological tenets of Jainism, Buddhism, Upanishads and the Bhagwatgita, as on the political theories of Tolstoy, Ruskin and Thureau.

Satyagraha: Definition and Method

Satyagraha is fundamentally a way of life, which guides the modes of political activism undertaken by the followers of its principle (or satyagrahis). On a personal front it involves a life committed to truth, chastity, non-attachment and hard-work. On the political front, satyagraha involves utilisation of nonviolent measures to curb the opponent, and ideally to convert him rather than to coerce him into submission. A satyagrahi wants to make the evildoers see the evil that they are indulging into, and realize their injustice. In an ideal way, it involves transforming them into acceptance of the right, and if that fails to come around, then at least to stop them from obstructing the right. Picketing, non-cooperation, peaceful marches and meetings, along with a peaceful disobedience of the laws of the land were typical modes of resistance adopted by satyagraha. Reverence to the opposition was one of the unique features of the satyagraha preached by Gandhi. Under no circumstance, should the opposition or the flag of the opposition be insulted in a Satyagraha movement. Resistance on the part of the authorities would be expected, but a true Satyagrahi had to bear all hardships, including physical assault with patience, not ever stooping to anger, and to defend the faith even at the cost of life. Gandhi believed that the Satyagrahis had to be extremely strong in inner strength and moral courage in order to do that, and also realized that could not be achieved unless the Satyagrahis maintained a pure and simple life. He made his own life a veritable example of his teachings, and also turned his ashram at Sabarmati as a haven for individuals who chose to maintain a life based on his teachings. Nonviolence of all forms were to be resisted and refrained from. Abuses and swearing were strictly prohibited and all forms of abstinence from sensual pleasures were highly advocated. Hard labour was an integral part of Satyagraha. Every one was meant to work for his or her food and the clothes. Khadi developed as the very mark of nationalism, and simple life became the order of the day. Absolute secularism and eradication of every shade of untouchability were also distinct characteristics of satyagraha. It was only in such a way, Gandhi believed, that the Indians would be strong enough to tread the paths of a truly nonviolent revolution.

Satyagraha in the Indian National Movement

Gandhi achieved success in the revolutions he led in South Africa by following the path of Satyagraha. He had an innate belief that it would succeed in India too. In fact, Gandhi had an innate belief that it would be the only effective way to fight the powerful British, because two centuries of colonial rule has financially and morally emasculated India to such a degree, that any other form of resistance was bound to fail. Gandhi's satyagraha methods had few takers in his early years at the Indian National Congress. However, under the able guidance of Gopal Krishna Gokhale, Gandhi's method gradually gained acceptance. Gandhi shot into political prominence by successfully employing methods of Satyagraha at the indigo planters revolution at Champaran in Bihar. The same method was repeated with similar results at Kheda in Gujarat against the raised taxes from the British authorities. Satyagraha became the foundation of the noncooperation movement of 1920, following the infamous Rowlatt Act. Noncooperation movement ended unceremoniously with the Chauri Chaura incident. However, it was during the Civil Disobedience movement that Gandhi re-inroduced satyagraha in a big way. His peaceful denial of government rules started with the celebrated Dandi march and the making of salt on 12th March 1930, defying the British Salt Law that prohibited the making of salt without government permission. Although ridiculed in the early years by a majority of the Western and particularly British press, the true power of satyagraha was soon realised by the British government, as all government endeavours and enterprises were in doldrums following mass boycott from Indians. Gandhis's satyagraha reached the pinnacle of success, and Indian Nationalist movement reached a feverish pitch, forcing the government to initiate procedures towards the Gandhi-Irwin pact, followed by the second round table conference, where Gandhi gave one of his greatest speeches exposing the evils of the British rule and endorsing the methods of satyagraha.

Satyagraha by that time has gained wide popularity, and there were committed satyagrahis all over the country. Quit India Movement reclaimed the ideals of satyagraha, which finally went a long in securing Indian independence.

The Legacy of Satyagraha

Gandhi had to pay for his ideals with his life, but he never veered from his innate faith in nonviolence and his belief in the methods of satyagraha. The significance of satyagraha was soon accepted worldwide. Martin Luther King adopted the methods of satyagraha in his fight against the racial discrimination of the American authorities in 1950.

Satyagraha is more than a political tool of resistance. It is a holistic approach towards life, based on the ideals of truth and moral courage. The similarity of the satyagraha to some of the greatest philosophical and religious tenets of the world have been observed and much written about. However, in the specific context of India, Satyagraha was an immense influence. It went a long way in instilling among the Indians a dignity for hard labour and mutual respect. In the traditional Indian society torn apart by caste and creed based discriminations, satyagraha stated that no work was lowly. It championed secularism and went a long way in eradicating untouchability from the heart of India's typically stratified society. Satyagraha glorified the role of women as an important member of the society. All in all, satyagraha instilled in the Indian mind a dignity and a self respect that is yet unprecedented in its modern history.

Salt Satyagraha

The Satyagraha was a campaign of nonviolent protest against the British salt tax in colonial India which began with the Salt March to Dandi on March 12, 1930. It was the first act of organized opposition to British rule after *Purna Swaraj*, the declaration of independence by the Indian National Congress. Mahatma Gandhi led the Dandi march from his Sabarmati Ashram to Dandi, Gujarat to produce salt without paying the tax, with growing numbers of Indians joining him along the way. When Gandhi broke the salt laws in Dandi at the conclusion of the march on April 6, 1930, it sparked large scale acts of civil disobedience against the British Raj salt laws by millions of Indians.

Gandhi was arrested on May 5, 1930, just days before his planned raid on the Dharasana Salt Works. The Dandi March and the ensuing Dharasana Satyagraha drew worldwide attention to the Indian independence movement through extensive newspaper and newsreel coverage. The satyagraha against the salt tax continued for almost a year, ending with Gandhi's release from jail and negotiations with Viceroy Lord Irwin at the Second Round Table Conference. Over 80,000 Indians were jailed as a result of the Salt Satyagraha. The campaign had a significant effect on changing world and British attitudes toward Indian independence, and caused large numbers of Indians to actively join the fight for the first time, but failed to win major concessions from the British.

The Salt Satyagraha campaign was based upon Gandhi's principles of nonviolent protest called *satyagraha*, which he loosely translated as "truth-force." In early 1930 the Indian National Congress chose satyagraha as their main tactic for winning Indian independence from British rule and appointed Gandhi to organize the campaign. Gandhi chose the 1882 British Salt Act as the first target of satyagraha. The Salt March to Dandi, and the beating of hundreds of nonviolent protesters in Dharasana, demonstrated the effective use of civil disobedience as a technique for fighting social and political injustice. The satyagraha teachings of Gandhi and the March to Dandi had a significant influence on American civil rights activist Martin Luther King, Jr., and his fight for civil rights for blacks and other minority groups in the 1960s.

Declaration of Independence

At midnight on December 31, 1929, the Indian National Congress raised the tricolour flag of India on the banks of the Ravi at Lahore. The Indian National Congress, led by Gandhi and Jawaharlal Nehru, publicly issued the Declaration of Independence, or *Purna Swaraj*, on January 26, 1930. The declaration included the readiness to withhold taxes, and the statement:

We believe that it is the inalienable right of the Indian people, as of any other people, to have freedom and to enjoy the fruits of their toil and have the necessities of life, so that they may have full opportunities of growth. We believe also that if any government deprives a people of these rights and oppresses them the people have a further right to alter it or abolish it. The British government in India has not only deprived the Indian people of their freedom but has based itself on the exploitation of the masses, and has ruined India economically, politically, culturally and spiritually. We believe therefore, that India must sever the British connection and attain *Purna Swaraj* or complete independence.

The Congress Working Committee gave Gandhi the responsibility for organizing the first act of civil disobedience, with Congress itself ready to take charge after Gandhi's expected arrest. Gandhi's plan was to begin civil disobedience with a satyagraha aimed at the British salt tax. The 1882 Salt Act gave the British a monopoly on the collection and manufacture of salt, limiting its handling to government salt depots and levying a salt tax. Violation of the Salt Act was a criminal offence. Even though salt was freely available to those living on the coast (by evaporation of sea water), Indians were forced to purchase it from the colonial government.

Gandhi's choice of the salt tax was met with incredulity by the Working Committee of the Congress, though Gandhi had his reasons for choosing the salt tax. The salt tax was a deeply symbolic choice, since salt was used by nearly everyone in India. It represented 8.2% of the British Raj tax revenue, and most significantly hurt the poorest Indians the most. Gandhi felt that this protest would dramatize Purna Swaraj in a way that was meaningful to the lowliest Indians. He also reasoned that it would build unity between Hindus and Muslims by fighting a wrong that touched them equally.

Satyagraha

Mahatma Gandhi, along with many members of the Congress Party, had a long-standing commitment to nonviolent civil disobedience, which he termed *satyagraha*, as the basis for achieving

Indian independence. Referring to the relationship between *satyagraha* and *Purna Swaraj,* Gandhi saw "an inviolable connection between the means and the end as there is between the seed and the tree." He wrote, "If the means employed are impure, the change will not be in the direction of progress but very likely in the opposite. Only a change brought about in our political condition by pure means can lead to real progress."

Satyagraha is a synthesis of the Sanskrit words *Satya* (truth) and *Agraha* (holding firmly to). For Gandhi, satyagraha went far beyond mere "passive resistance" and became strength in practicing nonviolent methods. In his words:

Truth (satya) implies love, and firmness (agraha) engenders and therefore serves as a synonym for force. I thus began to call the Indian movement Satyagraha, that is to say, the Force which is born of Truth and Love or nonviolence, and gave up the use of the phrase "passive resistance", in connection with it, so much so that even in English writing we often avoided it and used instead the word "satyagraha"....

His first significant attempt in India at leading mass satyagraha was the Noncooperation movement from 1920-1922. Even though it succeeded in raising millions of Indians in protest against the British created Rowlatt Acts, violence broke out at Chauri Chaura, where a mob killed 22 unarmed policemen. Gandhi suspended the protest, against the opposition of other Congress members. He decided that Indians were not yet ready for successful nonviolent resistance.

The Bardoli Satyagraha in 1928 was much more successful. It succeeded in paralysing the British government and winning significant concessions. More importantly, due to extensive press coverage, it scored a propaganda victory out of all proportion to its size. Gandhi later claimed that success at Bardoli confirmed his belief in Satyagraha and Swaraj: "It is only gradually that we shall come to know the importance of the victory gained at Bardoli...Bardoli has shown the way and cleared it. Swaraj lies on that route, and that alone is the cure..." Gandhi recruited heavily from the Bardoli Satyagraha participants for the Dandi march, which passed through many of the same villages that took part in the Bardoli protests.

Preparing to March

On February 5, newspapers reported that Gandhi would begin civil disobedience by defying the salt laws. The salt satyagraha would begin on March 12 and end in Dandi with Gandhi breaking the Salt Act on April 6. Gandhi chose April 6 to launch the mass breaking of the salt laws for a symbolic reason—it was the first day of "National Week", begun in 1919 when Gandhi conceived of the national hartal (strike) against the Rowlatt Act. Gandhi prepared the worldwide media for the march by issuing regular statements from Sabarmati, at his regular prayer meetings and through direct contact with the press. Expectations were heightened by his repeated statements anticipating arrest, and his increasingly dramatic language as the hour approached: "We are entering upon a life and death struggle, a holy war; we are performing an all-embracing sacrifice in which we wish to offer ourselves as oblation." Correspondents from dozens of Indian, European, and American newspapers, along with film companies, responded to the drama and began actively covering the event.

For the march itself, Gandhi wanted the strictest discipline and adherence to satyagraha and ahimsa. For that reason, he recruited the marchers not from Congress Party members, but from the residents of his own ashram, who were trained in Gandhi's strict standards of discipline. The 24 day march would pass through 4 districts and 48 villages. The route of the march, along with each evening's stopping place, was planned ahead of time based on recruitment potential, past contacts, and timing. Gandhi sent scouts to each village ahead of the march so he could plan his talks at each resting place, based on the needs of the local residents. Events at each village were scheduled and publicized in Indian and foreign press.

On March 2, 1930 Gandhi wrote to the Viceroy, Lord Irwin, offering to stop the march if Irwin met eleven demands, including reduction of land revenue assessments, cutting military spending, imposing a tariff on foreign cloth, and abolishing the salt tax. His strongest appeal to Irwin regarded the salt tax: If my letter makes no appeal to your heart, on the eleventh day of this month I shall proceed with such co-workers of the Ashram as I can take, to disregard the provisions of the Salt Laws. I regard this tax to be the most iniquitous of all from the poor man's standpoint. As the

Independence movement is essentially for the poorest in the land, the beginning will be made with this evil.

Irwin did not take the threat of a salt protest seriously, writing to London, "At present the prospect of a salt campaign does not keep me awake at night." After the Viceroy ignored the letter and refused to meet with Gandhi, the march was set in motion. The eve of the march brought thousands of Indians to Sabarmati to hear Gandhi speak at the regular evening prayer. An American academic writing for The Nation reported that "60,000 persons gathered on the bank of the river to hear Gandhi's call to arms. This call to arms was perhaps the most remarkable call to war that has ever been made."

March to Dandi

On March 12, 1930, Gandhi and 78 male satyagrahis set out on foot for the coastal village of Dandi, Gujarat, over 390 kilometres (240 mi) from their starting point at Sabarmati Ashram. According to The Statesman, the official government newspaper which usually played down the size of crowds at Gandhi's functions, 100,000 people crowded the road that separated Sabarmati from Ahmedabad. The first day's march of 21 kilometres (13 mi) ended in the village of Aslali, where Gandhi spoke to a crowd of about 4,000. At Aslali, and the other villages that the march passed through, volunteers collected donations, registered new satyagrahis, and received resignations from village officials who chose to end cooperation with British rule. As they entered each village, crowds greeted the marchers, beating drums and cymbals. Gandhi gave speeches attacking the salt tax as inhuman, and the salt satyagraha as a "poor man's battle." Each night they slept in the open, asking of the villagers nothing more than simple food and a place to rest and wash. Gandhi felt that this would bring the poor into the battle for independence, necessary for eventual victory.

Thousands of satyagrahis and leaders like Sarojini Naidu joined him. Every day, more and more people joined the march. At Surat, they were greeted by 30,000 people. When they reached the railhead at Dandi, more than 50,000 were gathered. Gandhi gave interviews and wrote articles along the way. Foreign journalists made him a household name in Europe and America.

The New York Times wrote almost daily about the Salt March, including two front page articles on April 6 and April 7. Near the end of the march, Gandhi declared, "I want world sympathy in this battle of Right against Might."

Upon arriving at the seashore on April 5, Gandhi was interviewed by an Associated Press reporter. He stated: I cannot withhold my compliments from the government for the policy of complete non interference adopted by them throughout the march.... I wish I could believe this non-interference was due to any real change of heart or policy. The wanton disregard shown by them to popular feeling in the Legislative Assembly and their high-handed action leave no room for doubt that the policy of heartless exploitation of India is to be persisted in at any cost, and so the only interpretation I can put upon this non-interference is that the British Government, powerful though it is, is sensitive to world opinion which will not tolerate repression of extreme political agitation which civil disobedience undoubtedly is, so long as disobedience remains civil and therefore necessarily nonviolent.... It remains to be seen whether the Government will tolerate as they have tolerated the march, the actual breach of the salt laws by countless people from tomorrow.

The following morning, after a prayer, Gandhi raised a lump of salty mud and declared, "With this, I am shaking the foundations of the British Empire." He then boiled it in seawater, producing illegal salt. He implored his thousands of followers to likewise begin making salt along the seashore, "wherever it is convenient" and to instruct villagers in making illegal, but necessary, salt.

Mass Civil Disobedience

Mass civil disobedience spread throughout India as millions broke the salt laws by making salt or buying illegal salt. Salt was sold illegally all over the coast of India. A pinch of salt made by Gandhi himself sold for 1,600 rupees (equivalent to $750 dollars at the time). In reaction, the British government incarcerated over sixty thousand people by the end of the month. What had begun as a Salt Satyagraha quickly grew into a mass Satyagraha. British cloth and goods were boycotted. Unpopular forest laws were defied in the Maharashtra, Carnatic (now Karnataka), and Central Provinces. Gujarati peasants refused to pay tax, under threat of losing their crops and land. In Midnapore, Bengalis took part by refusing to pay the chowkidar tax. The British responded with more laws, including censorship of correspondence and declaring the Congress and its associate organizations illegal. None of those measures slowed the civil disobedience movement.

In Peshawar, satyagraha was led by a Muslim Pashto disciple of Gandhi, Ghaffar Khan, who had trained a 50,000 member army of nonviolent activists called Khudai Khidmatgar. On April 23, 1930, Ghaffar Khan was arrested. A crowd of Khudai Khidmatgar gathered in Peshawar's Kissa Khani (Storytellers) Bazaar. The British ordered troops to open fire with machine guns on the unarmed crowd, killing an estimated 200-250. The Pashtun satyagrahis acted in accord with their training in nonviolence, willingly facing bullets as the troops fired on them. One British Indian Army regiment, troops of the renowned Royal Garhwal Rifles, refused to fire at the crowds. The entire platoon was arrested and many received heavy penalties, including life imprisonment.

The civil disobedience in 1930 marked the first time women became mass participants in the struggle for freedom. Thousands of women, from large cities to small villages, became active participants in satyagraha. Gandhi had asked that only men take part in the salt march, but eventually women began manufacturing and selling salt throughout India. Usha Mehta, an early Gandhian activist, remarked that "Even our old aunts and great-aunts and grandmothers used to bring pitchers of salt water to their houses and manufacture illegal salt. And then they would shout at the top of their voices: 'We have broken the salt law!'" The growing number of women in the fight for independence was a "new and serious feature" according to Lord Irwin. A government report on the involvement of women stated "thousands of them emerged....from the seclusion of their homes...in order to join Congress demonstrations and assist in picketing: and their presence on these occasions made the work the police was required to perform particularly unpleasant."

There were outbreaks of violence in Calcutta (now Kolkata), Karachi, and Gujarat. Unlike his suspension of satyagraha after violence broke out during the Noncooperation movement, this time Gandhi was "unmoved". Appealing for violence to end, at the same time Gandhi honoured those killed in Chittagong and congratulated their parents "for the finished sacrifices of their sons.... A warrior's death is never a matter for sorrow." British documents show that the British government was shaken by satyagraha. Nonviolent protest left the British confused about whether or not to jail Gandhi. John Court Curry, a British police officer stationed in India, wrote in his memoirs that he felt nausea every time he dealt with Congress demonstrations in 1930. Curry and others in British government, including Wedgwood Benn, Secretary of State for India, preferred fighting violent rather than nonviolent opponents.

Aftermath

Gandhi himself avoided further active involvement after the march, though he stayed in close contact with the developments throughout India. He created a temporary ashram near Dandi. From there, he urged women followers in Bombay (now Mumbai) to picket liquor shops and foreign cloth. He said that "a bonfire should be made of foreign cloth. Schools and colleges should become empty."

For his next major action, Gandhi decided on a raid of the Dharasana Salt Works in Gujarat. He wrote to Lord Irwin, again telling him of his plans. Around midnight of May 4, as Gandhi was sleeping on a cot in a mango grove, the District Magistrate of Surat drove up with two Indian officers and thirty heavily-armed constables. He was arrested under an 1827 regulation calling for the jailing of people engaged in unlawful activities, and held without trial near Poona (now Pune).

The Dharasana Satyagraha went ahead as planned, with Abbas Tyabji, a seventy-six year old retired judge, leading the march with Gandhi's wife Kasturba at his side. Both were arrested before reaching Dharasana and sentenced to three months in prison. After their arrests, the march continued under the leadership of Sarojini Naidu, a woman poet and freedom fighter, who warned the satyagrahis, "You must not use any violence under any circumstances. You will be beaten, but you must not resist: you must not even raise a hand to ward off blows." Soldiers began clubbing the satyagrahis with steel tipped lathis in an incident that attracted international attention. United Press correspondent Webb Miller reported that: Not one of the marchers even raised an arm to fend off the blows. They went down like ten-pins. From where I stood I heard the sickening whacks of the clubs on unprotected skulls. The waiting crowd of watchers groaned and sucked in their breaths in sympathetic pain at every blow. Those struck down fell sprawling, unconscious or writhing in pain with fractured skulls or broken shoulders. In two or three minutes the ground was quilted with bodies. Great patches of blood widened on their white clothes. The survivors without breaking ranks silently and doggedly marched on until struck down.

Vithalbhai Patel, former Speaker of the Assembly, watched the beatings and remarked, "All hope of reconciling India with the British Empire is lost forever." Following attempts by the British to censor Miller's story, it eventually appeared in 1,350 newspapers throughout the world, and was read into the official record of the United States Senate. Salt Satyagraha succeeded in drawing the attention of the world. Millions saw the newsreels showing the march. Time magazine declared Gandhi its 1930 Man of the Year, comparing Gandhi's march to the sea "to defy Britain's salt tax as some New Englanders once defied a British tea tax." Civil disobedience continued until early 1931, when Gandhi was finally released from prison to hold talks with Irwin. It was the first time the two held talks on equal terms. The talks would lead to the Second Round Table Conference at the end of 1931.

Long Term Impact

Salt Satyagraha produced scant progress toward dominion status or independence for India, and did not win any major concessions from the British. It also failed to attract Muslim support—many Muslims actively boycotted the satyagraha. Congress leaders decided to end satyagraha as official policy in 1934. Nehru and other Congress members drifted further apart from Gandhi, who withdrew from Congress to concentrate on his Constructive Programme, which included his efforts to end untouchability. Even though British authorities were again in control by the mid 1930s, Indian, British, and world opinion increasingly began to recognize the legitimacy of claims by Gandhi and the Congress Party for independence. The Satyagraha campaign of the 1930s also forced the British to recognize that their control of India depended entirely on the consent of the Indians — Salt Satyagraha was a significant step in the British losing that consent.

Nehru considered Salt Satyagraha the high water mark of his association with Gandhi, and felt that its lasting importance was in changing the attitudes of Indians: Of course these movements exercised tremendous pressure on the British Government and shook the government machinery. But the real importance, to my mind, lay in the effect they had on our own people, and especially the village masses....Non-cooperation dragged them out of the mire and gave them self-respect and self-reliance....They acted courageously and did not submit so easily to unjust oppression; their outlook widened and they began to think a little in terms of India as a whole....It was a remarkable transformation and the Congress, under Gandhi's leadership, must have the credit for it.

More than thirty years later, Satyagraha and the March to Dandi exercised a strong influence on American civil rights activist Martin Luther King, Jr., and his fight for civil rights for blacks in the 1960s: Like most people, I had heard of Gandhi, but I had never studied him seriously. As I read I became deeply fascinated by his campaigns of nonviolent resistance. I was particularly moved by his Salt March to the Sea and his numerous fasts. The whole concept of *Satyagraha* (*Satya* is truth which equals love, and *agraha* is force; *Satyagraha*, therefore, means truth force or love force) was profoundly significant to me. As I delved deeper into the philosophy of Gandhi, my skepticism concerning the power of love gradually diminished, and I came to see for the first time its potency in the area of social reform.

Re-enactment in 2005

To commemorate the Great Salt March, the Mahatma Gandhi Foundation proposed a re-enactment on the 75th anniversary. The event was known as the "International Walk for Justice and Freedom". Mahatma Gandhi's great-grandson Tushar Gandhi and several hundred fellow marchers followed the same route to Dandi. The start of the march on March 12, 2005 in Ahmedabad was attended by Sonia Gandhi, Chairperson of the National Advisory Council, as well as several Indian Cabinet Ministers, many of whom walked for the first few kilometres. The participants halted at Dandi on the night of April 5, with the commemoration ending on April 7. A series of commemorative stamps were issued on the 75th anniversary of the Dandi March—denomination INR 5, Date of Issue: April 5, 2005.

Power of Satyagraha

Victory of Satyagraha: ....a clear victory of Satyagraha is impossible so long as there is ill-will. But those who believe themselves to be weak are incapable of loving. Let, then, our first act every morning be to make the following resolve for the day: 'I shall not fear any one on earth. I shall fear God only; I shall not bear ill-will towards any one. I shall not submit to injustice from any one. I shall conquer untruth by truth and in resisting untruth I shall put up with all suffering. (SL NO. 14, 4-5-1919)

There is no time-limit for a Satyagrahi nor is there a limit to his capacity for suffering. Hence there is no such thing as defeat in Satyagraha. (YI, 19-2-1925, p. 61) It is not because I value life low that I countenance with joy thousands voluntarily losing their lives for Satyagraha, but because I know that it results, in the long run, in the least loss of life and, what is more, it ennobles those who lose their lives and morally enriches the world for their sacrifice. (YI, 8-10-1925, p. 345)

And when once it is set in motion, its effect, if it is intensive enough, can overtake the whole universe. It is the greatest force because it is the highest expression of the soul. (YI, 23-9-1926, p. 332)

My experience has taught me that a law of progression applies to every righteous struggle. But in the case of Satyagraha the law amounts to an axiom. As a Satyagraha struggle progresses onward, many another element helps to swell its current and there is a constant growth in the results to which it leads. This is really inevitable, and is bound up with the first principles of Satyagraha. For in Satyagraha the minimum is also the maximum, and as it is the irreducible minimum, there is no question of retreat, and the only movement possible is an advance. In other struggles, even when they are righteous, the demand is first pitched a little higher so as to admit of future reduction, and hence the law of progression does not apply to all of them without exception. (S, p. 319) To me it is one of the most active forces in the world, It is like the sun that rises upon us unfailingly from day to day. Only if we would but understand it, it is infinitely greater than a million suns put together. It radiates life and light and peace and happiness. (YI, 18-4-1929, p. 126)

One True Satyagrahi: If a single Satyagrahi holds out to the end, victory is certain. (SSA, p. xiv). Self-sacrifice of one innocent man is a million times more potent than the sacrifice of a million men who die in the act of killing others. The willing sacrificed of the innocent is the most powerful retort to insolent tyranny that has yet been conceived by God or man. (YI, 12-2-1925, p. 60) I have maintained that, even if there is one individual who is almost completely nonviolent, he can put out the conflagration...In this age of democracy, it is essential that desired results are achieved by the collective effort of the people. It will no doubt be good to achieve an objective through the effort of a supremely powerful individual, but it can never make the community conscious of its corporate strength. (H, 8-9-1940, p. 277)

I believe in walking alone. I came alone in this world, I have walked alone in the valley of the shadow of death and I shall quit alone when the time comes. I know I am quite capable of launching Satyagraha even if I am all alone. I have done so before. (YI, 21-7-1946, p. 227)

Application of Satyagraha: It is a force that may be used by individuals as well as by communities. It may be used as well in political as in domestic affairs. Its universal applicability is a demonstration of its permanence and invincibility. It can be used alike by men, women and children. It is totally untrue to say that it is a force to be used only by the weak so long as they are not capable of meeting violence by violence....

This force is to violence and, therefore, to all tyranny, all injustice, what light is to darkness. In politics, its use is based upon the immutable maxim that government of the people is possible only so long as they consent either consciously or unconsciously to be governed. (YI, 3-11-1927, 369) I have never claimed to be the one original Satyagrahi. What I have claimed is the application of that doctrine on an almost universal scale, and it yet remains to be seen and demonstrated that it is a doctrine which is capable of assimilation by thousands upon thousands of peoples in all ages and climes. (YI, 22-9-1927, p. 317)

The Nonviolent Sanction: Satyagraha is a law of universal application. Beginning with the family, its use can be extended to every other circle.

Supposing a landowner exploits his tenants and mulcts them of the fruit of their toil by appropriating it to his own use. When they expostulate with him he does not listen and raises objections that he requires so much for his wife, so much for his children and so on. The tenants or those who have espoused their cause and have influence will make an appeal to his wife to expostulate with her husband. She would probably say that for herself she does not need his exploited money. The children will say likewise that they would earn for themselves what they need.

Supposing further that he listens to nobody or that his wife and children combine against the tenants, they will not submit. They will quit if asked to do so, but they will make it clear that the land himself and he will have to give in to their just demands. It may, however, be that the tenants are replaced by others. Agitation short of violence will then continue till the replacing tenants see their error and make common cause with the evicted tenants.

Thus Satyagraha is a process of educating public opinion, such that it covers all elements of society and in the end makes itself irresistible. Violence interrupts the process and prolongs the real revolution of the whole social structure.

The conditions necessary for the success of Satyagraha are: (1) The Satyagrahi should not have any hatred in his heart against the opponent. (2) The issue must be true and substantial. (3) The Satyagrahi must be prepared to suffer till the end for his cause. (H, 31-3-1946, p. 64)

Training for Self-defence: I believe that every man and woman should learn the art of self-defence in this age. This is done through arms in the West. Every adult man is conscripted for army training for a definite period. The training for Satyagraha is meant for all, irrespective of age or sex. The more important part of the training here is mental, not physical. There can be no compulsion in mental training. The surrounding atmosphere no doubt acts on the mind, but that cannot justify compulsion... Satyagraha is always superior to armed resistance. This can only be effectively proved by demonstration, not by argument. It is the weapon that adorns the strong. It can never adorn the weak. By weak is meant the weak in mind and spirit, not in body. That limitation is a quality to be prized and not defect to be deplored. One ought also to understand one of its other limitations. It can never be used to defend a wrong cause.

Satyagraha brigades can be organized in every village and in every block of buildings in the cities. Each brigade should be composed of those persons who are well-known to the organizers. In this respect satyagraha differs from armed defence. For the latter the State impresses the service of everybody. For a Satyagraha brigade only those are eligible who believe in ahimsa and satya. Therefore, an intimate knowledge of the persons enlisted is necessary for the organizers. (H, 17-3-1946, pp. 45-46)

Duragraha: I can see nothing but catastrophe for India from methods of violence. Workmen would be committing suicide and India would have to suffer indescribable misery if workingmen were to vent their anger by criminal disobedience of the laws of the land.... When I began to preach Satyagraha and civil disobedience, it was never meant to cover criminal disobedience. My experience teaches me that truth can never be propagated by doing violence.

Those who believe in the justice of their cause need to possess boundless patience, and those alone are fit to offer civil disobedience who are above committing criminal disobedience or doing violence. A man cannot commit both civil and criminal disobedience at the same time, even as he cannot be both temperate and furious at the same time, and just as self-restraint is acquired only after one has been able to master his passions, so is the capacity for civil disobedience acquired after one has disciplined oneself in complete and voluntary obedience of the laws of the land.

Again, just as he alone can be said to be proof against temptations who, having been exposed to them, has succeeded in resisting them, so may we be said to have conquered anger when, having sufficient cause for it, we have succeeded in controlling ourselves. (YI, 28-4-1920, pp. 7-8) Some students have revived the ancient form of barbarity in the form of 'sitting dhurna'...I call it 'barbarity' for it is a crude way of using coercion. It is also cowardly, because one who sits dhurna knows that he is not going to be trampled over. It is difficult to call the practice violent, but it is certainly worse.

If we fight our opponent, we at least enable him to return the blow. But when we challenge him to walk over us, knowing that he will not, we place him in a most awkward and humiliating position. I know that the over-zealous students who sat dhurna never thought of the barbarity of the deed. But one who is expected to follow the voice of conscience and stand even single-handed in the face of odds cannot afford to be thoughtless.

There must be no impatience, no barbarity, no insolence, no undue pressure. If we want to cultivate a true spirit of democracy, we cannot afford to be intolerant. Intolerance betrays want of faith in one's cause. (YI, 2-2-1921, p. 33) I have not been able to understand the cause of so much excitement and disturbance that followed my detention. It is not Satyagraha. It is worse than Durgraha.

Those who join Satyagraha demonstrations were bound one and all to refrain at all hazard from violence, not to throw stones or in anyway whatever to injure anybody. But in Bombay we have been throwing stones. We have obstructed tram-cars by putting obstacles in the way. This is not Satyagraha. We have demanded the release of about 50 men who had been arrested for deeds of violence. Our duty is chiefly to get ourselves arrested. It is breach of religious duty to endeavour to secure the release of those who have committed deeds of violence. (SW, p. 474)

I have said times without number that Satyagraha admits of no violence, no pillage, no incendiarism; and still, in the name of Satyagraha, we have burnt buildings, forcibly captured weapons, extorted money, stopped trains, cut off telegraph wires, killed innocent people and plundered shops and private houses. If deeds such as these could save me from the prison-house or the scaffold, I should not like to be so saved. (ibid, p. 476)

....Heroism and sacrifice in a bad cause are so much waste of splendid energy and hurt the good cause by drawing away attention from it by the glamour of the misused heroism and sacrifice in a bad cause. (YI, 12-12-1925, p. 60)

....Indiscriminate resistance to authority must lead to lawlessness and unbridled license and consequent self-destruction. (YI, 2-4-1931, p. 58)

Non-Cooperation: Non-cooperation is an attempt to awaken the masses to a sense of their dignity and power. This can only be by enabling them to realize that they need not fear brute force if they would but know the soul within. (YI, 1-12-1920, p. 3)

Noncooperation is a protest against an unwitting and unwilling participation in evil....Non-cooperation with evil is as much a duty as cooperation with good. (YI, 1-6-1921, p. 172) Noncooperation is not a passive state, it is an intensively active state, more active than physical resistance or violence. Passive resistance is a misnomer. Noncooperation in the sense used by me must be nonviolent and therefore, neither punitive nor based on malice, ill-will or hatred. (YI, 25-8-1920, p. 322)

Religious Basis: I venture to submit that the Bhagavadgita is a gospel of Noncooperation between the forces of darkness and those of light. If it is to be literally interpreted, Arjuna representing a just cause was enjoined to engage in bloody warfare with the unjust Kauravas.

Tulasidas advises the sant (the good) to shun the asant (the evil doers). The Zend Avesta represents a perpetual duel between Ormuzd and Ahriman, between whom there is no compromise. To say of the Bible that it taboos Noncooperation is not to know Jesus, a prince among passive resisters, who uncompromisingly challenged the might of the Sadducees and the Pharisees and, for the sake of truth, did not hesitate to divide sons from their parents.

And what did the Prophet of Islam do? He non-co-operated in Mecca in a most active manner so long as his life was not in danger, and wiped the dust of Mecca off his faith when he found that he and his followers might have uselessly to perish, and fled to Medina and returned when he was strong enough to give battle to his opponents. The duty of Noncooperation with unjust men and kings is as strictly enjoined by all the religions as is the duty of cooperation with just men and kings. Indeed, most of the scriptures of the world seem even to go beyond Noncooperation and prefer violence to effeminate submission to a wrong. The Hindu religious tradition.....clearly proves the duty of

Noncooperation. Prahlad dissociated from his father, Meerabai from her husband, Bibhishan from his brutal brother. (YI, 4-8-1920, p. 4)

Basic Principle: The basic principle on which the practice of nonviolence rests is that what holds good in respect of oneself equally applies to the whole Universe. All mankind in essence are alike. What is therefore possible for me, is possible for everybody.... This is essence is the principle of nonviolent Noncooperation. It follows therefore that it must have its root in love. Its object should not be to punish the opponent or to inflict injury upon him. Even while non-co-operating with him, we must make him feel that in us he has a friend and we should try to reach his heart by rendering him humanitarian service whenever possible.

In fact, it is the acid test of nonviolence that in a nonviolent conflict there is no rancour left behind and, in the end, the enemies are converted into friends. That was my experience in South Africa with General Smuts. He started with being my bitterest opponent and critic. Today he is my warmest friend.

Enduring Quality: Times change and systems decay. But it is my faith that, in the result, it is only nonviolence and things that are based on nonviolence that will endure. Nineteen hundred years ago Christianity was born. The ministry of Jesus lasted for only three brief years. His teaching was misunderstood even during his own time and today Christianity is a denial of his central teaching [: "Love your enemy." But what are nineteen hundred years for the spread of the central doctrine of a man's teaching?] Six centuries rolled by and Islam appeared on the scene. Many Musalmans will not even allow me to say that Islam, as the word implies, it unadulterated peace. My reading of the Quran has convinced me that the basis of Islam is not violence.

But, here again, thirteen hundred years are but a speck in the cycle of Time. I am convinced that both these great faiths will life only to the extent that their followers imbibe the central teaching of nonviolence. But it is not a thing to be grasped through mere intellect, it must sink into our hearts. (H, 12-11-1938, p. 327) Although Noncooperation is one of the main weapons in the armoury of Satyagraha, it should not be forgotten that it is after all only a means to secure the cooperation of the opponent consistently with truth and justice. The essence of nonviolent technique is that it seeks to liquidate antagonisms but not the antagonists themselves. In nonviolent fight you have, to a certain measure, to conform to the tradition and conventions to the system you are pitted against. Avoidance of all relationship with the opposing power, therefore, can never be a Satyagrahi's object, but transformation or purification of that relationship. (H, 29-4-1939, p. 101)

Mission of Satyagraha

My mission is to teach by example and precept under sever restraint the use of the matchless weapon of Satyagraha; which is a direct corollary of nonviolence and truth. I am anxious, indeed I am impatient, to demonstrate that there is no remedy for the many ills of life save that of nonviolence.... When I have become incapable of evil and when nothing harsh or haughty occupies, be it momentarily, my thought-world, then, and not till then, my nonviolence will move all the hearts of all the world. I have placed before me and the reader no impossible ideal or ordeal. It is man's prerogative and birthright.

We have lost the paradise only to regain it. If it takes time, then it is but a speck in the complete time-circle. The Divine Teacher of the Gita knew when he said that millions of our days are equal to only a day of Brahma. (YI, 2-7-1925, p232)

Ahimsa is my God, and Truth is my God. When I look for ahimsa, Truth says 'Find it out through me'. When I look for Truth, ahimsa says 'Find it out through me'. (YI, 4-6-1925, p191) I believe myself to be saturated with ahimsa-non-violence. Ahimsa and Truth are as my two lungs. I cannot live without them. But I see every moment with more and more clearness the immense power of ahimsa and the littleness of man. Even the forest-dweller cannot be entirely free from violence, in spite of his limitless compassion. With every breath he commits a certain amount of violence.

The body itself is a house of slaughter, and, therefore, moksha and Eternal Bliss consist in perfect deliverance from the body, and therefore, all pleasure, save the joy of moksha, is evanescent, imperfect. That being the case, we have to drink, in daily life, many a bitter drought of violence. (YI, 21-10-1926, p364)

The Gospel of Satyagraha

Passive Resistance

Passive resistance is an all-sided sword; it can be used anyhow; it blesses him who uses it and him against whom it is used. Without drawing a drop of blood it produces far-reaching results. It never rusts and cannot be stolen. (Hs, p. 82)

I am quite sure that the stoniest heart will be melted by passive resistance...This is a sovereign and most effective remedy...It is a weapon of the purest type. It is not the weapon of the weak. It needs far greater courage to be a passive resister than a physical resister. It is the courage of a Jesus, a Daniel, a Crammer, a Latimer and a Ridley who could go calmly to suffering and death, and the courage of a Tolstoy who dared to defy the Czars of Russia, that stands out as the greatest. Indeed, one PERFECT resister is enough to win the battle of Right against Wrong. (YI, 10-11-1921, p. 362)

I claim...that the method of passive resistance...is the clearest and safest, because, if the cause is not true, it is the resisters and they alone who suffer. Jesus Christ, Daniel and Socrates represented the purest form of passive resistance or soul force. All these teachers counted their bodies as nothing in comparison to their soul. Tolstoy was the best and brightest (modern) exponent of the doctrine. He not only expounded it, but lived according to it. In India, the doctrine was understood and commonly practiced long before it came into vogue in Europe.

It is easy to see that soul force is infinitely superior to body force. If people in order to secure redress of wrongs resort to soul force, much of the present suffering will be avoided. In any case, the wielding of the force never causes suffering to others. So that whenever it is misused, It only injures the users and not those against whom it is used. Like virtue it has its own reward. There is no such thing as failure in the use of this kind of force. (SW, p. 165)

The Buddha fearlessly carried the war into the enemy's camp and brought down on its knees an arrogant priesthood. Christ drove out the money-changers from the temple of Jerusalem and drew down curses from Heaven upon he hypocrites and the

Pharisees. Both were for intensely direct action. But even as the Buddha and Christ chastised, they showed unmistakable gentleness and love behind every act of theirs. They would not raise a finger against their enemies, but would gladly surrender themselves rather than the truth for which they lived. The Buddha would have died resisting the priesthood, if the majesty of his love had not proved to be equal to the task of bending the priesthood. Christ died on the cross with a crown of thorns on his head, defying the might of a whole empire. And if I raise resistances of a nonviolent character, I simply and humbly follow in the footsteps of the great teachers... (YI, 12-5-1920, p. 3)

Civil Disobedience

Disobedience to be civil must be sincere, respectful, restrained, never defiant, must be based upon some well-understood principle, must not be capricious and, above all, must have no ill-will or hatred behind it. (YI, 24-3-1920, p. 4)

I hold the opinion firmly that civil disobedience is the purest type of constitutional agitation. Of course, it becomes degrading and despicable, if its civil, i.e., nonviolent character is a mere camouflage. If the honesty of nonviolence be admitted, there is no warrant for condemnation even of the fiercest disobedience, because of the likehood of its leading to violence. No big or swift movement can carried on without bold risks, and life will not be worth living if it is not attended with large risks. Does not the history of the world show that there would have been no romance in life if there had been no risks? (YI, 15-12-1921, p. 419)

Civil disobedience is the inherent right of a citizen. He dare not give it up without ceasing to be a man. Civil disobedience is never followed by anarchy. Criminal disobedience can lead to it. Every state puts down criminal disobedience by force. It perishes if it does not. (YI, 5-1-1922, p. 5)

A Satyagrahi obeys the laws of society intelligently and of his own free will, because he considers it to be his sacred duty to do so. It is only when a person has thus obeyed the laws of society scrupulously that he is in a position of judge as to which particular laws are good and just and which unjust and iniquitous. Only when does the right accrue to him of civil disobedience of certain laws in well-defined circumstances. (A, p. 347)

Condition Precedent

The first indispensable condition precedent to any civil resistance is that there should be surety against any outbreak of violence, whether on the part of those who are identified with civil resistance or on the part of the general public. It would be no answer in the case of an outbreak of violence that it was instigated by the State or other agencies hostile to civil resisters. It should be obvious that civil resistance cannot flourish in an atmosphere of violence. This does not mean that the resources of a satyagrahi have come to an end. Ways other than civil disobedience should be found out. (H, 18-3-1939, p. 53)

Character of Satyagraha

That is the beauty of Satyagraha. It comes up to oneself, one has not to go out in search for it. That is a virtue inherent in the principle itself.

A dharmayuddha, in which there are no secrete to be guarded, no scope for canning and no place for untruth, comes unsought; and a man of religion is ever ready for it. A struggle which has to be previously planned is not and it is only when the Satyagrahi feels quite helpless, is apparently on his last legs and finds utter darkness all around him, that God comes to the rescue. (SSA, p. xiv)

In the application of Satyagraha, I discovered, in the earliest stages, that pursuit of Truth did not admit of violence being inflicted on one's opponent, but that he must be weaned from error by patience and sympathy. For, what appears to be truth to the one may appear to be error to the other. And patience means self-suffering. So the doctrine came to mean vindication of Truth, not by infliction of suffering on the opponent but one's own self. (RCPS) Satyagraha and its off-shoots, noncooperation and civil resistance, are nothing but new names for the law of suffering. (YI, 11-8-1920, p. 3) With satya combined with ahimsa, you can bring the world to your feet. Satyagraha in its essence is nothing but the introduction of truth and gentleness in the political, i.e., the national, life. (YI, 10-3-1920, p. 3)

Satyagraha is utter self-effacement, greatest humiliation, greatest patience and brightest faith. It is its own reward. (YI, 26-2-1925, p. 73)

Satyagraha is a relentless search for truth and a determination to reach truth. (YI, 19-3-1925, p. 95)

It is a force that works silently and apparently slowly. In reality, there is no force in the world that is so direct or so swift in working. (YI, 4-6-1925, p. 189)

The word Satyagraha is often most loosely used and is made to cover veiled violence. But, as the author of the word, I may be allowed to say that it excludes every form of violence, direct or indirect, veiled or unveiled, and whether in thought, word or deed. It is breach of Satyagraha to with ill to an opponent or to say a harsh word to him or of him with the intention of harming him... Satyagraha is gentle, it never wounds. It must not be the result of anger or malice. It is never fussy, never impatient, never vociferous. It is the direct opposite of compulsion. It was conceived as a complete substitute for violence. (H, 15-4-1933, p. 8)

The fight of Satyagraha is for the strong in spirit, not the doubter or the timid. Satyagraha teaches us the art of living as well as dying. Birth and death are inevitable among mortals. What distinguishes the man from the brute is his conscious striving to realize the spirit within. (H, 7-4-1946, p. 74)

Evolving Science

I am myself daily growing in the knowledge of Satyagraha. I have no text-book to consult in time of need, not even the Gita which I have called my dictionary. Satyagraha as conceived by me is a science may prove to be no science at all and well prove to be the musings and doings of a fool, if not a madman. It may be that what is true in Satyagraha is as ancient as the hills. But it has not yet been acknowledged to be of any value in the solution of world problems or, rather, the one supreme problem or war. It may be that what is claimed to be new in it will prove to be really of no value in terms of that supreme problem. It may be that what are claimed to be victories of Satyagraha i.e., ahimsa, were really victories not of truth and nonviolence but of fear of violence. These possibilities have always been in front of me. I am helpless. All I present to the nation for adoption is an answer to prayer or, which is the same thing, constantly waiting on God. (H, 24-9-1938, p. 266)

The Technique of Satyagraha

Not to yield your soul to the conqueror means that you will refuse to do that which your conscience forbids you to do. Suppose the 'enemy' were to ask you to rub your nose on the ground or to pull your ears or to go through such humiliating performances, you would not submit to any of these humiliations. But if he robs you of your possessions, you will yield them because, as a votary of ahimsa, you have from the beginning decided that earthly possessions have nothing to do with your soul. That which you look upon as your own you may keep only so long as the world allows you to own it.

Not to yield your mind means that you will not give way to any temptation. Man is oftentimes weak-minded enough to be caught in the snare of greed and honeyed words. We see this happening daily in our social life. A weak-minded man can never be a Satyagrahi. The latter's 'no' is invariably a 'no' and his 'yes' an eternal 'yes'. Such a man alone has the strength to be a devotee of truth and ahimsa. But here one must know the difference between steadfastness and obstinacy. If, after having said 'yes' or 'no', one finds out that the decision was wrong and in spite of that knowledge clings to it, that is obstinacy and folly. It is necessary to think things out carefully and thoroughly before coming to any decision.

The meaning of refusal to own allegiance is clear. You will not bow to the supremacy of the victor, you will not help him to attain his object. Herr Hitler has never dreamt of possessing Britain. He wants the British to admit defeat. The victor can then demand anything he likes from the vanquished, and the latter has perforce to yield.

But if defeat is not admitted, the enemy will fight until he has killed his opponent. A Satyagrahi, however, is dead to his body even before the enemy attempts to kill him, i.e., he is free from attachment to his body and only lives in the victory of the soul. Therefore, when he is already thus dead, why would be yearn to kill anyone? To die in the act of killing is in essence to die defeated. Because, if the enemy is unable to get it after killing you. If, on the other hand, he realizes that you have not the remotest thought in your mind of raising your hand against him even for the sake of your life, he will lack the zest to kill you. Every hunter has had this experience. No one has ever heard of anyone hunting cows. (H, 18-8-1940, pp. 253-4)

Power of Suffering

The hardest heart and the grossest ignorance must disappear before the rising sun of suffering without anger and without malice. (YI, 19-2-1925, p. 61)

Suffering has its well-defined limits. Suffering can be both wise and unwise, and when the limit is reached, to prolong it would be not unwise but the height of folly. (YI, 12-3-1931, p. 30)

True suffering does not know itself and never calculates. It brings its own joy which surpasses all other joys. (YI, 19-3-1931, p. 41)

The conviction has been growing upon me that things of fundamental importance to the people are not secured by reason alone, but have to be purchased with their suffering. Suffering is the law of human beings; war is the law of the jungle. But suffering is infinitely more powerful than the law of the jungle for converting the opponent and opening his ears, which are otherwise shut, to the voice of reason. (YI, 5-11-1931, p. 341)

Code of Satyagraha

A Satyagrahi bids good-bye to fear. He is therefore, never afraid of trusting the opponent. Even if the opponent plays him false twenty times, the Satyagrahi is ready to trust him the twenty-first time, for an implicit trust in human nature is the very essence of his creed. (SSA, p. 159)

A Satyagrahi is nothing if not instinctively law-abiding, and it is his law-abiding nature which exacts from him implicit obedience to the highest law, that is the voice of conscience which overrides all other laws. (SW, p. 465)

Since Satyagraha is one of the most powerful methods of direct action, a Satyagrahi exhausts all other means before he resorts to Satyagraha. He will, therefore, constantly and continually approach the constituted authority, he will appeal to public opinion, educate public opinion, state his case calmly and coolly before everybody who wants to listen to him, and only after he has exhausted all these avenues will he resort to Satyagraha. But when he has found the impelling call of the inner voice within him and launches out upon Satyagraha, he has burnt his boats and there is no receding. (YI, 20-10-1927, p. 353)

The Satyagrahi, whilst he is ever ready for fight, must be equally eager for peace. He must welcome any honourable opportunity for peace. (YI, 19-3-1931, p. 40)

My advice is Satyagraha first and Satyagraha last. There is no other or better road to freedom. (H, 15-9-1946, p. 312)

In the code of the Satyagrahi there is no such thing as surrender to brute force. Or the surrender then is the surrender of suffering and not to the wielder of the bayonet. (YI, 30-4-1931, p. 93)

As a Satyagrahi I must always allow my cards to be examined and re-examined at all times and make reparation if an error is discovered. (H, 11-3-1939, p. 44)

Qualifications of a Satyagrahi

...The following qualifications....I hold are essential for every Satyagrahi in India:

He must have a living faith in God, for He is his only Rock. He must believe in truth and nonviolence as his creed and, therefore, have faith in the inherent goodness of human nature which he expects to evoke by his truth and love expressed through his suffering.

He must be leading a chaste life and be ready and willing, for the sake of his cause, to give up his life and his possessions. He must be a habitual Khadi-wearer and spinner. This is essential for India. He must be a teetotaler and be free from the use of other intoxicants in order that his reason may be always unclouded and his mind constant.

He must carry out with a willing heart all the rules or discipline as may be laid down from time to time. He should carry out the jail rules unless they are specially devised to hurt his self-respect. The qualifications are not to be regarded as exhaustive. They are illustrative only. (H, 25-3-1939, p. 64)

A Satyagrahi may not even ascend to heaven on the wings of Satan. (H, 15-4-1939, p. 86)

In Satyagraha there is no place for fraud or falsehood, or any kind of untruth. (BC, 9-8-1942)

A Satyagrahi never misses, can never miss, a chance of compromise on honourable terms, it being always assumed that, in the event of failure, he is ever ready to offer battle. He needs no previous preparation, his cards are always on the table. (YI, 16-4-1931, p. 77)

It is often forgotten that it is never the intention of a Satyagrahi to embarrass the wrongdoer. The appeal is never to his fear; it is, must, always to his heart. The Satyagrahi's object is to convert, not to coerce, the wrongdoer. He should avoid artificiality in all his doings. He acts naturally and from inward conviction. (H, 25-3-1939, p. 64)

Satyagraha is essentially a weapon of the truthful. A Satyagrahi is pledged to nonviolence and, unless people observe it in thought, word and deed, I cannot offer Satyagraha. (A, p. 345)

I have always held that it is only when one sees one's own mistakes with a convex lens, and does just the reverse in the case others, that one is able to arrive at a just relative estimate of the two. I further believe that a scrupulous and conscientious observance of this rule is necessary for one who wants to be a Satyagrahi. (ibid, p. 346)

A Satyagrahi relies upon God for protection against the tyranny of brute force... (H, 7-4-1946, p. 73)

No confirmed Satyagrahi is dismayed by the dangers, seen or unseen, from his opponent's side. What he must fear, as every army must, is the danger from within. (H, 14-7-1946, p. 220)

Satyagraha and Repression

Repression itself affords a training in Satyagraha, even as an unsought war affords a training for the soldier. Satyagrahis should discover the causes repression. They will find that repressed people are easily frightened by the slightest show of force and are unprepared for suffering and self-sacrifice. This is then the time for learning the first lessons of Satyagraha.

Those who know anything of this matchless force should teach their neighbours to bear repression not weakly and helplessly, but bravely and knowingly..... And yet they [the unexciting rules of preparation] are much the most important part of Satyagraha training. Potent and active nonviolence cannot be cultivated unless the candidate goes through the necessary stages which require a lot of plodding. (H, 8-4-1939, p. 80)

Training for Self-defence

I believe that every man and woman should learn the art of self-defence in this age. This is done through arms in the West. Every adult man is conscripted for army training for a definite period. The training for Satyagraha is meant for all, irrespective of age or sex. The more important part of the training here is mental, not physical. There can be no compulsion in mental training. The surrounding atmosphere no doubt acts on the mind, but that cannot justify compulsion...

Satyagraha is always superior to armed resistance. This can only be effectively proved by demonstration, not by argument. It is the weapon that adorns the strong. It can never adorn the weak. By weak is meant the weak in mind and spirit, not in body. That limitation is a quality to be prized and not defect to be deplored.

One ought also to understand one of its other limitations. It can never be used to defend a wrong cause.

Satyagraha brigades can be organized in every village and in every block of buildings in the cities. Each brigade should be composed of those persons who are well-known to the organizers. In this respect Satyagraha differs from armed defence. For the latter the State impresses the service of everybody. For a Satyagraha brigade only those are eligible who believe in ahimsa and satya. Therefore, an intimate knowledge of the persons enlisted is necessary for the organizers. (H, 17-3-1946, pp. 45-46)

Duragraha

I can see nothing but catastrophe for India from methods of violence. Workmen would be committing suicide and India would have to suffer indescribable misery if workingmen were to vent their anger by criminal disobedience of the laws of the land....

When I began to preach Satyagraha and civil disobedience, it was never meant to cover criminal disobedience. My experience teaches me that truth can never be propagated by doing violence.

Those who believe in the justice of their cause need to possess boundless patience, and those alone are fit to offer civil disobedience who are above committing criminal disobedience or doing violence.

A man cannot commit both civil and criminal disobedience at the same time, even as he cannot be both temperate and furious at the same time, and just as self-restraint is acquired only after one has been able to master his passions, so is the capacity for civil disobedience acquired after one has disciplined oneself in complete and voluntary obedience of the laws of the land. Again, just as he alone can be said to be proof against temptations who, having been exposed to them, has succeeded in resisting them, so may we be said to have conquered anger when, having sufficient cause for it, we have succeeded in controlling ourselves. (YI, 28-4-1920, pp. 7-8)

Some students have revived the ancient form of barbarity in the form of 'sitting dhurna'...I call it 'barbarity' for it is a crude way of using coercion. It is also cowardly, because one who sits dhurna knows that he is not going to be trampled over. It is difficult to call the practice violent, but it is certainly worse.

If we fight our opponent, we at least enable him to return the blow. But when we challenge him to walk over us, knowing that he will not, we place him in a most awkward and humiliating position. I know that the over-zealous students who sat dhurna never thought of the barbarity of the deed. But one who is expected to follow the voice of conscience and stand even single-handed in the face of odds cannot afford to be thoughtless. There must be no impatience, no barbarity, no insolence, no undue pressure. If we want to cultivate a true spirit of democracy, we cannot afford to be intolerant. Intolerance betrays want of faith in one's cause. (YI, 2-2-1921, p. 33)

I have not been able to understand the cause of so much excitement and disturbance that followed my detention. It is not Satyagraha. It is worse than Durgraha.

Those who join Satyagraha demonstrations were bound one and all to refrain at all hazard from violence, not to throw stones or in anyway whatever to injure anybody. But in Bombay we have been throwing stones. We have obstructed tram-cars by putting obstacles in the way. This is not Satyagraha. We have demanded the release of about 50 men who had been arrested for deeds of violence. Our duty is chiefly to get ourselves arrested. It is breach of religious duty to endeavour to secure the release of those who have committed deeds of violence. (SW, p. 474)

I have said times without number that Satyagraha admits of no violence, no pillage, no incendiarism; and still, in the name of Satyagraha, we have burnt buildings, forcibly captured weapons, extorted money, stopped trains, cut off telegraph wires, killed innocent people and plundered shops and private houses. If deeds such as these could save me from the prison-house or the scaffold, I should not like to be so saved. (ibid, p. 476)

....Heroism and sacrifice in a bad cause are so much waste of splendid energy and hurt the good cause by drawing away attention from it by the glamour of the misused heroism and sacrifice in a bad cause. (YI, 12-12-1925, p. 60)

....Indiscriminate resistance to authority must lead to lawlessness and unbridled license and consequent self-destruction. (YI, 2-4-1931, p. 58)

Fasting and Satyagraha

Fasting is a potent weapon in the Satyagraha armoury. It cannot be taken by every one. Mere physical capacity to take it is no qualification for it. It is of no use without a living faith in God. It should never be a mechanical effort or a mere limitation. It must come from the depth of one's soul. It is, therefore, always rare. (H, 18-3-1939, p. 56)

There can be no room for selfishness, anger, lack of faith or impatience in a pure fast....Infinite patience, firm resolve, single-mindedness of purpose, perfect calm, and no anger must of necessity be there. But since it is impossible for a person to develop all these qualities all at once, no one who has not devoted himself to following the laws of ahimsa should undertake a Satyagrahi fast. (H, 13-10-1940, p. 322)

[Fasting] is...fierce and not altogether free from danger. I myself have before condemned fasting when it seemed to me to be wrong or morally unjustified. But to shirk a fast where there is a clear moral indication is a dereliction of duty. Such a fast has to be based on unadulterated truth and ahimsa. (H, 28-7-1946, p. 235)

Fasting and Death

Fasting unto death is the last and the most potent weapon in the armoury of Satyagraha. It is a sacred thing. But it must be accepted with all its implication. It is not the fast itself, but what it implies that matters. (H, 18-8-1846, p. 262)

Fasting and the Way of Christ

Fasting cannot be undertaken mechanically. It is a powerful thing but a dangerous thing, if handled amateurishly. It requires complete self-purification, much more than what is required in facing death with retaliation even in mind. One such act of perfect sacrifice would suffice for the whole world. Such is held to be Jesus' example. (H, 27-10-1946, p. 272)

Of course, it is not to be denied that fasts can be really coercive. Such are fasts to attain a selfish object. A fast undertaken to wring money from a person or for fulfilling some such personal end would amount to the exercise of coercion or undue influence. I would unhesitatingly advocate resistance of such undue influence. I have myself successfully resisted it in the fasts that have been undertaken or threatened against me.

And if it is argued that the dividing line between a selfish and unselfish end is often very thin, I would urge that a person who regards the end of a fast to be selfish or otherwise base should resolutely refuse to yield to it, even though the refusal may result in the death of the fasting person. If people will cultivate the habit of disregarding fasts which, in their opinion, are taken for unworthy ends, such fasts will be robbed of the taint of coercion and undue influence. Like all human institutions, fasting can be both legitimately and illegitimately used. (H, 9-9-1931, p. 5)

If a man, however popular and great he may be, takes up an improper cause and fasts in defence of the impropriety, it is the duty of his friends (among whom I count myself), fellow-workers and relatives to let him die rather than that an improper cause should triumph so that he may live. Fairest means cease to be fair when the end sought is unfair. (H, 17-3-1946, p. 43)

Last Resort

One general principle, however, I would like to enunciate. A Satyagrahi should fast only as a last resort when all other avenues of redress have been explored and have failed. There is no room for imitation in fasts. He who has no inner strength should not dream of it, and never with attachment to success. But if a Satyagrahi once undertakes a fast from conviction, he must stick to his resolve whether there is a chance of his action bearing fruit or not. This does not mean that fasting cannot or can bear fruit. He who fasts in the expectation of fruit generally fails. And even if he does not seemingly fail, he loses all the inner joy which a true fast holds...

Ridiculous fasts spread like plague and are harmful. But, when fasting becomes a duty, it cannot be given up. Therefore, I do fast when I consider it to be necessary and cannot abstain from it on any score. What I do myself I cannot abstain from it on any score. What I do myself I cannot prevent others from doing under similar circumstances. It is common knowledge that the best of good things are often abused. We see this happening every day. (H, 21-4-1946, p. 93)

...When human ingenuity fails, the votary fasts. This fasting quickens the spirit of prayer, that is to say, the fasting is a spiritual act, and therefore, addressed to God. The effect of such action on the life of the people is that, where the person fasting is at all known to them, their sleeping conscience is awakened. But there is the danger that the people through mistaken sympathy may act against their will in order to save the life of the loved one. This danger has got to be faced. One ought not to be deterred from right action when one is sure of the rightness. It can best promote circumspection. Such a fast is undertaken in obedience to the dictates of the inner voice and, therefore, prevents haste. (H, 21-12-1947, p. 476).

4

Gandhi and Untouchables

As opposed to the popular perceptions, here you will see Gandhi's image from the eyes of a very famous untouchable leader, named, Dr. B. R. Ambedkar (1893-1956). Born and raised as an untouchable, Dr. Ambedkar received his masters and Ph. D. from Columbia University, which later on also conferred upon him the Doctor of Law. Dr. Ambedkar also received a D. Sc. degree from London School of Economics, and the Bar-at-Law from the Grays Inn, London. Suffice to say, Dr. Ambedkar's sharp intellect has provided us an insight into Gandhi, some of which we will like to share with you all. We recommend the following:

1. Nichols, Beverley. Verdict on India. New York: Harcourt, Brace and Company, 1944. A book we highly recommend. Beverley Nichols, a famous novelist, musician, playwright, essayist, reporter, and a journalist visited British India. During this visit, he met Dr. Ambedkar, who told him: "Gandhi is the greatest enemy the untouchables have ever had in India."

   So what did Ambedkar mean? Mr. Nichols explained it as follows: We can best explain it by a parallel. Take Ambedkar's remark, and for the word "untouchable" substitute the word "peace." Now imagine that a great champion of peace, like Lord Cecil, said, "Gandhi is the greatest enemy of peace the world has ever had." What would he mean, using these words of the most spectacular pacifist of modern times? He would mean that passive resistance—which is Gandhi's form of pacifism—could only lead to chaos and the eventual triumph of brute force; that to lie down and let people trample on you (which was

Gandhi's recipe for dealing with the Japanese) is a temptation to the aggressor rather than an example to the aggressed; and that in order to have peace you must organize, you must be strong, and that you must be prepared to use force. Mutatis mutandis, that is precisely what Ambedkar meant about the untouchables. He wanted them to be recognized and he wanted them to be strong. He rightly considered that the best way of gaining his object was by granting them separate electorates; a solid block of 60 million would be in a position to dictate terms to its oppressors. Gandhi fiercely opposed this scheme. "Give the untouchables separate electorates," he cried, "and you only perpetuate their status for all time." It was a queer argument, and those who were not bemused by the Mahatma's charm considered it a phoney one. They suspected that Gandhi was a little afraid that 60 million untouchables might join up with the 100 million Muslims—(as they nearly did)—and challenge the dictatorship of the 180 million orthodox Hindus. With such irreverent criticisms were made to him, Gandhi resorted to his usual tactics: he began to fast unto death. (As if that altered the situation by a comma or proved anything but his own obstinacy!) There was a frenzy of excitement, ending in a compromise on the seventh day of the fast. The untouchables still vote in the same constituencies as the caste Hindus, but a substantial number of seats are now reserved for them in the provincial legislatures. It is better than nothing, but it is not nearly so good as it would have been if Gandhi had not interfered. That is what Doctor Ambedkar meant. And I think that he was right.

2. Ambedkar, B. R. What Congress and Gandhi Have Done to the Untouchables. Bombay: Thacker & Co., Ltd, 2nd edition, 1946. Excerpts from this book were published in: Gandhi: Maker of Modern India? Edited by Martin Deming Lewis. Boston: D. C. Heath and Co., 1965. Here is the report which you must read in its entirety: Mr. Gandhi's views on the caste system—which constitutes the main social problem in India—were fully elaborated by him in 1921-22 in a Gujrati journal called Nava-Jivan. The article

is written in Gujrati. I give below an English translation of his views as near as possible in his own words. Says Mr. Gandhi:

(1) I believe that if Hindu Society has been able to stand it is because it is founded on the caste system.

(2) The seeds of Swaraj are to be found in the caste system. Different castes are like different sections of miliary division. Each division is working for the good of the whole.

(3) A community which can create the caste system must be said to possess unique power of organization.

(4) Caste has a ready made means for spreading primary education. Each caste can take the responsibility for the education of the children of the caste. Caste has a political basis. It can work as an electorate for a representative body. Caste can perform judicial functions by electing persons to act as judges to decide disputes among members of the same caste. With castes it is easy to raise a defense force by requiring each caste to raise a brigade.

(5) I believe that interdining or intermarriage are not necessary for promoting national unity. That dining together creates friendship is contrary to experience. If this was true there would have been no war in Europe.... Taking food is as dirty an act as answering the call of nature. The only difference is that after answering call of nature we get peace while after eating food we get discomfort. Just as we perform the act of answering the call of nature in seclusion so also the act of taking food must also be done in seclusion.

(6) In India children of brothers do not intermarry. Do they cease to love because they do not intermarry? Among the Vaishnavas many women are so orthodox that they will not eat with members of the family nor will they drink water from a common water pot. Have they no love? The caste system cannot be said to be bad because it does not allow interdining or intermarriage between different castes.

(7) Caste is another name for control. Caste puts a limit on enjoyment. Caste does not allow a person to transgress caste limits in pursuit of his enjoyment. That is the meaning of such caste restrictions as interdining and intermarriage.

(8) To destroy caste system and adopt Western European social system means that Hindus must give up the principle of hereditary occupation which is the soul of the caste system. Hereditary principle is an eternal principle. To change it is to create disorder. I have no use for a Brahmin if I cannot call him a Brahmin for my life. It will be a chaos if every day a Brahmin is to be changed into a Sudra and a Sudra is to be changed into a Brahmin.

(9) The caste system is a natural order of society. In India it has been given a religious coating. Other countries not having understood the utility of the caste system, it existed only in a loose condition and consequently those countries have not derived from caste system the same degree of advantage which India has derived. These being my views I am opposed to all those who are out to destroy the caste system.

In 1922, Mr. Gandhi was a defender of the caste system. Pursuing the inquiry, one comes across a somewhat critical view of the caste system by Mr. Gandhi in the year 1925. This is what Mr. Gandhi said on 3rd February 1925:

I gave support to caste because it stands for restraint. But at present caste does not mean restraint, it means limitations. Restraint is glorious and helps to achieve freedom. But limitation is like chain. It binds. There is nothing commendable in castes as they exist today. They are contrary to the tenets of the Shastras. The number of castes is infinite and there is a bar against intermarriage. This is not a condition of elevation. It is a state of fall.

In reply to the question: What is the way out? Mr. Gandhi said: The best remedy is that small castes should fuse themselves into one big caste. There should be four big castes so that we may reproduce the old system of four Varnas. In short, in 1925 Mr. Gandhi became an upholder of the Varna system. The old Varna system prevalent in ancient India had the society divided into four orders: (1) Brahmins, whose occupation was learning; (2) Kshatriyas, whose occupation was warfare; (3) Vaishyas, whose occupation was trade and (4) Sudras, whose occupation was service of the other classes. Is Mr. Gandhi's Varna system the same as this old Varna system of the orthodox Hindus? Mr. Gandhi explained his Varna system in the following terms:

(1) I believe that the divisions into Varna is based on birth.

(2) There is nothing in the Varna system which stands in the way of the Sudra acquiring learning or studying military art of offence or defence. Contra it is open to a Kshatriya to serve. The Varna system is no bar to him. What the Varna system enjoins is that a Sudra will not make learning a way of earning a living. Nor will a Kshatriya adopt service as a way of learning a living. (Similarly a Brahmin may learn the art of war or trade. But he must not make them a way of earning his living. Contra a Vaishya may acquire learning or may cultivate the art of war. But he must not make them a way of learning his living.)

(3) The Varna system is connected with the way of earning a living. There is no harm if a person belonging to one Varna acquires the knowledge or science and art specialized in by persons belonging to other Varnas. But as far as the way of earning his living is concerned he must follow the occupation of the Varna to which he belongs which means he must follow the hereditary profession of his forefathers.

(4) The object of the Varna is to prevent competition and class struggle and class war. I believe in the Varna system because it fixes the duties and occupations of persons.

(5) Varna means the determination of a man's occupation before he is born.

(6) In the Varna system no man has any liberty to choose his occupation. His occupation is determined for him by heredity.

The social life of Gandhism is either caste or Varna. Though it may be difficult to say which, there can be no doubt that the social ideal of Gandhism is not democracy. For, whether one takes for comparison caste or Varnaboth are fundamentally opposed to democracy. That Mr. Gandhi changed over from the caste system to the Varna system does not make the slightest difference to the charge that Gandhism is opposed to democracy. In the first place, the idea of Varna is the parent of the idea of caste. If the idea of caste is a pernicious idea it is entirely because of the viciousness of the idea of Varna. Both are evil ideas and it matters very little whether one believes in Varna or in caste.

Turning to the field of economic life, Mr. Gandhi stands for two ideals. One of these is the opposition to machinery... evidenced by his idolization of Charkha (the spinning wheel) and by insistence upon hand-spinning and hand-weaving. His opposition to machinery and his love for Charkha are not matter of accident. They are a matter of his philosophy of life.

The second ideal of Mr. Gandhi is the elimination of class war and even class struggle in the relationship between employers and employees and between landlords and tenants.... Mr. Gandhi does not wish to hurt the propertied class. He is even opposed to a campaign against them. He has no passion for economic equality. Referring to the propertied class Mr. Gandhi said quite recently that he does not wish to destroy the hen that lays the golden egg. His solution for the economic conflict between the owners and the workers, between the rich and the poor, between the landlords and the tenants and between the employers and the employees is very simple. The owners need not deprive themselves of their property. All they need do is to declare themselves trustees for the poor. Of course, the trust is to be a voluntary one carrying only a spiritual obligation.

Is there anything new in the Gandhian analysis of economic ills? Are the economics of Gandhism sound? What hope does Gandhism hold out to the common man, to the down and out? Does it promise him a better life, a life of joy and culture, a life of freedom, not merely freedom from want but freedom to rise, to grow to the full stature which his capacities can reach?

There is nothing new in the Gandhian analysis of economic ills, insofar as it attributes them to machinery and the civilization that is built upon it. That machinery and modern civilization help to concentrate management and control into relatively few hands, and with the aid of banking and credit facilitate the transfer into still fewer hands of all materials and factories and mills in which millions are bled white in order to support huge industries thousands of miles away from their cottages, maimings and cripplings far in excess of the corresponding injuries by war, and are responsible for disease and physical deterioration due directly and indirectly to the development of large cities with their smoke, dirt, noise, foul air, lack of sunshine and outdoor life, slums, prostitution and unnatural living which they bring about, are all old and worn-out arguments. There is nothing new in them. Gandhism is merely repeating the views of Rousseau, Ruskin, Tolstoy and their school.

The ideas which go to make up Gandhism are just primitive. It is a return to nature, to animal life. The only merit is their simplicity. As there is always a large corps of simple people who are attracted by them, such simple ideas do not die, and there is always some simpleton to preach them. There is, however, no doubt that the practical instincts of men—which seldom go wrong—have found them unfruitful and which society in search of progress has thought it best to reject.

The economics of Gandhism are hopelessly fallacious. The fact that machinery and modern civilization have produced many evils may be admitted. But these evils are no argument against them. For the evils are not due to machinery and modern civilization. They are due to wrong social organization, which has made private property and pursuit of personal gain, matters of absolute sanctity. If machinery and civilization have not benefited everybody, the remedy is not to condemn machinery and civilization but to alter the organization of society so that the benefits will not be usurped by the few but will accrue to all.

In Gandhism, the common man has no hope. It treats man as an animal and no more. It is true that man shares the constitution and functions of animals, nutritive, reproductive, etc. But these are not distinctively human functions. The distinctively human function is reason, the purpose of which is to enable man to observe, meditate, cogitate, study and discover the beauties of the Universe and enrich his life and control the animal elements in his life. Man thus occupies the highest place in the scheme of animate existence. If this is true what is the conclusion that follows: The conclusion that follows is that while the ultimate goal of a brute's life is reached once his physical appetites are satisfied, the ultimate goal of man's existence is not reached unless and until he has fully cultivated his mind. In short, what divides the brute from man is culture. Culture is not possible for the brute, but it is essential for man. That being so, the aim of human society must be to enable every person to lead a life of culture, which means the cultivation of mind as distinguished from the satisfaction of mere physical wants. How can this happen?

Both for society as well as for individual(s) there is always a gulf between merely living and living worthily. In order that one may live worthily one must first live. The time and energy spent upon mere life, upon gaining of subsistence detracts from that available for activities of a distinctively human nature and which go to make up a life of culture. How then can a life of culture be made possible? It is not possible unless there is sufficient leisure. For, it is only when there is leisure that a person is free to devote himself to a life of culture.

The problem of all problems, which human society has to face, is how to provide leisure to every individual. What does leisure mean? Leisure means the lessening of the toil and effort necessary for satisfying the physical wants of life. How can leisure be made possible? Leisure is quite impossible unless some means are found whereby the toil required for producing goods necessary to satisfy human needs is lessened. What can lessen such toil? Only when machine takes the place of man. There is no other means of producing leisure. Machinery and modern civilization are thus indispensable for emancipating man from leading the life of a brute, and for providing him with leisure and for making a life of culture possible. The man who condemns machinery and modern civilization simply does not understand their purpose and the ultimate aim which human society must strive to achieve.

Gandhism may well be well suited to a society which does not accept democracy as its ideal. A society which does not believe in democracy may be indifferent to machinery and the civilization based upon it. But a democratic society cannot. The former may well content itself with a life of leisure and culture for the few and a life of toil and drudgery for the many. But a democratic society must assure a life of leisure and culture to each one of its citizens. If the above analysis is correct then the slogan of a democratic society must be machinery, and more machinery, civilization and more civilization. Under Gandhism the common man must keep on toiling ceaselessly for a pittance and remain a brute. In short, Gandhism with its call of back to nature, means back to nakedness, back to squalor, back to poverty and back to ignorance for the vast mass of the people.

Gandhism insists upon class structure. It regards the class structure of society and also the income structure as sacrosanct with the consequent distinctions of rich and poor, high and low, owners and workers, as permanent parts of social organization. From the point of view of social consequences, nothing can be more pernicious.... It is not enough to say that Gandhism believes in a class structure. Gandhism stands for more than that. A class structure which is a faded, jejune, effete thing—a mere sentimentality, a mere skeleton is not what Gandhism wants. It wants class structure to function as a living faith. In this there is nothing to be surprised at. For, class structure in Gandhism is not a mere accident. It is its official doctrine.

The idea of trusteeship, which Gandhism proposes as a panacea and by which the moneyed classes will hold their properties in trust for the poor, is the most ridiculous part of it. All that one can say about it is that if anybody else had propounded it the author would have been laughed at as a silly fool, who had not known the hard realities of life and was deceiving the servile classes by telling them that a little dose of moral rearmament to the propertied classes—those who by their insatiable cupidity and indomitable arrogance have made and will always make this world a vale of tears for the toiling millions—will recondition them to such an extent that they will be able to withstand the temptation to misuse the tremendous powers which the class structure gives them over servile classes.

Mr. Gandhi sometimes speaks on social and economic subjects as though he was a blushing Red. Those who will study Gandhism will not be deceived by the occasional aberrations of Mr. Gandhi in favour of democracy and against capitalism. For, Gandhism is in no sense a revolutionary creed. It is conservatism in excelsis. So far as India is concerned, it is a reactionary creed blazoning on its banner the call of Return to Antiquity. Gandhism aims at the resuscitation and reanimating of India's dread, dying past.

Gandhism is a paradox. It stands for freedom from foreign domination, which means the destruction of the existing political structure of the country. At the same time, it seeks to maintain intact a social structure which permits the domination of one class by another on a hereditary basis which means a perpetual domination of one class by another....

The first special feature of Gandhism is that its philosophy helps those who want to keep what they have and to prevent those who have not from getting what they have a right to get. No one who examines the Gandhian attitude to strikes, the Gandhian reverence for caste and the Gandhian doctrine of Trusteeship by the rich for the benefit of the poor can deny that this is an upshot of Gandhism. Whether this is the calculated result of a deliberate design or whether it is a matter of accident may be open to argument. But the fact remains that Gandhism is the philosophy of the well-to-do and the leisure class. The second special feature of Gandhism is to delude people into accepting their misfortunes by presenting them as best of good fortunes. One or two illustrations will suffice to bring out the truth of this statement.

The Hindu sacred law penalized the Sudras (Hindus of the fourth class) from acquiring wealth. It is a law of enforced poverty unknown in any other part of the world. What does Gandhism do? It does not lift the ban. It blesses the Sudra for his moral courage to give up property. It is well worth quoting Mr. Gandhi's own words. Here they are: The Sudra who only serves (the higher caste) as a matter of religious duty, and who will never own any property, who indeed has not even the ambition to own anything, is deserving of thousand obeisance... The very Gods will shower flowers on him.

Another illustration in support is the attitude of Gandhism towards the scavenger. The sacred law of the Hindus lays down that a scavenger's progeny shall live by scavenging. Under Hinduism scavenging was not a matter of choice, it was a matter of force. What does Gandhism do? It seeks to perpetuate this system by praising scavenging as the noblest service to society! Let me quote Mr. Gandhi: As a President of a Conference of the Untouchables, Mr. Gandhi said: I do not want to attain Moksha. I do not want to be reborn. But if I have to be reborn, I should be born an untouchable, so that I may share their sorrows, sufferings and the affronts levelled at them, in order that I endeavour to free myself and them from that miserable condition. I, therefore prayed that if I should be born again, I should do so not as a Brahmin, Kshatriya, Vaishya, or Sudra, but as an Atishudra.... I love scavenging. In my Ashram, an eighteen-years-old Brahmin lad is doing the scavenger's work in order to teach the Ashram scavenger cleanliness. The lad is no reformer. He was born and bred in orthodoxy.... But he felt that his accomplishments were incomplete until he had become also a perfect sweeper, and that, if he wanted the Ashram sweeper to do his work well, he must do it himself and set an example. You should realize that you are cleaning Hindu Society.

Can there be a worse example of false propaganda than this attempt of Gandhism to perpetuate evils which have been deliberately imposed by one class over another? If Gandhism preached the rule of poverty for all and not merely for the Sudra the worst that could be said about it is that it is mistaken idea. But why preach it as good for one class only?... In India a man is not a scavenger because of his work. He is a scavenger because of his birth irrespective of the question whether he does scavenging or not. If Gandhism preached that scavenging is a noble profession with the object of inducing those who refuse to engage in it, one could understand it. But why appeal to the scavenger's pride and vanity in order to induce him and him only to keep on to scavenging by telling him that scavenging is a noble profession and that he need not be ashamed of it? To preach that poverty is good for the Sudra and for none else, to preach that scavenging is good for the Untouchables and for none else and to make them accept these onerous impositions as voluntary purposes of life, by appeal to their failings is an outrage and a cruel joke on the helpless classes which none but Mr. Gandhi can perpetrate with equanimity and impunity.

Criticism apart, this is the technique of Gandhism to make wrongs done appear to the very victim as though they were his privileges. If there is an "ism" which has made full use of religion as an opium to lull the people into false beliefs and false security, it is Gandhism. Following Shakespeare, one can well say: Plausibility! Ingenuity! Thy name is Gandhism. Such is Gandhism.

Having known what is Gandhism the answer to the question, "Should Gandhism become the law of the land what would be the lot of the Untouchables under it?" cannot require much scratching of the brain.... In India even the lowest man among the caste Hindus—why even the aboriginal and the Hill Tribe man—though educationally and economically not very much above the Untouchables. The Hindu society accepts him claim to superiority over the Untouchables. The Untouchable will therefore continue to suffer the worst fate as he does now namely, in prosperity he will be the last to be employed and in depression the first to be fired.

What does Gandhism do to relieve the Untouchables from this fate? Gandhism professes to abolish Untouchability. That is hailed as the greatest virtue of Gandhism. But what does this virtue amount to in actual life? To assess the value of this anti-Untouchability which is regarded as a very big element in Gandhism, it is necessary to understand fully the scope of Mr. Gandhi's programme for the removal of Untouchability. Does it mean anything more than that the Hindus will not mind touching the Untouchables? Does it mean the removal of the ban on the right of the Untouchables to education? It would be better to take the two questions separately.

To start wit the first question. Mr. Gandhi does not say that a Hindu should not take a bath after touching the Untouchables. If Mr. Gandhi does not object to it as a purification of pollution then it is difficult to see how Untouchability can be said to vanish by touching the Untouchables. Untouchability centres round the idea of pollution by contact and purification by bath to remove the pollution. Does it mean social assimilation of the Untouchables with the Hindus? Mr. Gandhi has most categorically stated that removal of Untouchability does not mean interdining or intermarriage between the Hindus and the Untouchables. Mr. Gandhi's anti-Untouchability means that the Untouchables will be classes as Sudras instead of being classed as Atishudras (*i.e.,* "beyond Sudras").

There is nothing more in it. Mr. Gandhi has not considered whether the old Sudras will accept the new Sudras into their fold. If they don't then the removal of Untouchability is a senseless proposition for it will still keep the Untouchables as a separate social category. Mr. Gandhi probably knows that the abolition of Untouchability will not bring about the assimilation of the Untouchables by the Sudras. That seems to be the reason why Mr. Gandhi himself has given a new and a different name to the Untouchables. The new name registers by anticipation what is likely to be the fact. By calling the Untouchables Harijans, Mr. Gandhi has killed two birds with one stone. He has shown that assimilation of the Untouchables by the Sudras is not possible. He has also by his new name counteracted assimilation and made it impossible.

Regarding the second question, it is true that Gandhism is prepared to remove the old ban placed by the Hindu Shastras on the right of the Untouchables to education and permit them to acquire knowledge and learning. Under Gandhism the Untouchables may study law, they may study medicine, they may study engineering or anything else they may fancy. So far so good. But will the Untouchables be free to make use of their knowledge and learning? Will they have the right to choose their profession? Can they adopt the career of lawyer, doctor or engineer? To these questions the answer which Gandhism gives is an emphatic "no." The untouchables must follow their hereditary professions. That those occupations are unclean is no excuse. That before the occupation became hereditary it was the result of force and not volition does not matter.

The argument of Gandhism is that what is once settled is settled forever even it was wrongly settled. Under Gandhism the Untouchables are to be eternal scavengers. There is no doubt that the Untouchables would much prefer the orthodox system of Untouchability. A compulsory state of ignorance imposed upon the Untouchables by the Hindu Shastras made scavenging bearable. But Gandhism which compels an educated Untouchable to do scavenging is nothing short of cruelty. The grace in Gandhism is a curse in its worst form. The virtue of the anti-Untouchability plant in Gandhism is quite illusory. There is no substance in it.

What else is there in Gandhism which the Untouchables can accept as opening a way for their ultimate salvation? Barring this illusory campaign against Untouchability, Gandhism is simply another form of Sanatanism which is the ancient name for militant orthodox Hinduism. What is there in Gandhism which is not to be found in orthodox Hinduism? There is caste in Hinduism, there is caste in Gandhism. Hinduism believes in the law of hereditary profession, so does Gandhism. Hinduism enjoins cow-worship. So does Gandhism. Hinduism upholds the law of karma, predestination of man's condition in this world, so does Gandhism. Hinduism accepts the authority of the Shastras. So does Gandhism. Hinduism believes in idols. So does Gandhism. All that Gandhism has done is to find a philosophic justification for Hinduism and its dogmas. Hinduism is bald in the sense that it is just a set of rules which bear on their face the appearance of a crude and cruel system. Gandhism supplies the philosophy which smoothens its surface and gives it the appearance of decency and respectability and so alters it and embellishes it as to make it even more attractive.

What hope can Gandhism offer to the Untouchables? To the Untouchables, Hinduism is a veritable chamber of horrors. The sanctity and infallibility of the Vedas, Smritis and Shastras, the iron law of caste, the heartless law of karma and the senseless law of status by birth are to the Untouchables veritable instruments of torture which Hinduism has forged against the Untouchables. These very instruments which have mutilated, blasted and blighted the life of the Untouchables are to be found intact and untarnished in the bosom of Gandhism. How can the Untouchables say that Gandhism is a heaven and not a chamber of horrors as Hinduism has been? The only reaction and a very natural reaction of the Untouchables would be to run away from Gandhism.

Gandhists may say that what I have stated applies to the old type of Gandhism. There is a new Gandhism, Gandhism without caste. This has reference to the recent statement of Mr. Gandhi that caste is an anachronism. Reformers were naturally gladdened by this declaration of Mr. Gandhi. And who would not be glad to see that a man like Mr. Gandhi having such terrible influence over the Hindus, after having played the most mischievous part of a social reactionary, after having stood out as the protagonist of the caste system, after having beguiled and befooled the unthinking Hindus with arguments which made no distinction between what is fair and foul should have come out with this recantation? But is this really a matter for jubilation? Does it change the nature of Gandhism? Does it make Gandhism a new and a better "ism" than it was before? Those who are carried away by this recantation of Mr. Gandhi, forget two things. In the first place, all that Mr. Gandhi has said is that caste is an anachronism. He does not say it is an evil. He does not say it is anathema. Mr. Gandhi may be taken to be not in favour of caste, but Mr. Gandhi does not say that he is against the Varna system. And what is Mr. Gandhi's Varna system? It is simply a new name for the caste system and retains all the worst features of the caste system.

The declaration of Mr. Gandhi cannot be taken to mean any fundamental change in Gandhism. It cannot make Gandhism acceptable to the Untouchables. The untouchables will still have ground to say: "Good God! Is this man Gandhi our Saviour?"

Gandhi and Racism

To understand Gandhi's role towards the blacks, one requires a knowledge of Hinduism. Within the constraints, a few words on Hinduism will suffice: The caste is the bedrock of Hinduism. The Hindu term for caste is varna; which means arranging the society on a four-level hierarchy based on the skin colour: The darker-skinned relegated to the lowest level, the lighter-skinned to the top three levels of the apartheid scale called the Caste System. The race factor underlies the intricate workings of Hinduism, not to mention the countless evil practices embedded within. Have no doubt, Gandhi loved the Caste system.

Gandhi lived in South Africa for roughly twenty one years from 1893 to 1914. In 1906, he joined the military with a rank of Sergeant-Major and actively participated in the war against the blacks. Gandhi's racist ideas are also evident in his writings of these periods. One should ask a question: Were our American Black leaders including Dr. King aware of Gandhi's anti-black activities? Painfully, we have researched the literature and the answer is, no. For this lapse, the blame lies on the Afro-American newspapers which portrayed Gandhi in ever glowing terms, setting the stage for African-American leaders Howard Thurman, Sue Baily Thurman, Reverend Edward Carroll, Benjamin E. Mays, Channing H. Tobias, and William Stuart Nelson to visit India at different time periods to meet Gandhi in person. None of these leaders had any deeper understanding of Hinduism, British India, or the complexities of Gandhi's convoluted multilayered Hindu mind.

Frankly speaking, these leaders were no match to Gandhi's deceit; Gandhi hoodwinked them all, and that too, with great ease. Understanding of Hindu India with our black leaders never really improved even considering years later in March 1959, much after Gandhi's death, Dr. Martin Luther King, Jr., his wife, and Professor Lawrence D. Reddick visited India and to our way of analysis, they fared no better than their predecessors. We are certain, had Dr. King known Gandhi's anti-black and other criminal activities, he would have distanced his civil-rights movement away from the name of Gandhi. We recommend the following:

1. Grenier, Richard. The Gandhi Nobody Knows published in Commentary March 1983; pages 59 to 72. This is the best article on Gandhi briefly outlining his war activities against the blacks.
2. Kapur, Sudarshan. Raising up a Prophet: The African-American Encounter with Gandhi; Boston: Beacon Press, 1992 Excellent research book into the perspective of distant American blacks with respect to their new hero, Gandhi. However, this book has one major flaw: The author seems to be unaware of Gandhi's anti-black activities in South Africa.
3. Huq, Fazlul. Gandhi: Saint or Sinner? Bangalore: Dalit Sahitya Akademy, 1992.

Superb book. Really gets into the Gandhi's anti-black ideology with a sense of history setting intact. This book's second chapter-Gandhi's Anti-African Racismóis a superb analysis of Gandhi's anti-black thinking. We bring to you the whole chapter for your review: Gandhi was not a whit less racist than the white racists of South Africa. When Gandhi formed the Natal Indian Congress on August 22, 1894, the no. 1 objective he declared was: "To promote concord and harmony among the Indians and Europeans in the Colony." (Collected Works (CW)1 pp. 132-33) He launched his Indian Opinion on June 4 1904: "The object of Indian Opinion was to bring the European and the Indian subjects of the King Edward closer together." (CW. IV P. 320)

What was the harm in making an effort to bring understanding among all people, irrespective of colour, creed or religion? Did not Gandhi know that a huge population of blacks and coloured lived there? Perhaps to Gandhi they were less than human beings.

Addressing a public meeting in Bombay on Sept. 26 1896 (CW II p. 74), Gandhi said: Ours is one continued struggle against degradation sought to be inflicted upon us by the European, who desire to degrade us to the level of the raw Kaffir, whose occupation is hunting and whose sole ambition is to collect a certain number of cattle to buy a wife with, and then pass his life in indolence and nakedness.

In 1904, he wrote (CW. IV p. 193): It is one thing to register natives who would not work, and whom it is very difficult to find out if they absent themselves, but it is another thing-and most insulting-to expect decent, hard-working, and respectable Indians, whose only fault is that they work too much, to have themselves registered and carry with them registration badges.

In its editorial on the Natal Municipal Corporation Bill, the Indian Opinion of March 18 1905 wrote: Clause 200 makes provision for registration of persons belonging to uncivilized races (meaning the local Africans), resident and employed within the Borough. One can understand the necessity of registration of Kaffirs who will not work, but why should registration be required for indentured Indians who have become free, and for their descendants about whom the general complaint is that they work too much? (Italic portion is added)

The Indian Opinion published an editorial on September 9 1905 under the heading, "The relative Value of the Natives and the Indians in Natal". In it Gandhi referred to a speech made by Rev. Dube, a most accomplished African, who said that an African had the capacity for improvement, if only the Colonials would look upon him as better than dirt, and give him a chance to develop self-respect. Gandhi suggested that "A little judicious extra taxation would do no harm; in the majority of cases it compels the native to work for at least a few days a year." Then he added:

Now let us turn our attention to another and entirely unrepresented community-the Indian. He is in striking contrast with the native. While the native has been of little benefit to the State, it owes its prosperity largely to the Indians. While native loafers abound on every side, that species of humanity is almost unknown among Indians here.

Nothing could be further from the truth, that Gandhi fought against Apartheid, which many propagandists in later years wanted people to believe. He was all in favour of continuation of white domination and oppression of the blacks in South Africa.

In the Government Gazette of Natal for Feb. 28 1905, a Bill was published regulating the use of firearms by the natives and Asiatics. Commenting on the Bill, the Indian Opinion of March 25 1905 stated: In this instance of the firearms, the Asiatic has been most improperly bracketed with the natives. The British Indian does not need any such restrictions as are imposed by the Bill on the natives regarding the carrying of firearms. The prominent race can remain so by preventing the native from arming himself. Is there a slightest vestige of justification for so preventing the British Indian?

Here is the budding Mahatma telling the white racists how they can perpetuate their Nazi domination over the vast majority of Africans. In the British imperialist scheme, one important strategy was to divide and rule. Gandhi advised Indians not to align with other political groups in either coloured or African communities. In 1906 the coloured people in the colonies of Good Hope, the Transvaal and the Orange River colony, addressed a petition to the King Emperor demanding franchise rights. The petitioners showed clearly that, in one part of South Africa, namely the Cape of Good Hope, they had enjoyed the franchise ever since the introduction of representative institutions. Commenting on the petition, the Indian Opinion of March 24 1906, declaring that "British Indians have, in order that they may never be misunderstood, made it clear that they do not aspire to any political power," added:

It seems that the petition is being widely circulated, and signatures are being taken of all coloured people in the three colonies named. The petition is non-Indian in character, although British Indians, being coloured people, are very largely affected by it. We consider that it was a wise policy on the part of the British Indians throughout South Africa, to have kept themselves apart and distinct from the other coloured communities in this country.

In a statement made in 1906 to the Constitution Committee, the British Indian Association led by Gandhi (CW. V p. 335) said:

The British Indian Association has always admitted the principle of white domination and has, therefore, no desire, on behalf of the community it represents, for any political rights just for the sake of them. Commenting on a court case, the Indian Opinion of 2, June 1906, in its Gujrati section, stated: You say that the magistrate's decision is unsatisfactory because it would enable a person, however unclean, to travel by a tram, and that even the Kaffirs would be able to do so. But the magistrate's decision is quite different. The Court declared that the Kaffirs have no legal right to travel by tram. And according to tram regulations, those in an unclean dress or in a drunken state are prohibited from boarding a tram. Thanks to the Court's decision, only clean Indians (meaning upper caste Hindu Indians) or coloured people other than Kaffirs, can now travel in the trams. (Italic portion is added)

Apartheid defended: Gandhi accepted racial segregation, not only because it was politically expedient as his Imperial masters had already drawn such a blueprint, it also conformed with his own attitude to the caste system. In his own mind he fitted Apartheid into the caste system: whites in the position of Brahmins, Indian merchants and professionals as Sudras, and all other non-whites as Untouchables. Though Gandhi was strongly opposed to the comingling of races, the working-class Indians did not share his distaste. There were many areas where Indians, Chinese, Coloured, Africans and poor whites lived together. On February 15 1905, Gandhi wrote to Dr. Porter, the Medical Officer of Health, Johannesburg (CW. IV p. 244, and "Indian Opinion" 9 April 1904):

Why, of all places in Johannesburg, the Indian location should be chosen for dumping down all kaffirs of the town, passes my comprehension. Of course, under my suggestion, the Town Council must withdraw the Kaffirs from the Location. About this mixing of the Kaffirs with the Indians I must confess I feel most strongly. I think it is very unfair to the Indian population, and it is an undue tax on even the proverbial patience of my countrymen.

Dr. Porter replied that it was the Indians who sub-let to Africans. Commenting on the White League's agitation, Gandhi wrote in his Indian Opinion of September 24 1903: We believe as much in the purity of race as we think they do, only we believe that they would best serve these interests, which are as dear to us as to them, by advocating the purity of all races, and not one alone. We believe also that the white race of South Africa should be the predominating race.

Again, on December 24 1903, Indian Opinion stated: The petition dwells upon `the comingling of the coloured and white races'. May we inform the members of the Conference that so far as British Indians are concerned, such a thing is particularly unknown. If there is one thing which the Indian cherishes more than any other, it is the purity of type.

In his farewell speech at a meeting held in the house of Dr. Gool in Capetown, which was reported in the Indian Opinion of July 1 1914, Gandhi said: The Indians knew perfectly well which was the dominant and governing race. They aspired to no social equality with Europeans. They felt that the path of their development was separate. They did not even aspire to the franchise, or, if the aspiration exists, it was with no idea of its having a present effect.

Gandhi joined in the orgy of Zulu slaughter when the Bambata Rebellion broke out. It is essential to discuss the background of the Bambata Rebellion, to place Gandhi's Nazi war crime in its proper perspective.

The Bambatta Rebellion—Background

The spiritual foundation of Nazism was the superiority of the Aryan race or its modern version, the Anglo-Saxon race. When Disraeli was Prime Minister, Britain enunciated a doctrine, like the Monroe Doctrine, warning other European powers that Africa would be a British preserve, and that from the Cape to the Limpopo, if not to Cairo, only white people would have local political power. Successive British Governments pursued this policy.

In the 1870s, the Zulu Kingdom was by far the most powerful African State of the Limpopo. Cetewayo, who succeeded his father in 1872, was an able and popular ruler. He united the kingdom and built up a most efficient army. He followed a policy of alliance with the British Colony of Natal. The Zulu Kingdom and the Boer Republic of the Transvaal had been feuding for a long time. The Zulus were defeated twice by the Boers, in 1838 and 1840. By 1877 Cetewayo was ready to invade the Transvaal. But the British stepped in and annexed the Transvaal in 1877, only to prevent

Cetewayo from doing it first and becoming powerful and a challenge to white supremacy.

Some contemporary reports throw light on the relative strength of the Zulus and their Boer enemies. Colonel A. W. Durnford wrote in a memorandum on July 5 ("The Secret History of South Africa" by Abercrombe. The Central News Agency Ltd., Johannesburg South Africa. 1951 p. 6): About this time (April 10th) Cetewayo had massed his forces in three corps on the borders, and would undoubtedly have swept the Transvaal, at least up to the Vaal River if not to Pretoria itself, had the country not been taken over by the English. In my opinion he would have cleared the country to Pretoria.

Shepstone, the British Administrator, himself wrote concerning the reality of the danger on Dec. 25 1877: The Boers are still flying, and I think by this time there must be a belt of more than a hundred miles long and thirty broad in which, with three insignificant exceptions, there is nothing but absolute desolation. This will give some idea of the mischief which Cetewayo's conduct has caused. (Ibid p.7).

The above facts explode the myth that the British protected the Zulus from the Boers. British barbarity on Blacks: After annexing the Transvaal, Shepstone turned his attention to destroying all the independent African states in that region, particularly the Zulu Kingdom. Before annexation of the Transvaal, Shepstone sided with the Zulus in their border disputes with the Transvaal. After annexation he made a volte-face and used those disputes as excuses to invade Zululand. The British public was told that the Zulu War was to liberate the Zulu people from a tyrannical ruler, and South Africa from a menace to "Christianity and civilisation".

In 1879, the British invaded the Zulu Kingdom and defeated Cetawayo. Then they started their complete subjugation. First the army was broken, thus destroying their ability to defend themselves. The country was then split into thirteen separate units under the nominal control of the chiefs, salaried by the Government. The white magistrates supplanted the chiefs as the most powerful men in their districts. Most important of all, the land was partitioned. Before the war, Shepstone had expressed the hope that Cetewayo's warriors would be "changed to labourers working for wages". It makes a sad story, how this was accomplished. In 1902-4, the Land Commission delineated a number of locations for the Zulus, and threw open the rest of the country to white settlement. Out of a total acreage of more than 12 million acres, the Africans held some 2 million acres. They numbered, at the lowest reckoning, over three hundred thousand.

The Europeans, who were less than 20, 000, owned most of the best land. A large proportion of the African population was forced to live upon land to which it had no legal claim. Where the Africans lived upon private or crown lands, they lived there entirely upon sufferance and without legal title. By this time, other independent African states in that region were also destroyed by the British army. Wheresoever, they marched, in Basutoland, Zululand or Bechuanaland, the Queen's horses and the Queen's men were like unto a "Salvation Army" ministering to the welfare of the colonists. The sufferers were the Africans.

Gandhi wrote in his Satyagraha in South Africa (p. 15): The Boers are simple, frank and religious. They settle in the midst of extensive farms. We can have no idea of the extent of these farms. A farm with us means generally an acre or two, and sometimes even less. In South Africa, a single farmer has hundreds or thousands of acres of land in his possession. He is not anxious to put all this under cultivation at once, and if any one argues with him he will say, `Let it lie fallow; lands which are now fallow will be cultivated by our children'.

Also in his Indian Opinion (March 15 1913), he wrote: General Botha has thousands of acres of land... (there is) a big company in Natal which has hundreds of thousands of acres of land.

Thou shalt not steal but rob. It did not seem to occur to Gandhi how these people came into possession of thousands of acres of land, whereas Africans were cooped in locations like chicken in pens.

Grabbing the land was not enough: it needed manpower to cultivate that land. The cry of the farmers was for labour. Naturally it found a favourite response from Shepstone, whose dream it was to convert Cetewayo's warriors into labourers for white men. His native policy was to meet the demands of the European farmers.

He agreed that Europeans could not expand or grow in wealth unless they could draw more fully upon the reservoirs of labour in the African reserves.

In the process of European colonisation, the swiftly expanding land-hungry Europeans turned the bulk of the African population into a proletariat. Due to the congestion and landlessness in the reserves, created deliberately by the white rulers, their agricultural return was not sufficient for bare existence. Then there were the taxes on huts, cattle and what not. On the other hand, working for white men did not provide them with adequate sustenance. In Natal, the sugar farmers of the coast relied upon the Indian indentured labour, whereas the stock farmers of the interior relied exclusively on Africans, and regarded the failure of Africans to work for them as a criminal offence.

In a report to the Chief Commissioner of Police in 1903, the Police Inspector W. F. Fairley wrote: "With regard to crime, the principal complaints made by Dutch farmers to patrols was of the refusal to work on the part of the natives." (Department Reports 1903 p. 67 cited "Reluctant Rebellion" by Marks p. 17. Clarendon Press, Oxford 1970). Complaints about the shortage of African labour were voiced in all parts of the country. The farmers were later joined by the mining industries. The most obvious change was the broadening of the economic base from being entirely agricultural to one in which mining played a more and more important part. Diamond, gold, coal became major industries, and with this development, the deeper involvement of the big finance houses, particularly Rothschilds. So the fate of the Africans as the source of cheap labour, and the fat dividends derived from mining by the British ruling class, became interlinked. This still continues in a modified form. Now it is Anglo-American corporations.

Cheap labour from India: Europeans assumed that Africans lived only to meet their requirements of cheap labour, and as such they had no right to establish themselves as self-sufficient and independent farmers because this conflicted with European interests. Famines in India facilitates the recruitment of indentured Indian labourers for white employers in the Colonies. It was no different in relation to Africans. In a Report of the Native Affairs Commission, (Native Affairs Commission Report 1939-40 cited "Oxford History of South Africa" p. 182. Clarendon Press,

Oxford, 1969) it was admitted that "African reserves were regarded by whites as reservoirs of labour, and congestion, landlessness and crop failure were welcomed as stimulants to the labour supply".

Similar situations among whites were viewed as national calamities. The Government lent millions of pounds to white farmers, gave them tax relief in times of famine, paid subsidies, facilitated the export of their produce, and wrote off their debts. But what about Africans? Famine would be rampant, crops ruined, food exhausted, thousands of Africans and their cattle would starve to death, but the government would not raise a finger.

The whites not only stole the land from the Africans, and used them as cheap labour, but also looked to them for revenue. They drew a relatively large and growing income from the Africans. "The Native population of Natal", Shepstone admitted ("Imperial Factor" by De Kieweit p. 193. Clarendon Press, Oxford 1970), "contribute to the revenue annually a sum equal, at least, to that necessary to maintain the whole fixed establishment of the Colony for the government of the whites as well as themselves." Taxation is a financial measure to gather revenue to meet the expenditure of the state. But in South Africa it was used to reduce Africans to slavery. The sole motive behind the extra taxation imposed on Africans was to force the Africans to work on terms dictated by the whites.

Always there was resentment against any measure which would allow the Africans to settle in locations instead of keeping them as labourers. It was not only the farmers' conferences, the press owned by the mining magnates joined the outcry of the farmers to enact special laws to compel the Africans to come out of their locations and work for the whites. The press was in the forefront to arouse the sentiments that Africans not in European service were necessarily living in idleness. Gandhi's Indian Opinion played second fiddle to the white press in this respect. To Gandhi, the imposition of taxes upon the Africans to compel them to work for the white employers was "gentle persuasion".

By a stroke of the pen, the major part of the available land was taken away from the Zulus and given to Europeans. Some of the dispossessed Zulus were allotted locations and others remained on the land of European landlords on sufferance. Bambata was one of these unfortunate chiefs. He became Chief in 1890 and he and his people were placed in private locations on very high rents. The land was useless for any agricultural purpose. To make things worse, the Boer farmers suspected Bambata of informing the British about their pro-Boer activities, and naturally they tried to victimise him and his people. But after the war, the British rulers leaned backwards and went out of their way to kiss and hug the Boers. So Bambata was caught in a cleft stick. By 1905 the tension between Bambata and his white landlords reached crisis point. The Assistant Magistrate of Greytown, H. Von Gerard, wrote to the Under Secretary of Native Affairs recommending the allocation of a location for his people. Gerard described how people were being oppressed and squeezed by the landlords, what useless land it was for agricultural purposes, and how summons after summons was being issued against people who were unable to pay high rents. Finally he remarked ("Reluctant Rebellion" by Marks. P. 201):

A most desperate state of affairs, the more so as there seems no remedy for it.... My sympathies with Bambata's people... but I see no way out of the difficulty. The military and civilian leaders of Natal were consciously developing a picture as if an uprising was imminent. Not that they could foresee one, but they wanted to foresee one because that would give them a golden opportunity to inflict severe punishments on Zulus who, according to the colonists, were growing insolent. They drew up a plan to deal with this imaginary uprising swiftly, and all agreed that was the way they could save not only Natal but North Africa from the "barbarities which only the savage mind can conceive." (Ibid p. xvii)

Zulu Revolt: But outside Natal, people were not so sure. Styne, President of the Orange Free State, called it "hysteria". Smuts, Botha and Merriman expressed concern as to whether the whites of Natal would spur a rebellion. Some churchmen and many radical humanitarians in Natal, as well as England, produced volumes of irrefutable evidence proving that it was a conspiracy to goad the Zulus into rebellion and then massacre them. In this, Hariette Colenso, the famous daughter of a famous father, Bishop Colenso, made the most outstanding contribution. There was a cry of imminent native revolt in the press long before active rebellion broke out.

As far back as 1902, Lieu. G. A. Mills in his report (GH18/ 02. Cited "Reluctant Rebellion" p. 158) to the Chief of Staff, Natal, on July 1 informed him: Every Boer expresses the most bitter hatred of the Zulus. They all express a wish that the Zulus would rise now while the British troops are in the country so that they may be practically wiped out. The Boers all say that in the event of the rising, every one of them would join the British troops in order to have a chance of paying off old scores against the Zulus. When I first came here, I visited farms and asked the Boers what they thought of the advisability of keeping troops here. They all said it was most necessary, as they were afraid of the Kaffirs and it would not be safe to stay on their farms if the troops withdrew.... Taking everything into consideration, I cannot help being forced to the opinion that many Boers intend to provoke a Zulu rising if they can do so.

It was Colonel Mackenzie, the military supremo before the rebellion, who was prophesying a native uprising and cleaning the barrels of his guns to use the "golden opportunity" to inflict "the most drastic punishment" on leading natives he found guilty of treason, and to "instill a proper respect for the white man". (C. O. 179/233/12460. Dispatch 9. 3. 06 cited "Reluctant Rebellion" p. 188).

On June 14, Charles Saunders, Chief Magistrate and Civil Commissioner in Zululand (1899-1909) wrote to C. J. Hignet, the magistrate of Nqutu ("Reluctant Rebellion" p. 241): I quite agree with your conclusions as to our men trying to goad the whole population into rebellion, and you have no idea of the difficulties we had in Nkandha in trying to protect people one knew perfectly well were faithful to us.

In his communication of July 10 1906 to the Prime Minister, (PM 61/15/66 Governor to PM 10. 7. 06) the Governor described the "sweeping actions and the mopping-up operations as continued slaughter. Fred Graham, a permanent civil servant in the Colonial Office, in his Minute of July 10, described it as "massacre". Nazism & racism: The most revealing was the long letter of July 24 1906 (CO 179/236/24787 minute 10-7-06) sent by the Anglican Archdeacon, Charles Johnson, from St. Augustine's in Nqutu division, to the Society for the Propagation of the Gospels in London. He was a man of the British establishment and not known to have excessive zeal for standing up for the rights of the Africans. He wrote (cited "Reluctant Rebellion" p. 241): Many thinking people have been asking themselves, what are we going to do with his teeming population? Some strong-handed men have thought the time was ripe for solving the great question. They knew that there was a general widespread spirit of disaffection among the natives of Natal, the Free State and the Transvaal, but specially in Natal, and they commenced the suppression of the rebellion in the fierce hope that the rebellion might so spread throughout the land and engender a war of practical extermination. I fully believe that they were imbued with the conviction that this was the only safe way of dealing with the native question, and they are greatly disappointed that the spirit of rebellion was not strong enough to bring more than a moiety of the native peoples under the influence of the rifle. Over and over again it was said, 'They are only sitting on the fence, it shall be our endeavour to bring them over'; and again, speaking of the big chiefs, 'We must endeavour to bring them in if possible! Yes, they have been honest and outspoken enough-the wish being father to the thought-they prophesied the rebellion would spread throughout South Africa; had they been true prophets, no doubt the necessity of solving the native question would have been solved for this generation at least.

John Merriman was a veteran Cape politician. He was one of those so-called liberals who accepted Nazism as a doctrine, or in other words Anglo-Saxon superiority, but regretted its consequent atrocities and thus fumigated their consciences. He wrote to Goldwin Smith (Merriman papers NHo. 202, 16. 9. 06 cited "Reluctant Rebellion" p. 246) in September 1906: We have had a horrible business in Natal with the natives. I suppose the whole truth will never be known, but enough comes out to make us see how thin the crust is that keeps our Christian civilisation from the old-fashioned savagery-machine-guns and modern rifles against knobsticks and assagais are heavy odds and do not add much to the glory of the superior race.

In the letter of the Archdeacon the expression "practical extermination", and in a letter of Lieutenant Mills "practically wiped out", have been used. This was what the German Nazis wanted to do to the Jews: to exterminate them. Does it make any difference whether the victims of racial slaughter are Jews or blacks? Conspiracy to massacre Blacks: Gandhi was well aware of the conspiracy to massacre the Africans. When there was war hysteria in the colonial press, this prophet of nonviolence did not apply his mind as to how to stop such a conflict. On the contrary, he did not want Indians to be left behind, but wanted them to take a full part in this genocide.

In his editorial in the Indian Opinion of Nov. 18 1905, long before the actual rebellion broke out, Gandhi complained that the Government simply did not wish to give Indians an opportunity of showing that they were as capable as any other community of taking their share in the defence of the colony. He suggested that a volunteer corps should be formed from colonial-born Indians, which would be useful in actual service.

Indentured Indians lived in conditions worse than slavery. Gandhi during his 20 years' stay in South Africa, did not raise a finger to ease their sufferings. But he was quick to suggest using them as cannon fodder for racists against Africans. In his Indian Opinion in Dec. 2 1905 he referred to Law 25 of 1875 which was specially passed to increase "the maximum strength of the volunteer force in the colony adding thereto a force of Indian immigrant volunteer infantry". To assure the Europeans that such Indians would only kill Africans, he pointed out that "section 83 of the Militia Act states that no ordinary member of the coloured contingent shall be armed with weapons of precision, unless such contingent is called to operate against other than Europeans".

Gandhi defends massacre: Many years later, he wrote (p. 233) in his autobiography: The Boer War had not brought home to me the horrors of war with anything like the vividness that the `rebellion' did. This was no war but a man-hunt, not only in my opinion but also in that of many Englishmen with whom I had occasion to talk. To hear every morning reports of the soldiers' rifles exploding like crackers in innocent hamlets, and to live in the midst of them, was a trial.

Then to justify his participation in this massacre, he went on (Autobiography p. 231): I bore no grudge against the Zulus, they had harmed no Indian. I had doubts about the `rebellion' itself, but I then believed that the British Empire existed for the welfare of the world. A genuine sense of loyalty prevented me from even wishing ill to the Empire. The righteness or otherwise of the `rebellion' was therefore not likely to affect my decision.

What about the Nazi war criminals? Did they not have a genuine sense of loyalty to Hitler and Nazism? In Great Britain another storm of protest was raised against the atrocities perpetrated in Natal. The only time Gandhi mentioned the Zulu suppression was on August 4 1906, when he wrote in his Indian Opinion: A controversy is going on in England about what the Natal Army did during the Kaffir rebellion. The people here believe that the whites of Natal perpetrated great atrocities on the Kaffirs. In reply to such critics, the Star has pointed to the doings of the Imperial Army in Egypt. Those among the Egyptian rebels who had been captured were ordered to be flogged. The flogging was continued to the limits of the victim's endurance; it took place in public and was watched by thousands of people. Those sentenced to death were also hanged at the same time. While those sentenced to death were hanging, the flogging of others was taken up. While the sentences were being executed, the relatives of the victims cried and wept until many of them swooned. If this is true, there is no reason why there should be such an outcry in England against Natal outrages.

One may notice that the article was very cleverly written. First Gandhi stated that people in England believed that the whites of Natal perpetrated great atrocities on Africans, as if he himself did not know what happened, and also gave the impression that it was the local Natal Army and not the Imperial Army which was involved in the atrocities, which is not true. Even at this stage, he was not willing to tell the simple truth, that atrocities were committed. Then he borrowed the description of hanging and flogging in Egypt from the Star as if he did not know about that either. Did or did not Gandhi know that those Egyptians were not common criminals to be flogged and hanged-that they were the patriots, the flowers of the Egyptian nation?

If Gandhi unequivocally accepted or found out that the Imperial Army committed those atrocities, then he could not claim that he believed the British Empire existed for the welfare of mankind. The last and the vilest of all was the subtle suggestion that if the Imperial Army did what they were accused of doing, then there was no reason why there should be such an outcry in England against the Natal outrage. Why could this Imperialist-manufactured Mahatma not say clearly that both were crimes against humanity?

Untouchables: Subordination, Poverty and the State in Modern India

Untouchability has played an important role in Indian history and still affects many millions of Indians. The Untouchables focuses on its connections with poverty and state politics, with a primarily political and historical focus, but also looks at its social construction and effects on the lives of individuals. With a broad approach not burdened with too much theory, it will interest scholars, students, and lay readers of history, politics, religion, economics, sociology, and other disciplines.

Mendelsohn and Vicziany begin with the vexed question of the identity of "the Untouchables" and an explanation for their choice of that term for their title, over Harijan, Dalit, or Scheduled Caste. (They use all these terms and others in the text.) There has been a long-running debate over the nature of Untouchable identity and its relationship with Hindu culture. For Mendelsohn and Vicziany the key issue is "whether the Untouchables share a social situation that is sufficiently common to be the basis or potential basis for their mobilisation as a distinct unit for some important purposes.... There is indeed something of a `hard bar' separating Untouchables from the rest of Indian society, and Untouchables themselves have come to see that bar as the basis for a certain amount of common consciousness and action."

The category as it exists now may be a recent construction, a response to British actions and Muslim/Hindu rivalry, but it was constructed on long-standing foundations: evidence from the Bhakti literary tradition shows that Untouchable ritual subordination existed in medieval times.

Recent violence against Untouchables-the so-called "Harijan atrocities"-has brought the issue of Untouchability to prominence. Mendelsohn and Vicziany argue "that the incidence of violence involving Untouchables has increased significantly over the post-Independence period". The violence can be divided into "traditional" forms and others that are responses to Untouchable resistance to ritual subordination, often taking the form of organised retaliatory violence by caste Hindus, sometimes abetted by the police and state apparatus. There are marked regional variations in such violence and it is often tied up with broader political violence, associated with mainstream electoral contests as well as with class conflict and Naxalite revolutionaries.

Early Untouchable politics involved Hindu reform movements, often motivated by the threat, however nugatory, of Untouchable conversion to Christianity or Islam. Early organisation by Untouchables themselves was on a caste and regional basis, and relationships between different Untouchable castes were often difficult. The 1930s saw key struggles between Gandhi and Ambedkar, most notably over whether Untouchables would have separate electorates or joint electorates with reserved seats. Congress was the only national organisation with a large Untouchable following, but Gandhi failed to gain their commitment. Ambedkar, an Untouchable himself, developed a deeper analysis of Untouchability, but lacked a workable political strategy: his conversion to Buddhism in 1956, along with millions of followers, highlighted the failure of his political endeavours.

In the years since 1956 Ambedkarite political organisations have been riven by internal conflicts, notably between young, modernist, and urban elements and older, rural, and often Buddhist ones. But Ambedkar's legacy remains fruitful. Maharashtra and Karnataka have produced a Dalit literary movement, while there have been political success in northern India. In Uttar Pradesh, the Bahujana Samaj party lead by Kanshi Ram has, through alliances of convenience with other parties, attained minority government, installing Mayawati as Chief Minister. Though their achievements in power were limited, this illustrates how Dalits are now using their voting power directly rather than as simple vote banks at the service of mainstream parties. Public policy on Untouchability has been "abstract and unrealistic" but not completely ineffective. One strand has been action against adverse discrimination. Discrimination against Untouchables is still widespread in rural areas in the private sphere, in ritual matters such as access to eating places and water sources. It has largely disappeared, however, in urban areas and in the public sphere, in rights of movement and access to schools. Mendelsohn and Vicziany argue, however, that this has been part of a broader movement towards a new civic culture rather than the result of legislative action: "court enforcement of the anti-disabilities legislation has not been a powerful force in bringing about an abatement of the practice of Untouchability".

Compensatory discrimination has been more controversial. One success of Ambedkar's was the creation of quotas within public service for Scheduled Castes, though targets set after Independence are only being attained now. Complaints about this system are that it benefits an elite group of well-off Untouchables, that particular castes or regions benefit more, and that those in office do little to help their fellows. Compensatory discrimination in education, through scholarships and reserved places, has had some effects but has generally been poorly implemented. Despite this, basic literacy amongst Untouchables is gradually catching up to that of the broader population.

Brief biographies of some Scheduled Caste politicians, national and state, show that they have indeed come from the better off among their communities. But their advantages have often been very slight: family ownership of a cow, for example, or a small plot of land-just enough to alleviate the desperation of poverty and allow an opportunity for education. Along with public service reservations, scholarships (however small and corruptly administered) and the "Harijan hostels" associated with colleges have helped them overcome the barriers of poverty and Untouchability. While Scheduled Caste politicians have not been effective in representing Untouchables generally, Mendelsohn and Vicziany find little evidence of a "Harijan elite".

Other public policy initiatives of key importance to the Untouchables have been the anti-poverty programs: famine prevention, land reform, food-for-work schemes, and the Integrated Rural Development Program, among others. Apart from the first, these have had limited success. There has been considerable regional variation in alleviation of Untouchable poverty. Along with the population generally, Untouchables in Kerala score extremely well on social indicators such as literacy, education, health, and fertility, but they face high unemployment and lack of opportunity. For contrast Mendelsohn and Vicziany look in detail at the village of Behror, located in a relatively affluent "Green Revolution" area midway between Delhi and Jaipur. Different Untouchable communities here exhibit great variation in their employment patterns and economic success.

The Faisalabad stone quarries, just outside Delhi, provide an example of the new Untouchable proletariat being created through urbanisation and migration: eight out of ten workers there are Untouchable and most of the rest are tribals. A case to have welfare legislation enforced and end bonded labour was taken to the Supreme Court by activist Swami Agnivesh, but ostensible success was vitiated by the failure of governments and employers to implement court directives and by an excessive focus on bonded labour. And union organisation amongst Untouchables faces many obstacles.

The negotiations between Gandhi, Ambedkar, and the British in the late 20s and early 30s had a key role in shaping subsequent Untouchable history. But the greatest changes have been gradual, brought about by improvements in education and possession of the franchise. Mendelsohn and Vicziany foresee no end to Untouchable poverty: with the decline of ritual discrimination, "Untouchables will become decreasingly differentiated from other Indians" in their poverty.

Gandhi's Attitude to Class, Caste and Untouchability

One of the major difficulties in any analysis of Gandhi's attitude towards untouchability, class and caste must be his inconsistency in many areas. However this is hardly surprising since Gandhi regarded consistency as the "refuge of fools."1 For Gandhi it was adherence to' Truth' that was important, thus if one realised that ones held opinions were false then they should be dropped even at the expense of appearing foolish or inconsistent. In Gandhi's history it is apparent that the attitudes that he publicly expressed towards class and caste changed radically between 1915, when he returned to India from South Africa and 1948 when he was shot.

Gandhi's attitude towards untouchability appears to have been fairly consistent in that he rejected it from childhood. In a letter to Charles Freer Andrews he wrote "I used to laugh at my mother for making us bath when we brothers touched any pariah."2 He continued to play with an untouchable boy even though his mother had forbidden it. Later in South Africa he associated with untouchables and had untouchable friends and clients. Gandhi even lodged an untouchable in his own home.

On his return to India in 1915 he started an ashram called the Satyagraha Ashram. Right from the beginning Gandhi made it clear that if a suitable untouchable candidate came forward admission would be instant.3 An untouchable family was admitted to the ashram and Gandhi adopted their daughter Lakshmi as his own. He also began cleaning toilets which was the work of untouchables. His disciples voluntarily emulated him so there were no untouchables in the ashram since all did the work of untouchables. This disregard for traditional Hindu mores was reinforced by Gandhi's rule that "food and water should always be handled and therefore polluted, by untouchables. Thus no one could live at the ashram who would not give way at least slightly on the orthodox taboo."

Gandhi said little publicly on untouchability until he had begun to take action against it himself. On 25th May 1921 in 'Young India' he wrote, "Swaraj is a meaningless term if we desire to keep a fifth of India under perpetual subjection... Inhuman ourselves we may not plead before the Throne for the deliverance from the inhumanity of others." 5 In 1928 Gandhi urged untouchables to clean up their habits and to caste Hindus he asserted, "this blot (untouchability) poisons the whole (caste) system, even as a drop of arsenic would poison a tankful of milk." Gandhi regarded untouchability as an "inhuman boycott of human beings" and thought that its removal was a prerequisite for the attainment of home-rule. He once said, "if it is proved to me that it, (untouchability) is an essential part of Hinduism I for one would declare myself an open rebel against Hinduism itself." As far as Gandhi was concerned untouchability was not a part of early Hinduism and he regarded untouchability as a corruption of Hinduism.

Gandhi's attitude to class and caste was more complex than his straightforward opposition to untouchability. Typically class is seen as being the four varnas (literally colours) these being the divisions of society outlined in the Vedic literature. Castes are usually understood as being the many divided social groups in

Indian society often believed to be derived from subdivision of the four varnas, although it is questionable as to whether there was time when Indian society was actually divided into four sections. However Gandhi redefined his terms so that when he spoke of 'caste' he meant the traditional divisions of Brahmins, Ksatriyas, Vaisyas and Sudras. He saw the division of Indian society into inummerable subcastes as being a corruption of Hindu society.

In 1920 Gandhi said, "I consider the four divisions to be fundamental, natural and essential." At this time Gandhi envisaged an India with four castes of equal status separated only by their traditional occupations. In "Young India" October 1921 he wrote, "Hinduism does most emphatically discourage interdining and intermarriage between divisions... Prohibitions against intermarriage and interdining is essential for the rapid evolution of the soul." At that time Gandhi's position was a very orthodox one. Subsequently Gandhi's attitude was to change completely.

In 1927 his son Devadas fell in love with the daughter of a Brahman and asked to marry her. At first Gandhi objected to the intercaste marriage eventually the two fathers agreed that iftheir two children still wished to marry after five years then they would allow them to marry. On Novemeber the 4th 1932, five years later, Gandhi said" Restriction on intercaste dining and intercaste marriage is no part of the Hindu religion. It crept into Hinduism when perhaps it was in decline..." His son married the Brahmans daughter Lakshmi on the 16th of June 1933 after waiting almost six years.

Gandhi went even further than this in his rejection of caste restrictions. In the Hindu Standard January 4th 1946 he wrote, "I therefore tell all the boys and girls who want to marry at Sevagram Ashram unless one of the parties is a Harijan (untouchable)." Finally we see in 1946 that Gandhi took his rejection of the orthodox view of caste to its logical conclusion when we read Louis Fisher's report that, "He said that he was trying to create a classless and casteless India. He yearned for the day when there would only be one caste and Brahmans would marry Harijans."

It is clear that over the period of 1921-46 Gandhi's public stance on caste and class was completely reversed. From acclaiming the caste system of the four varnas and stating that prohibitions against inter-dining and intermarriage were essential, he went on to completely reject any restrictions in inter-dining and intermarriage which he once believed had held Indian society together and prevented its disintegration.

Gandhi's defence of caste restrictions, on inter-dining, in the twenties, is made all the more puzzling by the fact that he seems to have thought little of restrictions concerning inter-dining from his youth. Before leaving India for London, to study law, Gandhi's caste told him they forbade him to go abroad, since in doing so he would have to eat and drink with Europeans. This they regarded as being against their religion. However even at the early age of nineteen Gandhi had sufficient conviction in his own beliefs to argue that he did not think that it was against his religion to go to England. In disregarding the orders of his caste he was made an outcaste. "He never sought readmission to his caste. This experience, he said, led him to a broader view of the system than most Hindus held. He was never 'troubled by castes.'" William Shirer, a reporter who spent some time with Gandhi in the 1930's, recounting his experiences of Gandhi in 1931 wrote, "In his ashrams, or on the road, he shared a meal with 'any and everybody' – Hindus of all castes, untouchables, Moselems, English, Americans, Europeans."

Clearly then for some time before 1932, when Gandhi said that restrictions on inter-dining and intermarriage were no part of Hinduism, He had in fact been ignoring the restrictions on inter-dining even before 1921 when he said that such restrictions were essential for the evolution of the soul. What reasons could Gandhi have had for perpetrating this apparent hypocrisy?

It is possible that Gandhi kept quiet in public about his thoughts on caste and untouchability in order to consolidate his political strength. Certainly as he gained political influence he became much more outspoken about his controversial views on the unacceptability of untouchabilty and on caste with its concomitant restrictions on inter-dining and intermarriage. Conceivably Gandhi may have held these extreme views all along and may simply have been waiting for the right moment to be outspoken. This possibility is compromised to a certain extent in the light of his attempts to prevent the marriage of his son, which he eventually allowed. From his decisions about the marriage it would appear likely that Gandhi genuinely decided that caste restrictions on intermarriage were not a part of Hinduism between 1927 and 1932.

Gandhi was a curious mixture of politician and saint. These two aspects of his personality are highlighted in the way that he dealt with the issue of caste and class. Shrewd politician that he was, he carefully chose the times when he spoke out against something. Thus upon arriving in India in 1915 he did not start out immediately campaigning for untouchable rights or criticizing the caste system. Gandhi may well have refrained from such immediate action for political reasons, knowing that he was unlikely to achieve much success if he immediately started challenging the traditions of India before he had obtained the respect of the people of India.

Another possibility is that Gandhi may have felt unworthy in himself to criticize Indian society of that which he was guilty himself. He may well have been attempting to purify himself of prejudice towards untouchables before he spoke out against untouchability and the same may apply in the apparent change in his views towards caste. Rather that waiting for the politically correct moment to reveal his views Gandhi may well have been searching within himself to ensure that he was free from the faults that he was about to draw attention to in society.

There is something of a logical progression in Gandhi's initial rejection of the contemporary caste system as a whole with his subsequent support of what he saw as the more egalitarian system of the four varnas. It is hardly surprising that from supporting mingling with untouchables Gandhi moved on to supporting inter-dining and intermarriage. The fact that Gandhi took such a long time to reject caste completely, indicates the extent to which he was influenced by tradition. Perhaps it is something of an indication of the mans devotion to the truth that he was able, near the end of his life, to turn around and refute all that he had said on the issue of caste and class.

On the issue of inter-dining Gandhi probably displayed political shrewdness in not being initially outspoken but as regards the issue of intermarriage it seems likely that he underwent a genuine change in his point of view. This may well have been due to events in his personal life, such as his sons wish to marry outside his caste.

Gandhi never tried to present a coherent philosophy of life, his was the way of action or Karma Yoga, his worship was the service of humanity and he believe himself to be guided by his pursuit of 'Absolute Truth.' It is due to this approach to life that we may perceive many inconsistencies in the things that Gandhi said and did. But to reiterate a point that I made earlier, Gandhi considered consistency to be the 'refuge of fools' and when making decisions he did what he felt to be right at that moment and strove to be free of the influence of what he had said and done in the past.

Somewhat paradoxically Gandhi's inconsistencies regarding the matters of caste and class are consistent within the context of his approach to life. If we view Gandhi as being primarily a religious man with political leanings then his inconsistencies make sense. His changing opinions then, rather than showing political shrewdness, reflect Gandhi's own attempts to free himself from 'the canker of untruth.' In his search for the pure essence of Hinduism, Gandhi seems to have concluded that class, caste and untouchability are in fact no part of Hinduism or were perhaps only temporary measures to prevent the disintegration of Hindu society.

By 1946 Gandhi was saying that he hoped for a classless and casteless India. At the time he said, "Violence is bred by inequality, non violence by equality." From this it may be inferred that Gandhi had concluded that any divisions in society would lead to inequality and this inequality would in turn lead to violence. Gandhi's final hope for a classless and casteless India reflected his religious strivings towards ahimsa and the realisation of unity, both of which he saw as being essential prerequisites for the realisation of 'Truth.'

5

Gandhi and Sarvodaya

Sarvodaya is a term meaning 'universal uplift' or 'progress of all'. The term was first coined by Mohandas Gandhi as the title of his 1908 translation of John Ruskin's tract on political economy, *Unto This Last,* and Gandhi came to use the term for the ideal of his own political philosophy. Later Gandhians, like the Indian nonviolence activist Vinoba Bhave, embraced the term as a name for the social movement in post-independence India which strove to ensure that self-determination and equality reached all strata of India society.

Origins and Gandhi's Political Ideal

Gandhi received a copy of Ruskin's *Unto This Last* from a British friend, Mr.Henry Polak, while working as a lawyer in South Africa in 1904. In his *Autobiography,* Gandhi remembers the twenty-four hour train ride to Durban(from when he first read the book, being so in the grip of Ruskin's ideas that he could not sleep at all: "I determined to change my life in accordance with the ideals of the book."

As Gandhi construed it, Ruskin's outlook on political-economic life extended from three central tenets:

1. That the good of the individual is contained in the good of all.
2. That a lawyer's work has the same value as the barber's in as much as all have the same right of earning their livelihood from their work.
3. That a life of labour, i.e., the life of the tiller of the soil and the handicraftsman is the life worth living.

The first of these I knew. The second I had dimly realized. The third had never occurred to me. *Unto This Last* made it clear as daylight for me that the second and third were contained in the first. I arose with the dawn, ready to reduce these principles to practice. " Four years later, in 1908, Gandhi rendered a paraphrased translation of Ruskin's book into his native tongue of Gujarati. He entitled the book *Sarvodaya*, a compound (sandhi) he invented from two Sanskrit roots: *sarva* (all) and *udaya* (uplift) — "the uplift of all" (or as Gandhi glossed it in his autobiography, "the welfare of all"). Although inspired by Ruskin, the term would for Gandhi come to stand for a political ideal of his own stamp. (Indeed Gandhi was keen to distance himself from Ruskin's more conservative ideas.) The ideal which Gandhi strove to put into practice in his ashrams was, he hoped, one that he could persuade the whole of India to embrace, becoming a light to the other nations of the world. The Gandhian social ideal encompassed the dignity of labour, an equitable distribution of wealth, communal self-sufficiency and individual freedom.

Sarvodaya Movement

Gandhi's ideals have lasted well beyond the achievement of one of his chief projects, Indian independence (*swaraj*). His followers in India (notably, Vinoba Bhave) continued working to promote the kind of society that he envisioned, and their efforts have come to be known as the Sarvodaya Movement. Anima Bose has referred to the movement's philosophy as "a fuller and richer concept of people's democracy than any we have yet known." Sarvodaya workers associated with Vinoba, J. P. Narayan, Dada Dharmadhikari, Dhirendra Mazumdaar, Shankarrao Deo, K. G. Mashruwala undertook various projects aimed at encouraging popular self-organisation during the 1950s and 1960s, including *Bhoodan* and *Gramdan* movements. Many groups descended from these networks continue to function locally in India today.

The Gospel of Sarvodaya

Unity of Man

I do not believe...that an individual may gain spiritually and those who surround him suffer. I believe in advaita, I believe in the essential unity of man and, for that matter, of all that life's. Therefore, I believe that if one man gains spiritually, the whole world gains with him and, if one man falls, the whole world falls to that extent. (YI, 4-12-1924, p. 398)

I do not believe that the spiritual law works on a field of its own. On the contrary, it expresses itself only through the ordinary activities of life. It thus affects the economic, the social and the political fields. (YI, 3-9-1925, p. 304)

If we would serve Him or become one with Him, our activity must be as unwearied as His. There may be momentary rest in store for the drop which is separated from the ocean, but not for the drop in the ocean, which knows no rest. The same is the case with ourselves.

As soon as we become one with the ocean in the shape of God, there is no more rest for us, nor indeed do we need rest any longer. Our very sleep is action. For we sleep with the thought of God in our hearts. This restlessness constitutes true rest. This never-ceasing agitation holds the key to peace ineffable. This supreme state of total surrender is difficult to describe, but not beyond the bounds of human experience. It has been attained by many dedicated souls, and may be attained by ourselves as well. (FYM, p. 47)

Identification with Poor

I cannot imagine anything nobler or more national than that for, say, one hour in the day, we should all do the labour that the poor must do, and thus identify ourselves with them and through them with all mankind. I cannot imagine better worship of God than that, in His name, I should labour for the poor even as they do. (YI, 20-10-1921, p. 329)

God demands nothing less than self-surrender as the price for the only real freedom that is worth having. And when a man thus loses himself, he immediately finds himself in the service of God's creation. (YI, 20-12-1928, p. 420)

All our activity should be centred in Truth. Truth should be the very breath of our life. When once this stage in the pilgrim's progress is reached, all other rules of correct living will come without effort, and obedience to them will be instinctive. But without Truth it is impossible to observe any principles or rules in life. (FYM, p. 2)

Faith in Providence

A seeker after Truth, a follower of the Law of Love, cannot hold anything against tomorrow. God never provides for the morrow; He never creates more than what is strictly needed from day to day. If, therefore, we repose faith in His Providence, we should rest assured that He will give us every day our daily bread, supplying enough that we require. (YI, 4-9-1930, p. 1)

Service of Man

Man's ultimate aim is the realization of God, and all his activities, social, political, religious, have to be guided by the ultimate aim of the vision of God. The immediate service of all human beings becomes a necessary part of the endeavour simply because the only way to find God is to see Him in His creation and be one with it. This can only be done by service of all. I am a part and parcel of the whole and I cannot find Him apart from the rest of humanity. My countrymen are my nearest neighbours. They have become so helpless, so resourceless, so inert that I must concentrate myself on serving them. If I could persuade myself that I could find Him in a Himalayan cave, I would proceed there immediately. But I know that I cannot find Him apart from humanity. (H, 29-8-1936, p. 226)

My God is myriad-formed and, while sometimes I see Him in the spinning-wheel, at other times I see Him in communal unity; then again in the removal of untouchability and that is how I establish communion with Him according as the spirit moves me. (H, 8-5-1937, p. 99)

Charkha a Means

He who spins before the poor, inviting them to do likewise, serves God as no one else does. 'He who gives me even a trifle as a fruit or a flower or even a leaf in the spirit of bhakti is my servant', says the Lord in the Bhagvad Gita. And He hath His footstool where live the humble, the lowliest and the lost. Spinning, therefore, for such is the greatest prayer, the greatest worship, the greatest sacrifice. (YI, 24-9-1925, pp. 331-2)

The world is weary of the after-effects of the War. Even as the Charkha is India's comforter today, it may be the world's tomorrow, because it stands, not for the greatest good of the greatest number, but for the greatest good of all. (YI, 10-2-1927, pp. 43-44)

I stand by what is implied in the phrase, 'Unto This Last'. That book marked the turning in my life. We must do even unto this last as we would have the world do by us. All must have equal opportunity. Given the opportunity, every human being has the same possibility for spiritual growth. That is what the spinning wheelsymbolizes. (H, 17-11-1946, p. 404)

Self-purification

Identification with everything that lives is impossible without self-purification; without self-purification the observance of the law of ahimsa must remain an empty dream; God can never be realized by one who is not pure of heart. Self-purification, therefore, must mean purification in all the walks of life. And purification being highly infectious, purification of oneself necessarily leads to the purification of one's surroundings. But the path of purification is hard and steep. To attain to perfect purity one has to become absolutely passion-free in thought, speech and action; to rise above the opposing currents of love and hatred, attachment and repulsion. I know that I have not in me as yet that triple purity, in spite of constant ceaseless striving for it. That is why the world's praise fails to move me, indeed, it very often stings me. To conquer the subtle passions seems to me to be harder far than the physical conquest of the world by the force of arms....I have had experiences of the dormant passions lying hidden within me. The knowledge of them has made me feel humiliated, though not defeated. The experiences and experiments have sustained me and given me great joy. But I know that I have still before me a difficult path to traverse. I must reduce myself to zero. So long as a man does not of his own free will put himself last among his fellow-creatures, there is no salvation for him. Ahimsa is the farthest limit of humility. (A, p. 371)

Ends and Means

Means and ends are convertible terms in my philosophy of life. (YI, 26-12-1946, p. 424)

The means may be likened to a seed, the end to a tree; and there is just the same inviolable connection between the means and the end as there is between the seed and the tree. (HS, p. 71)

No Separation

They say, 'means are after all means'. I would say, 'means are after all everything'. As the means so the end.... There is no wall of separation between the means and the end. Indeed, the Creator has given us control (and that, too, very limited) over means, none over the end. Realization of the goal is in exact proportion to that of the means. This is a proposition that admits of no exception. (YI, 17-7-1924, p. 236-7)

Providence has its appointed hour for everything. We cannot command results; we can only strive. And so far as I am concerned, it is enough satisfaction for me to know that I have striven my utmost to discharge the duty that rested on me. (H, 6-5-1939, p. 112)

Rights and Duties

The true source of rights is duty. If we all discharge our duties, rights will not be far to seek. If leaving duties unperformed we run after rights, they will escape us like a will-o'-the-wisp. The more we pursue them, the farther will they fly. The same teaching has been embodied by Krishna in the immortal words: 'Action alone is thine. Leave thou the fruit severely alone.' Action is duty; fruit is the right. (YI, 8-1-1925, pp.15-16)

Rights accrue automatically to him who duly performs his duties. In fact, the right to perform one's duties is the only right that is worth living for the dying for. It covers all legitimate rights. All the rest is grab under one guise or another and contains in it seeds of himsa. The capitalist and the zamindar talk of their rights, the labourer on the other hand of his, the prince of his divine right to rule, the ryot of his to resist it. If all simply insist on rights and no duties, there will be utter confusion and chaos. (H, 27-5-1939, p. 143)

If, instead of insisting on rights, everyone does his duty, there will immediately be the rule of order established among mankind....I venture to suggest that rights that do not flow directly from duty well performed are not worth having. They will be usurpations, sooner discarded the better. A wretched parent who claims obedience from his children without first doing his duty by them excites nothing but contempt. It is distortion of religious precepts for a dissolute husband to expect compliance in every respect from his dutiful wife. But the children who flout their parent who is ever ready to do his duty towards them would be considered ungrateful and would harm themselves more than their parent. The same can be said about husband and wife.

If you apply this simple and universal rule to employers and labourers, landlords and tenants, the princes and their subjects or the Hindus and the Muslims, you will find that the happiest relations can be established in all walks of life without creating disturbances in and dislocation of life and business which you see in India as in other parts of the world. What I call the law of Satyagraha is to be deduced from an appreciation of duties and the rights flowing therefore. (H, 6-7-1947, p. 217)

6

Gandhi and Swadeshi

Meaning of Swadeshi

Spirit of Swadeshi: Swadeshi is that spirit in us which restricts us to the use and service of our immediate surroundings to the exclusion of the more remote. Thus, as for religion, in order to satisfy the requirements of the definition, I must restrict myself to my ancestral religion.

That is, the use of my immediate religious surrounding. If I find it defective, I should serve it by purging it of its defects. In the domain of politics, I should make use of the indigenous institutions and sere them by curing them of their proved defects. In that of economics I should use only things that are produced by my immediate neighbours and serve those industries by making them efficient and complete where they might be found wanting. It is suggested that such Swadeshi, if reduced to practice, will lead to the millennium.....

Religion: ...Hinduism has become a conservative religion and, therefore, a mighty force because of the Swadeshi spirit underlying it. It is the most tolerant because it is non-proselytizing and it is as capable of expansion today as it has been found to be in the past. It has succeeded not in driving out, as I think it has been erroneously held, but in absorbing Buddhism. By reason of the Swadeshi spirit, a Hindu refuses to change his religion, not necessarily because he considers it to be the best, but because he knows that he can complement it by introducing reforms. And what I have said about Hinduism is, I suppose, true of the other great faiths of the world, only it is held that it is specially so in the case of Hinduism.

Education: We have laboured under a terrible handicap owing to an almost fatal departure from the Swadeshi spirit. We, the educated classes, have received our education through a foreign tongue. We have, therefore, not reacted upon the masses. We want to represent the masses, but we fail. They recognize us not much more than they recognize the English officers. Their hearts are an open book to neither. Their aspirations are not ours. Hence there is a break. And you witness not, in reality, failure to organize but want of correspondence between the representatives and the represented. If during the last fifty years we had been educated through the vernaculars, our elders and our servant and our neighbours would have partaken of our knowledge; the discoveries of Bose or a Ray would have been household treasures as are the RAMAYAN and the MAHABHARAT. As it is, so far as the masses are concerned, those great discoveries might as well have been made by foreigners. Had instruction in all the branches of learning been given through the vernaculars, I make bold to say that they would have enriched wonderfully.....

Economic Life: Much of the deep poverty of the masses is due to the ruinous departure from Swadeshi in the economic and industrial life. If not an article of commerce had been brought from outside India, she would be today a land flowing with milk and honey. But that was not to be. We were greedy and so was England. The connection between England and India was based clearly upon an error.... If we follow the Swadeshi doctrine, it would be your duty and mine to find out neighbours who can supply our wants and to teach them to supply them where they do not know how to proceed, assuming that there are neighbours who are in want of healthy occupation. Then every village of India will almost be a self-supporting and self-contained unit, exchanging only such necessary commodities with other villages as are not locally producible.

This may all sound nonsensical. Well, India is a country of nonsense. It is nonsensical to parch one's throat with thirst when a kindly Mohammedan is ready to offer pure water to drink. And yet thousands of Hindus would rather die of thirst than drink water from a Mohammedan household. These nonsensical men can also, once they are convinced that their religion demands that they should wear garments manufactured in India only clothing or eat any other food...

Religious Discipline: It has often been urged that India cannot adopt Swadeshi, in the economic life at any rate. Those who advance this objection do not look upon Swadeshi, as a rule of life. With them it is a mere patriotic effort-not to be made if it involved any self-denial. Swadeshi, as defined here, is a religious discipline to be undergone in utter disregard of the physical discomfort it may cause to individuals. Under its spell the deprivation of a pin or a needle, because these are not manufactured in India, need cause no terror. A Swadeshist will learn to do without hundreds of things which today he considers necessary.... I would urge that Swadeshi is the only doctrine consistent with the law of humility and love. It is arrogance to think of launching out to serve the whole of India when I am hardly able to serve even my own family. It were better to concentrate my effort upon the family and consider that through them I was serving the whole nation and, if you will, the whole of humanity. This is humility and it is love.

The motive will determine the quality of the act. I may serve my family regardless of the sufferings I may cause to theirs. As, for instance, I may accept an employment which enables me to extort money from people. I enrich myself thereby and then satisfy many unlawful demands of the family. Here I am neither serving the family nor the State. Or I may recognize that God has given me hands and feet only to work with for my sustenance and for that of those who may be dependent upon me. I would then at once simplify my life and that of those whom I can directly reach. In this instance, I would have served the family without causing injury to anyone else. Supposing that every one followed this mode of life, we should have at once an ideal state. All will no reach that state at the same time. But those of us who, realizing its truth, enforce it in practice, will clearly anticipate and accelerate the coming of that happy day. (SW, pp.336-44)

Service of Neighbours: My definition of Swadeshi is well known. I must not serve my distant neighbour at the expense of the nearest. It is never vindictive or punitive. It is in no sense narrow, for I buy from every part of the world what is needed for my growth. I refuse to buy from anybody anything, however nice or beautiful, if it interferes with my growth or injures those whom Nature has made my first care. I buy useful healthy literature from every part of the world. I buy surgical instruments from England, pins and pencils from Austria and watches from Switzerland. But I will not buy and inch of the finest cotton fabric from England or Japan or any other part of the world because it has injured and increasingly injures the million of the inhabitants of India.

I hold it to be sinful for me to refuse to buy the cloth spun and woven by the needy million of India's paupers and to buy foreign cloth although it may be superior in quality to the Indian hand-spun. My Swadeshi, therefore, chiefly centres round the hand-spun Khaddar and extends to everything that can be and is produced in India. (YI. 12-3-1925, p. 88)

[The votary of Swadeshi will,] as a first duty, dedicate himself to the service of his immediate neighbours. This involves exclusion or even sacrifice of the interests of the rest, but the exclusion or the sacrifice would be only in appearance. Pure service of our neighbours can never, from its very nature, result in disservice to those who are far away, but rather the contrary. 'As with the individual, so with the universe' is an unfailing principle which we would do well to lay to heart. On the other hand, a man who allows himself to be lured by 'the distant scene', and runs to the ends of the earth for service, is not only foiled in his ambition, but also fails in his duty towards his neighbours..... (FYM, pp. 62-63)

I believe in the truth implicitly that a man can serve his neighbours and humanity at the same time, the condition being that the service of the neighbours is in no way selfish or exclusive, *i.e.*, does not in any way involve the exploitation of any other human being. The neighbours will then understand the spirit in which such service is given. They will also know that they will be expected to give their services to their neighbours. Thus considered, it will spread like the proverbial snowball gathering strength geometrical progression, encircling the whole earth. It follows that Swadeshi is that spirit which dictates man to serve his next-door neighbour to the exclusion of any other. The condition that I have already mentioned is that the neighbour, thus served, has, in his turn, to serve his own neighbour. In this sense, Swadeshi is never exclusive. It recognizes the scientific limitation of human capacity for service. (H, 23-7-1947, p. 79)

No Chauvinism: Under this plan of life, in seeming to serve India to the exclusion of every other country, I do not harm any other country. My patriotism is both exclusive and inclusive. It is exclusive in the sense that, in all humility, I confine my attention to the land of my birth, but is inclusive in the sense that my service is not of a competitive or antagonistic nature. SIC UTERE TUO UT ALIENUM NON LAEDAS is not merely a legal maxim, but it is a grand doctrine of life. It is the key to proper practice of ahimsa or love. (SW, p. 344)

I have never considered the exclusion of everything foreign under every conceivable circumstance as a part of Swadeshi. The broad definition of Swadeshi is the use of all home-made things to the exclusion of foreign things, in so far as such use is necessary for the protection of home industry, more especially those industries without which India will become pauperized. In my opinion, therefore, Swadeshi which excludes the use of everything foreign, no matter how beneficial it may be, and irrespective of the fact that it impoverishes nobody, is a narrow interpretation of Swadeshi. (YI, 17-6-1926, p. 218)

Even Swadeshi, like any other good thing, can be ridden to death if it is made a fetish. That is a danger that must be guarded against. To reject foreign manufactures, merely because they are foreign and to go on wasting national time and money in the promotion in one's country of manufactures for which it is not suited would be criminal folly and a negation of the Swadeshi spirit. A true votary of Swadeshi will never harbour ill-will towards the foreigner; he will not be actuated by antagonism towards anybody on earth. Swadeshism is not a cult of hatred. It is a doctrine of selfless service that has its roots in the purest AHIMSA, *i.e.*, love. (FYM, p. 66)

The Gospel of the Charkha

I think of the poor of India every time that I draw a thread on the wheel. The poor of India today have lost faith in God, more so than the middle classes or the rich. For a person suffering from the pangs of hunger, and desiring nothing but to fill his belly is his God. To him any one who gives him his bread is his Master. Through him he may even see God. To give alms to such persons, who are sound in all their limbs, is to debase oneself and them.

What they need is some kind of occupation, and the occupation that will give employment to millions can only be hand-spinning.

.... I have described my spinning as a penance or sacrament. And, since I believe that where there is pure and active love for the poor there is God also, I see God in every thread that I draw on the spinning-wheel. (YI, 20-5-1926, p. 187)

...The spinning-wheel enables us to identify ourselves with cores. The millionaires imagine that money can bring them anything in the world. But it is not so. At any moment death might come and snuff them out.... Losing one's life...is not the same thing as shedding 'self'. One has to learn to efface self or the ego voluntarily and as a sacrifice in order to find God. The spinning-wheel rules out exclusiveness. It stands for all inclusiveness. It stands for all including the poorest. It, therefore, requires us to be humble and to cast away pride completely. (H, 13-10-1946, p. 345)

Revival of the cottage industry, and not cottage industries, will remove the growing poverty. When once we have revived the one industry, all the other industries will follow.... I would make the spinning-wheel the foundation on which to build a sound village life. I would make the wheel the centre round which all other activities will revolve. (YI, 21-5-1925, pp. 176, 177)

Message of the Charkha

I ... claim for the Charkha the honour of being able to solve the problem of economic distress in a most natural, simple, inexpensive and business like manner..... It is the symbol of the nation's prosperity and, therefore, freedom. It is a symbol not of commercial war but of commercial peace. (YI, 8-12-1921, p. 406)

The message of the spinning-wheel is much wider than its circumference. Its message is one of simplicity, service of mankind, living so as not to hurt others, creating an indissoluble bond between the rich and the poor, capital and labour, the prince and the peasant. That larger message is naturally for all. (YI, 17-9-1925, p. 321)

The message of the spinning-wheel is, really, to replace the spirit of exploitation by the spirit of service. The dominant not in the West is the note of exploitation. I have no desire that our country should copy that spirit or that note. (YI, 2-2-1928, p. 34)

I do feel that it has message for the U.S.A. and the whole world. But it cannot be until India has demonstrated to the world that it has made the spinning-wheel its own, which it has not done today. The fault is not of the wheel. I have not the slightest doubt that the saving of India and of the world lies in the wheel. If India becomes the slave of-the machine, then, I say, heaven save the world? (H, 17-11-1946, p. 404)

Return to Simplicity

If I preach against the modern artificial life of sensual enjoyment, and ask men and women to go back to the wimple life epitomized in the Charkha, I do so because I know that, without an intelligent return to simplicity, there is no escape from our descent to a state lower than brutality. (YI, 21-7-1921, pp. 228-9)

I believe that no other path but that of nonviolence will suit India. The symbol of that DHARMA for India is the spinning-wheel as it alone is the friend of the distressed and the giver of plenty for the poor. The law of love knows no bounds of space or time. My Swaraj, therefore, takes note of Bhangis, Dublas and the weakest of the weak, and except the spinning-wheel I know no other thing which befriends all these. (YI, 8-1-1925, p. 18)

Wheel of Life

Take to spinning [to find peace of mind]. The music of the wheel will be as balm to your soul. I believe that the yarn we spin is capable of mending the broken warp and woof of our life. The Charkha is the symbol of nonviolence on which all life, if it is to be real life, must be based. (H, 27-4-1947, p. 122)

Some will recall through the wheel the name of that Prince of Peace, Ashoka, the founder of an empire, who ultimately gave up the pomp and circumstance of power to become the undisputed Emperor of the hearts of men and became the representative of all the then known faiths. We would call it a legitimate interpretation of the wheel to seek in it he Wheel of Law ascribed to that living store of mercy and love.

The spinning-wheel thus interpreted adds to its importance in the life of billions of mankind to liken it to and to derive it from the Ashoka disc is to recognize in the insignificant-looking Charkha the necessity of obeying the ever-moving Wheel of the Divine Law of Love. (H, 3-8-1947, p. 266)

... Spinning has become a part and parcel of the Ashram prayer. The conception of spinning as sacrifice has been linked with the idea of God, the reason being that we believe that in the Charkha and what it stands for lies the only hope of salvation of the poor. (H, 18-8-1946, p. 263)

It is my claim that the universalization of hand-spinning with a full knowledge of all that it stands for alone can bring that [conquest of inertia] in a subcontinent so vast and varied as India. I have compared spinning to the central sun and the other village crafts to the various constellations in the solar system. The former gives light and warmth to the latter and sustains them. Without it they would not be able to exist. (H, 31-3-1946, p. 58)

Duty of Spinning

Just as every one of us must eat and drink and clothe himself, even so everyone of us must spin himself. (YI, 28-5-1925, p. 182)

I do not know whether I am a Karmayogi or any other Yogi. I know that I cannot live without work. I crave to die with my hand at the spinning-wheel. I one has to establish communion with God through some means, why not through the spinning wheel? Him who worships Me, says the Lord in the Gita, I guide along the right path and see to his needs. (H, 8-5-1937, p. 99)

If every woman in India spins, then a silent revolution will certainly be created, of which a Jawaharlal [Nehru] can make full use. Unless steam generated is put to proper use, the engine will not run and the person generating the steam may himself be scalded by it even unto death. (H, 14-4-1946, p. 88). A scientific study of the spinning-wheel will lead on to Sociology. The spinning-wheel will not become a power for the liberation of India in our hands unless we have made a deep study of the various sciences related to it. It will then not only make India free, but point the way to the whole world. (H, 31-3-1946, p. 59)

'Livery of Freedom'

...While Khadi is good for the poor as an honourable occupation for earning bread, it has an additional and far greater value as an instrument of winning Swaraj through nonviolence means. (H, 28-4-1946, p. 104)

In 1908, in South Africa, I conceived the idea that, if poverty-stricken India were to be freed form the alien yoke, India must learn to look upon the spinning-wheel and hand-spun yarn as the symbol, not of slavery, but of freedom. It should also mean butter to bread. (H, 22-9-1946, p. 320)

Khadi to me is the symbol of unity of Indian humanity, of its economic freedom and equality and, therefore, ultimately, in the poetic expression of Jawaharlal Nehru, "the livery of India's freedom." Moreover, Khadi mentality means decentralization of the production and distribution of the necessaries of life. Therefore, the formula so far evolved is, every village to produce all its necessaries and a certain percentage in addition for the requirements of the cities.Heavy industries will needs be centralized and nationalized. But they will occupy the least part of the vast national activity which will mainly be in the villages..... Since the wanton destruction of this central village industry and the allied handicrafts, intelligence and brightness have fled from the villages, leaving them inane, lusterless, and reduced almost to the state of their ill-kept cattle. (CP, p. 12)

Economic Regeneration

I feel convinced that the revival of hand-spinning and hand-weaving will make the largest contribution to the economic and the moral regeneration of India. The millions must have a simple industry to supplement agriculture. Spinning was the cottage industry years ago, and if the millions are to be saved from starvation, they must be enabled to introduce spinning in their homes, and every village must repossess its own weaver. (YI, 21-7-1920, p. 4)

It bears not a message of ill-will towards the nations of the earth but of goodwill and self-half. It will not need the protection of a navy threatening a world's peace and exploiting its resources, but it needs the religious determination of millions to spin their yarn in their own homes as today they cook their food in their own homes. I may deserve the curses of posterity for many mistakes of omission and commission, but I am confident of earning its blessing for suggesting a revival of the Charkha. I stake my all on it. For every revolution of the wheel spins peace, goodwill and love. And with all that, inasmuch as the loss of it brought about India's slavery. Its voluntary revival with all its implications must mean India's freedom. (YI, 8-12-1921, p. 406)

Hope of Rural Masses

I have often said that, if the seven lakhs of the villages of India were to be kept alive, and if peace that is at the root of all civilization is to be achieved, we have to make the spinning-wheel the centre of all handicrafts. (H, 19-2-1938, p. 11)

The spinning-wheel represents to me the hope of the masses. The masses lost their freedom, such as it was, with the loss of the Charkha. The Charkha supplemented the agriculture of the villagers and gave it dignity. It was the friend and solace of the widow. It kept the villagers from idleness. For the Charkha included all the anterior and posterior industries-ginning, carding, warping, sizing, dyeing and waving. These in their turn kept the village carpenter and the blacksmith busy.

The Charkha enabled the seven hundred thousand villages to become self-contained. With the exit of the Charkha went the other village industries, such as the oil press. Nothing took the place of these industries.

Therefore, the villages were drained of their varied occupations and their creative talent and what little wealth these brought them.... Hence, if the villages are to come into their own, the most natural thing that suggests itself is the revival of the Charkha and all it means. (H, 13-4-1940, p. 85)

I have no doubt in my mind that the wheel can serve as the instrument of earning one's livelihood and, at the same time, enable the worker to render useful service to his neighbours.... In order to ply the wheel intelligently, he should now all the processes that precede and succeed spinning. (H,17-3-1946, p. 42)

The conviction dawned upon me even before I came to India that the revival of hand-spinning alone could restore India to its pristine glory. I have since compared the spinning-wheel to the central sun round which the solar system of our village economy revolves. It provides the golden bridge between the rich and the poor. (H, 21-7-1946, p. 231)

The Charkha is not like either the small or large machines of the West. There cores of watches are produced in a few special places. They are sold all over the world. The same tale applies to the sewing machine.

These things are symbols of one civilization. The Charkha represents the opposite. We do not to universalize the Charkha through mass production in one place. Our ideal is to make the Charkha and all its accessories in the locality where the spinners live. Therein lies the value of the spinning-wheel. Anything that goes wrong with it should be put right on the spot and the spinners should be taught how to do so. (H, 20-10-1946, pp. 363-4)

Mill Industry

Our mills cannot today spin enough for our wants, and if they did, they will not keep down prices unless they were compelled. They are frankly money-makers and will not, therefore, regulate prices according to the needs of the nation. Hand-spinning is therefore designed to put millions of rupees in the hands of the poor villagers. Every agriculrural country requires a supplementary industry to enable the peasants to utilize the spare hours. Such industry for India has always been spinning. Is it such a visionary ideal-an attempt to revive an ancient occupation whose destruction has brought on slavery, pauperism and disappearance of the inimitable artistic talent which was once all expressed in the wonderful fabric of India which was the envy of the world? (YI, 16-2-1921, pp. 50-51)

Do I seek to destroy the mill-industry, I have often been asked. If I did, I should not have pressed for the abolition of the excise duty. I want the mill-industry to prosper-only I do not want it to prosper at the expense of the country. On the contrary, If the interests of the country demand that the industry should go, I should let it go without the slightest compunction. (YI, 24-2-1927, p. 58)

In my opinion, the mill-hands are as much the proprietors of their mills as the shareholders, and when the mill-owner realize that the mill-hand are as much mill-owners as they, there will be no quarrel between them. (YI, 4-8-1927, p. 248)

Meaning and Spirit of Swadeshi

Swadeshi is that spirit in us which restricts us to the use and service of our immediate surroundings to the exclusion of the more remote. Thus, as for religion, in order to satisfy the requirements of the definition, I must restrict myself to my ancestral religion. That is, the use of my immediate religious surrounding. If I find it defective, I should serve it by purging it of its defects. In the domain of politics, I should make use of the indigenous institutions and serve them by curing them of their proved defects. In that of economics I should use only things that are produced by my immediate neighbours and serve those industries by making them efficient and complete where they might be found wanting. It is suggested that such Swadeshi, if reduced to practice, will lead to the millennium.....

Religion

...Hinduism has become a conservative religion and, therefore, a mighty force because of the Swadeshi spirit underlying it. It is the most tolerant because it is non-proselytizing and it is as capable of expansion today as it has been found to be in the past. It has succeeded not in driving out, as I think it has been erroneously held, but in absorbing Buddhism. By reason of the Swadeshi spirit, a Hindu refuses to change his religion, not necessarily because he considers it to be the best, but because he knows that he can complement it by introducing reforms. And what I have said about Hinduism is, I suppose, true of the other great faiths of the world, only it is held that it is specially so in the case of Hinduism.

Education

We have laboured under a terrible handicap owing to an almost fatal departure from the Swadeshi spirit. We, the educated classes, have received our education through a foreign tongue. We have, therefore, not reacted upon the masses. We want to represent the masses, but we fail. They recognize us not much more than they recognize the English officers. Their hearts are an open book to neither. Their aspirations are not ours. Hence there is a break. And you witness not, in reality, failure to organize but want of correspondence between the representatives and the represented.

If during the last fifty years we had been educated through the vernaculars, our elders and our servant and our neighbours would have partaken of our knowledge; the discoveries of Bose or a Ray would have been household treasures as are the RAMAYAN and the MAHABHARAT. As it is, so far as the masses are concerned, those great discoveries might as well have been made by foreigners. Had instruction in all the branches of learning been given through the vernaculars, I make bold to say that they would have enriched wonderfully.....

Economic Life

Much of the deep poverty of the masses is due to the ruinous departure from Swadeshi in the economic and industrial life. If not an article of commerce had been brought from outside India, she would be today a land flowing with milk and honey. But that was not to be. We were greedy and so was England. The connection between England and India was based clearly upon an error.... If we follow the Swadeshi doctrine, it would be your duty and mine to find out neighbours who can supply our wants and to teach them to supply them where they do not know how to proceed, assuming that there are neighbours who are in want of healthy occupation. Then every village of India will almost be a self-supporting and self-contained unit, exchanging only such necessary commodities with other villages as are not locally producible.

This may all sound nonsensical. Well, India is a country of nonsense. It is nonsensical to parch one's throat with thirst when a kindly Mohammedan is ready to offer pure water to drink. And yet thousands of Hindus would rather die of thirst than drink water from a Mohammedan household. These nonsensical men can also, once they are convinced that their religion demands that they should wear garments manufactured in India only clothing or eat any other food...

Religious Discipline

It has often been urged that India cannot adopt Swadeshi, in the economic life at any rate. Those who advance this objection do not look upon Swadeshi, as a rule of life. With them it is a mere patriotic effort-not to be made if it involved any self-denial.

Swadeshi, as defined here, is a religious discipline to be undergone in utter disregard of the physical discomfort it may cause to individuals. Under its spell the deprivation of a pin or a needle, because these are not manufactured in India, need cause no terror. A Swadeshist will learn to do without hundreds of things which today he considers necessary.... I would urge that Swadeshi is the only doctrine consistent with the law of humility and love. It is arrogance to think of launching out to serve the whole of India when I am hardly able to serve even my own family. It were better to concentrate my effort upon the family and consider that through them I was serving the whole nation and, if you will, the whole of humanity. This is humility and it is love.

The motive will determine the quality of the act. I may serve my family regardless of the sufferings I may cause to theirs. As, for instance, I may accept an employment which enables me to extort money from people. I enrich myself thereby and then satisfy many unlawful demands of the family. Here I am neither serving the family nor the State. Or I may recognize that God has given me hands and feet only to work with for my sustenance and for that of those who may be dependent upon me. I would then at once simplify my life and that of those whom I can directly reach. In this instance, I would have served the family without causing injury to anyone else. Supposing that every one followed this mode of life, we should have at once an ideal state. All will no reach that state at the same time. But those of us who, realizing its truth, enforce it in practice, will clearly anticipate and accelerate the coming of that happy day. (SW, pp.336-44)

Service of Neighbours

My definition of Swadeshi is well known. I must not serve my distant neighbour at the expense of the nearest. It is never vindictive or punitive. It is in no sense narrow, for I buy from every part of the world what is needed for my growth. I refuse to buy from anybody anything, however nice or beautiful, if it interferes with my growth or injures those whom Nature has made my first care. I buy useful healthy literature from every part of the world. I buy surgical instruments from England, pins and pencils from Austria and watches from Switzerland. But I will not buy and inch of the finest cotton fabric from England or Japan or any other part of the world because it has injured and increasingly injures the million of the inhabitants of India.

I hold it to be sinful for me to refuse to buy the cloth spun and woven by the needy million of India's paupers and to buy foreign cloth although it may be superior in quality to the Indian hand-spun. My Swadeshi, therefore, chiefly centres round the hand-spun Khaddar and extends to everything that can be and is produced in India. (YI. 12-3-1925, p. 88)

[The votary of Swadeshi will,] as a first duty, dedicate himself to the service of his immediate neighbours. This involves exclusion or even sacrifice of the interests of the rest, but the exclusion or the sacrifice would be only in appearance. Pure service of our neighbours can never, from its very nature, result in disservice to those who are far away, but rather the contrary. 'As with the individual, so with the universe' is an unfailing principle which we would do well to lay to heart. On the other hand, a man who allows himself to be lured by 'the distant scene', and runs to the ends of the earth for service, is not only foiled in his ambition, but also fails in his duty towards his neighbours..... (FYM, pp. 62-63)

I believe in the truth implicitly that a man can serve his neighbours and humanity at the same time, the condition being that the service of the neighbours is in no way selfish or exclusive, i.e., does not in any way involve the exploitation of any other human being. The neighbours will then understand the spirit in which such service is given. They will also know that they will be expected to give their services to their neighbours. Thus considered, it will spread like the proverbial snow-ball gathering strength in geometrical progression, encircling the whole earth. It follows that Swadeshi is that spirit which dictates man to serve his next-door neighbour to the exclusion of any other. The condition that I have already mentioned is that the neighbour, thus served, has, in his turn, to serve his own neighbour. In this sense, Swadeshi is never exclusive. It recognizes the scientific limitation of human capacity for service. (H, 23-7-1947, p. 79)

No Chauvinism

Under this plan of life, in seeming to serve India to the exclusion of every other country, I do not harm any other country. My patriotism is both exclusive and inclusive. It is exclusive in the sense that, in all humility, I confine my attention to the land of my birth, but is inclusive in the sense that my service is not of a competitive or antagonistic nature. SIC UTERE TUO UT ALIENUM NON LAEDAS is not merely a legal maxim, but it is a grand doctrine of life. It is the key to proper practice of ahimsa or love. (SW, p. 344)

I have never considered the exclusion of everything foreign under every conceivable circumstance as a part of Swadeshi. The broad definition of Swadeshi is the use of all home-made things to the exclusion of foreign things, in so far as such use is necessary for the protection of home industry, more especially those industries without which India will become pauperized. In my opinion, therefore, Swadeshi which excludes the use of everything foreign, no matter how beneficial it may be, and irrespective of the fact that it impoverishes nobody, is a narrow interpretation of Swadeshi. (YI, 17-6-1926, p. 218)

Even Swadeshi, like any other good thing, can be ridden to death if it is made a fetish. That is a danger that must be guarded against. To reject foreign manufactures, merely because they are foreign and to go on wasting national time and money in the promotion in one's country of manufactures for which it is not suited would be criminal folly and a negation of the Swadeshi spirit. A true votary of Swadeshi will never harbour ill-will towards the foreigner; he will not be actuated by antagonism towards anybody on earth. Swadeshism is not a cult of hatred. It is a doctrine of selfless service that has its roots in the purest AHIMSA, i.e., love. (FYM, p. 66)

Swadeshi: True and False

All those who have studied the Industrial Arts of India unite in recognizing and deploring their profound decay, and in very many cases, their practical extinction. Investigation invariably shows that goods that ought to be, and once were, common in the market, are now only to be seen in museums. One hundred, or even fifty years ago, it would have been possible to fill many museums worthily with the everyday handiwork of Indian artisans: now this would be only possible after years of patient collecting in remote districts. During the nineteenth century India has in fact, ceased to excel in those Industrial arts which provided the bulk of her exports, the main source of her wealth (after agriculture), and of the refined luxury of her homes during a period of time that must be counted in millenniums.

During this period—if we are to judge from the wreckage of her Industrial arts remaining to us—we must rank the civilisation of India indeed highly, for it could have been truly said that in her homes, whether of rich or poor, there could be found nothing that was not either useful or beautiful. In exchange for this world of beauty that was our birthright, the nineteenth century has made of our country a 'dumping--ground' for all the vulgar superfluities of European over-production; and all that the Swadeshi movement of the twentieth century has done is to provide us with many spurious imitations of these unlovely inutilities.

It could hardly have been otherwise, for behind the Swadeshi movement there is no serious and consistent ideal. Its leaders have had but one thought before them—to save money. The movement has lacked almost totally in those constructive elements which we meet with in similar movements in other countries, such as Denmark or Ireland. Never have I seen in any Swadeshi literature the wish expressed to preserve Indian manufactures on account of their intrinsic excellence, or because the presence amongst us of these highly skilled craftsmen represented an important element in the national culture, or because these craftsmen still worked under conditions of life still infinitely superior, physically and spiritually, to those of the European factory-slaves.

Too often the leaders of our political movement have forgotten (as men forgot in the early days of the development of European industrialism) that elementary principle of statecraft, that *men are of more account than things.* They have forgotten that the goal of all material civilisation is not labour but leisure, and that industry without art only brutalises and degrades. For *things* then—things economic, political, temporary—they have been willing to undermine both our immemorial industrial culture, and to degrade the status and destroy the physique of those artisans who once served us so faithfully and who even now if we would let them would make our cities and our houses beautiful again. I know no sign more ominous for the future of the Indian civilisation, than our utter indifference to social industrial idealism, and the heartless callousness with which we have cast aside the services of those who built our homes, and clothed and wrought for us in the days before we learned to despise our own culture,— leaving them to eke out a precarious living by making petty trivialities-for tourists, curio-collectors, and for Anglo-Indian bungalows, or to drift into the ranks of menial labourers or factory hands. Do you think that we can thus degrade the status of so many men without impairing the vitality of our national life and without injuring the basis of its possible prosperity?

We, who think that we are educated and progressive, we, who attend conferences and sit on legislative councils, who are rulers of states, or earn more princely incomes in courts of law, we ourselves have despised and hated everything Indian, and it is by that hatred that we have destroyed our industries and degraded the status of our artisans. And when at last our pockets were touched—then so far from realising what we had done, we set ourselves to form Swadeshi companies for making enamelled cufflinks (with pansies on them), for dyeing yarn (with German dyes), or making uncomfortable furniture (for Anglo-Indians). We never thought that the fault was in ourselves. We lived in caricatured English villas, and studied the latest fashion in collars and ties arid sat on the verandahs of Collectors bungalows and strove to preserve our respectability by listening to gramophone records of the London music halls instead of living Indian singers— we learned to sit on chairs and eat with spoons and to adorn our walls with German oleographs and our floors with Brussels carpets: and then we thought to save our souls by taking shares in some Swadeshi company for making soap.

True Swadeshi is none of these things: it is a way of looking at life. It is essentially sincerity. Seek first this, learn once more the *art of living*, and you will find that our ancient civilisation, industrial no less than spiritual, will re-arise from the ashes of our vulgarity and parasitism of today.

I do not think we fully realise the depth of our present intellectual poverty. If everything produced in India during the nineteenth century were to be suddenly miraculously destroyed, the world would be very little the poorer. The creative force in us has died, because we had no faith in ourselves—we could only learn to be intellectual parasites: to make, as has been said, of our country a mere suburb of Birmingham and Paris. It is imperative that we should recognize our real position, if we could reconstruct our national life. To this end, years of patient labour in the field of National Education is needed. So long as this education is based on the assumption that all true light and learning must come from Europe, so long will the restoration of industrial prosperity for India be impossible.

The first thing that must always strike a critical visitor examining Indian work exposed for sale in shops, or at an Industrial exhibition, is the extraordinary and consistent contrast between old and modern work. The latter almost always shows marked degeneration in respect of technique or intention or both. The place of those things which used to be common but now are rare is taken by cheap substitutes and by imitations of the imported superfluities of European overproduction. The most significant phenomenon is the change of application of all the more elaborate arts, such as enamelling, wood carving, and embroidery, from the real service of the daily needs, domestic and ceremonial, of the people of the country, to the production of trinkets and curiosities for tourists and foreign markets. It is this fact which accounts for an often criticised feature in the modern work—the faulty construction or overloading of ornaments which are so often combined with patient and devoted labour and the use of fine and traditional designs. One may instance the ill-fitting hinges of inlaid glove boxes: the elaborate carving of the tops of tables, making them useless *as tables,* exquisite embroidery for blouses applied to cheap materials which do not last, or worked in colours which do not wash. This state of affairs results from the facts that the craftsman does not use, and has little or nothing to do with persons who do use, glove-boxes, tables, and blouses, and there can be no serious change in the position of the Industrial arts of India until the present *Indian* boycott of the *Indian* craftsman is replaced by something more like that intelligent boycott of worthless importations from Europe (and their imitations made in India) which Lord Curzon so passionately advocated at Delhi.

No less than forty years ago Sir George Birdwood wrote "Indian Native Gentlemen and Ladies should make it a point of culture never to wear any clothing or ornaments but of native manufacture and strictly native design." How we should have scoffed at this idea then! Even now there are Bengali gentlemen who bring home trunks full of English dresses for their wives after completing their studies at the English bar: and it is not ten years since the students of the Calcutta School of Art went on strike, and were strongly supported in doing so by the Bengali press, because an Englishman dared to think that real Indian art instead of second rate European might be made the basis of the teaching in the school. It is true that things have changed during the last ten years, and a change once begun progresses swiftly: but the amount of change is still insignificant, and we are only to a small extent less parasitic than the last generation. It is a marvel to me how any self-respecting people can endure for a day, not the system of government,—but the system of education from which we suffer, a system which is a far deeper and more perpetual insult to our culture than any of the incidents in railway trains of which we hear so much. The Education Court at the late United Provinces Exhibition, for instance was little more than a gigantic advertisement of English schoolmasters and Messrs Macmillan. There was practically nothing Indian about it. It is not surprising that the products of such education do not care for Indian art. It would be more surprising if they did.

Let me now briefly analyse the chief causes of decline in Indian industrial art. Every one knows that architecture is a synthesis of all the arts and that their prosperity is bound up with that of the art of building. Modern Indian architecture** however, domestic or palatial, is at the very lowest ebb. The average modern house is a cross between a suburban villa and a Government barrack. The new palaces of most of the rulers of native States are, as Sir George Birdwood has remarked, like anything in the world except a habitation fit for kings. While European architecture is nominally the model, in India, "the essence of European architecture is supposed to consist in a reckless disregard of all recognized canons of ornament and proportion".

It is very true, as Mr. Lockwood Kipling remarked in the first volume of the *Journal of Indian* Art—"It is on the architecture of today that the preservation of Indian Art semblance of healthy life now hinges." Yet so far as I am aware it has never occurred to any Swadeshist politician to demand from Government that in public buildings Indian architecture should be the rule, and Indian architects employed or that the State should again patronise and foster Indian artistic industries. These things are still done in some of the native States: but not in all of these—Baroda, for instance, affords a conspicuously objectionable example of Anglicisation and total disregard of Indian artistic tradition. Nearly everywhere in India there are still living hereditary and most capable working architects— such as no other country in the world still possesses—but like other craftsmen they are being starved by neglect and forced to adopt menial or agricultural work for a bare living.

Living in pseudo-European homes naturally and logically involves and corresponds to the using of European furniture, clothes and finally, to an entire dependence on imported apparatus of material comfort and amusement—a dependence upon boxes of sardines and upon gramophones and on all that lies between them. In this process an accelerating touch is given by employing slightly educated Eurasian governesses to teach our daughters the use of knives and forks. I should like to say in passing, that in speaking thus I do not mean in any way to disparage things European, as such. Nothing is further from my thoughts than that absurd notion which is expressed in the not uncommon saying, "that *our* ancestors were civilised when Europeans were 'dressed' in woad." As a matter of fact early Keltic and Teutonic Europe was much more civilised in some respects than we are today—at least it cared more for creative and imaginative art. What I do wish to point out is that *our imitations,* whether in Swadeshi factories or in our lives, of things European are and must always be for ourselves socially and industrially disintegrating, and for the rest of the world wholly valueless.

Nor do I mean that we should never assimilate or adopt any foreign idea or custom. On the contrary I believe that even in such things as music and the plastic arts, and still more in sociology we have some things to learn from others, as well as to recover from our own past: only we do not show our progress in these things by taking to harmoniums, by buying German oleographs, or by adopting the crudest and least considered phases of a foreign culture. But let us recognise that by doing these things we offend both against the higher and the lower ideal of Swadeshi—the higher which is in our hearts, and the lower in our pockets.

Let us now study the process of disintegration further, passing from architecture, the main setting of our lives, to all the lesser elements of our environment. "Not in Benares only" says Sir G. Watt, "but throughout India the fine old art designs that have been attained after centuries of evolution are being abandoned and models utterly unsuited and far inferior artistically are being substituted. The writer can confidently affirm that he found in at least fifty percent of the important silversmiths shops in India, the illustrated trade catalogues of European firms and stores being employed as the pattern books upon which their silver plate was being modelled." The natural result is that when you want a Polo Trophy, you have to go to England for it—for we know that our Swadeshi imitations of European industrial art are never as good as the originals and are never likely to be. Swadeshi as we *now* understand it—i.e., erecting factories for naturalising European manufactures—is simply accepting for ourselves a permanent inferiority of environment, and irremediably lowering the standard of living amongst us.

The modern amongst us can already tolerate an environment of cheap hideousness and tawdry, expensive discomfort, which would have disgusted the poorest in the days of Hindu or Mughal civilisation. Take Benares brass at Delhi: "all but one or two pieces were bad in design and worse in execution."

Take enamelling: "Formerly every attention was given to effect, and a background or field colour was regularly employed, most frequently a rich creamy white. Within the past few decades this has been discontinued, and complex and intricate designs substituted in which it can hardly be said there is a field colour at all. The result is distinctly inferior and may be described as garish rather than artistic."

A Benares Kinkhab manufacturer, asked to show a treasured pattern book, produced a sample book of English wallpapers—"This at once explained the monstrous degeneration perceived in the Benares Kinkhabs." The value of gold thread imported into India is now 44 lacs. It is much inferior to India handmade gold thread, now going out of use. The author of a monograph on Indian Gold lace remarks: "In such seemingly minor and unimportant details the true cause of the artistic degeneracy of Indian weaving is to be found."

Exactly the same conclusion may be drawn from the imports of aniline dyes. In such cases we actually pay money out of pocket, to ruin our own industrial arts. It would be useless to multiply examples here: those who wish may find them in the pages of all, Indian or English, who have written upon the industrial arts of India. I think no one will deny that these Industrial arts are in a nearly hopeless state. No one can ultimately deny that the main cause of this is our own deficient artistic understanding. It is, I repeat, far more necessary to cease our own boycott of the Indian craftsman, than for us to carry on a boycott of foreign imports.

In attempting to establish factories for the imitation of European imported goods we overlook one thing—the relative value of men and things. True Swadeshi would have attempted to preserve the status of our skilled artisans and village craftsmen, for the sake of the value to our country of men *as men*. Already it is being recognized in Europe that the general substitution of machines for men must invariably lower the whole intellectual and moral status of the working population: and we need not hope to avoid this result by tinkering at compulsory education. A False Swadeshi does not object to crowding the craftsmen into factories, where drunkenness, physical degeneration and all other natural results of the factory system follow. One has but to read the reports of factory inspectors to understand—"The legal hours of rest for women are constantly exceeded:" "sanitary arrangements are horrible:" "children are often puny, probably owing to overwork." "Nearly every factory is a constant offender." Such are the facts recorded in the last report of the Director of Industries 11 the Punjab. The moral should be clear. Yet we find the members of the late Factory Commission lamenting the absence of a pure factory class, totally severed from village life, in Western India. The whole endeavour of a True Swadeshi should be to restore, not to destroy, the organic life of the village communities. It is not that we learn too much from foreign countries. We learn too little. If we learnt more, we should not want to repeat the experiments in *Laissez faire* of early Victorian England.

To sum up our conclusions—Who are the natural patrons of our Industrial Arts? Not tourists, I think you will agree. The sumptuary arts of India, the decline of which we are discussing, are those which naturally most depend, like architecture itself, on the tastes and patronage of the educated, aristocratic and wealthy classes amongst us and of the courts and have always so depended: and unless we can restore the fine aesthetic culture which these classes in India once possessed, we cannot hope that our Industrial Arts will flourish. Mr. Burns the other day remarked that out of two hundred wedding presents which he had the opportunity of seeing at an Indian wedding, only some sixteen were Indian in point of character and origin: and the same state of affairs may be observed in the houses of almost all our prosperous lawyers and Deputy Collectors. Now the situation is this—that a mere desire to save money for our country will never remedy this state of affairs, neither will a wish to achieve political revenge. But artistic education, the setting of men before things in our own estimation, and the ideal of nationality as service may achieve, what lesser motives cannot. What is necessary is that we should let the real love of our country allow us to realize that Her gifts are (with the rarest exceptions) really and intrinsically better than those which we can import—that our dyes, our handmade gold thread, our designs, our ways of dressing and building, our jewellery, our carpets and all that goes to make the daily environment of our lives are better than the things we import from Europe—more beautiful, more enduring, more vital in response and more a part of our real life. Then it will not be so difficult perhaps to spend a little more in the first instance on such things. But all this is not a matter of political platforms, it is simply and solely a matter of National Education, the sort of education that will help us some day to prefer a living singer to what an Indian friend of mine has very aptly called 'the voice of the living dead'. Then we shall be saved not only the expense of importing gramophones, but all the bother of trying to make them in local factories, with indifferent success. This is a parable of all the other Industrial Arts.

Secondly, the great manufacturers can take care of themselves. Business men will not fail to discover where money can be made. It is hardly necessary for us to assist them in becoming millionaires by bringing to their aid the whole weight of Swadeshi sentimentality. We have only to see that they injure as little as possible the physique and morale of the workers. Temporary cheapness is no guarantee of ultimate value from the standpoint of national evolution or even of private advantage on the part of the individual purchaser. Swadeshi does not consist in imitating new productions recently imported—this may be left to the speculative businessman, who has his due place—but in restoring the status and the prosperity of the skilled artisan and the village craftsman. It is these artisans who most need the help of our national idealism. It is these skill craftsmen also whom we as a nation most need as members of our body politic. We have enough of agricultural labourers and are like to have too many factory hands, and perhaps too many lawyers and clerks. To assist the skilled artisan and the village craftsman may seem too simple, too unromantic a thing for nationalists to undertake. Even national education requires half a century to bear its fruits. Yet it is assuredly only by such personal activity and gradual recovery of social cooperation that an end so great as the restoration of our status amongst the nations of the world can be achieved. And it is almost waste of time to work for ends that may or may not be achieved in ten or fifteen years: the greatest work is done by those who scarcely look to see its fruits within their own lifetime.

7

Gandhi and Nonviolence

The Nonviolent Society

I hold that nonviolence is not merely a personal virtue. It is also a social virtue to be cultivated like the other virtues. Surely society is largely regulated by the expression of nonviolence in its mutual dealings. What I ask for is an extension of it on a larger, national and international scale. (H, 7-1-1939, p417)

All society is held together by nonviolence, even as the earth is held in her position by gravitation. But when the law of gravitation was discovered, the discovery yielded results of which our ancestors had no knowledge. Even so, when society is deliberately constructed in accordance with the law of nonviolence, its structure will be different in material particulars from what it is today. But I cannot say in advance what the government based on nonviolence will be like. What is happening today is disregard of the law of nonviolence and enthronement of violence as if it were an eternal law. (H, 11-12-1939, p8)

Society based on nonviolence can only consist of groups settled in villages in which voluntary cooperation is the condition of dignified and peaceful existence. (H, 13-1-1940, pp410-11)

Democracy and Nonviolence

Science of war leads one to dictatorship pure and simple. Science of nonviolence can alone lead one to pure democracy. (H, 15-10-1938, p290)

Democracy and violence can ill go together. The State that are today nominally democratic have either to become frankly totalitarian, or if they are to become truly democratic, they must become courageously nonviolent. (H, 12-11-1938, p328)

Holding the view that, without the recognition of nonviolence on a national scale, there is no such thing as a constitutional or democratic government, I devote my energy to the propagation of nonviolence as the law of our life, individual, social, political, national and international.

I fancy that I have seen the light, though dimly. I write cautiously for I do not profess to know the whole of the Law. If I know the success of my experiments, I know also my failures. But the successes are enough to fill me with undying hope. I have often said that if one takes care of the means, the end will take care of itself. Nonviolence is the means, the end for everyone is complete independence. There will be an international League only when all the nations, big or small, composing it are fully independent. The nature of that independence will correspond to the extent of nonviolence assimilated by the nations concerned. One thing is certain. In a society based on nonviolence, the smallest nation will feel as tall as the tallest. The idea of superiority and inferiority will be wholly obliterated.

...The conclusion is irresistible that for one like me, wedded to nonviolence, constitutional or democratic government is a distant dream so long as nonviolence is not recognized as a living force, an inviolable creed, not a mere policy. While I prate about universal nonviolence, my experiment is confined to India. If it succeeds, the world will accept it without effort. There is however a bit BUT. The pause does not worry me. My faith is brightest in the midst of impenetrable darkness. (H, 11-12-1939, p8)

Use of Power: By its very nature, nonviolence cannot 'seize' power, nor can that be its goal. But nonviolence can do more; it can effectively control and guide power without capturing the machinery of government. That is its beauty.

There is an exception, of course. If the nonviolent Noncooperation of the people is so complete that the administration ceases to function or if the administration crumbles under the impact of a foreign invasion and a vacuum results, the people's representatives will then step in and fill it. Theoretically that is possible. But the use of power need not necessarily be violent. A father wields power over his children; he may even punish but not by inflicting violence. The most effective exercise of power is that which irks least. Power rightly exercised must sit light as a flower; no one should feel the weight of it.

The people accepted the authority of the Congress willingly. I was on more than one occasion invested with the absolute power of dictatorship. But everybody knew that my power rested on their willing acceptance.

They could set me aside at any time and I would have stepped aside without a murmur. Prophets and supermen are born only once in an age. But if even a single individual realizes the ideal of ahimsa in its fullness, he covers and redeems the whole society. Once Jesus had blazed the trail, his twelve disciples could carry on his mission without his presence.

It needed the perseverance and genius of so many generations of scientists to discover the laws of electricity, but today everybody, even children use electric power in their daily life. Similarly, it will not always need a perfect being to administer an ideal State once it has come into being. What is needed is a thorough social awakening to begin with. The rest will follow. To take an instance nearer home, I have presented to the working class the truth that true capital is not silver or gold, but the labour of their hands and feet and their intelligence. Once labour develops that awareness, it would not need my presence to enable it to make use of the power that it will release. (TNH, pp91-93)

Training For Nonviolence

"How are we to train individuals or communities in this difficult art?" There is no royal road, except through living the creed in your life which must be a living sermon. Of course, the expression in one's own life presupposes great study, tremendous perseverance, and thorough cleansing of one's self of all the impurities. If for mastering of the physical sciences you have to devote a whole life-time, how many lifetimes may be needed for mastering the greatest spiritual force that mankind has known? But why worry even if it means several lifetimes? For, if this is the only permanent thing in life, if this is the only thing that counts, then whatever effort you bestow on mastering it is well spent. Seek ye first the Kingdom of Heaven and everything else shall be added unto you. The Kingdom of Heaven is ahimsa. (H, 14-3-1936, p39)

Arms are surely unnecessary for a training in ahimsa. In fact the arms, if any, have to be thrown away, as the Khansaheb did in the Frontier Province. Those who hold that it is essential to learn violence before we can learn nonviolence, would hold that only sinners can be saints.

Fearlessness the Prerequisite

Just as one must learn the art of killing in the training for violence, so one must learn the art of dying in the training for nonviolence. Violence does not mean emancipation from fear, but discovering the means of combating the cause of fear. Nonviolence, on the other hand, has no cause for fear. The votary of nonviolence has to cultivate the capacity for sacrifice of the highest type in order to be free from fear. He racks not if he should lose his land, his wealth, his life. He who has not overcome all fear cannot practice ahimsa to perfection.

The votary of ahimsa has only one fear, that is of God. He who seeks refuge in God ought to have a glimpse of the Atman that transcends the body; and the moment one has a glimpse of the Imperishable Atman, one sheds the love of the perishable body. Training in nonviolence is thus diametrically opposed to training in violence. Violence is needed for the protection of things external, nonviolence is needed for the protection of the Atman, for the protection of one's honour.

This nonviolence cannot be learnt by staying at home. It needs enterprise. In order to test ourselves we should learn to dare danger and death, mortify the flesh, and acquire the capacity to endure all manner of hardships. He who trembles or take to his heels the moment he sees two people fighting is not nonviolent, but a coward. A nonviolent person will lay down his life in preventing such quarrels. The bravery of the nonviolent is vastly superior to that of the violent. The badge of the violent is his weapon-spear, or sword, or rifle. God is the shield of the nonviolent. This is not course of training for one intending to learn nonviolence. But it is easy to evolve one from the principles I have laid down. (H, 1-9-1940, p268)

Nonviolence of the Brave

Nonviolence does not require any outside or outward training. It simply requires the will not to kill even in retaliation and the courage to face death without revenge. This is no sermon on ahimsa but cold reason and the statement of a universal law. Given the unquenchable faith in the law, no provocation should prove too great for the exercise of forbearance. This I have described as the nonviolence of the brave. (H, 8-9-1946, p296)

That nonviolence which only an individual can use is not of much use in terms of society. Man is a social being. His accomplishments to be of use must be such as any person with sufficient diligence can attain. That which can be exercised only among friends is of value only as a spark of nonviolence. It cannot merit the appellation of ahimsa. 'Enmity vanishes before ahimsa' is a great aphorism. It means that the greatest enmity requires an equal measure of ahimsa for its abatement.

Cultivation of this virtue may need long practice, ever extending to several births. It does not become useless on that account. Travelling along the route, the pilgrim will meet richer experiences from day to day, so that he may have a glimpse of the beauty he is destined to see at the top. This will add to his zest. No one is entitled to infer from this that the path will be a continuous carpet of roses without thorns. A poet has sung that the way to reach God accrues only to the very brave, never to the fainthearted.

The atmosphere today is so much saturated with poison that one refuses to recollect the wisdom of the ancients and to perceive the varied little experience of ahimsa in action. 'A bad turn is neutralized by a good',is a wise saying of daily experience in practice. Why can we not see that if the sum total of the world's activities was destructive, it would have come to an end long ago? Love, otherwise, ahimsa, sustains this planet of ours. This much must be admitted. The precious grace of life has to be strenuously cultivated, naturally so because it is uplifting. Descent is easy, not so ascent. A large majority of us being undisciplined, our daily experience is that of fighting or swearing at one another on the slightest pretext. This, the richest grace of ahimsa, will descend easily upon the owner of hard discipline. (H, 14-12-1947, p468)

Application of Nonviolence

If one does not practice nonviolence in one's personal relations with others, and hopes to use it in bigger affairs, one is vastly mistaken. Nonviolence like charity must begin at home. But if it is necessary for the individual to be trained in nonviolence, it is even more necessary for the nation to be trained likewise. One cannot be nonviolent in one's own circle and violent outside it. Or else, one is not truly nonviolent even in one's own circle; often the nonviolence is only in appearance. It is only when you meet with resistance, as for instance, when a thief or a murderer appears, that your nonviolence is put on its trail. You either try or should try to oppose the thief with his own weapons, or you try to disarm him by love. Living among decent people, your conduct may not be described as a nonviolent.

Mutual forbearance is nonviolence. Immediately, therefore, you get the conviction that nonviolence is the law of life, you have to practice it towards those who act violently towards you, and the law must apply to nations as individuals. Training no doubt is necessary. And beginnings are always small. But if the conviction is there, the rest will follow. (H, 28-1-1939, pp441-2)

Universality of Nonviolence

Nonviolence to be a creed has to be all-pervasive. I cannot be nonviolent about one activity of mine and violent about others. (H, 12-10-1935, p376)

It is a blasphemy to say that nonviolence can only be practiced by individuals and never by nations which are composed of individuals. (H, 12-11-1938, p328)

In my opinion, nonviolence is not passivity in any shape or form. Nonviolence, as I understand it, is the most active force in the world...Non-violence is the supreme law. During my half a century of experience, I have not yet come across a situation when I had to say that I was helpless, that I had no remedy in terms of nonviolence. (H, 24-12-1938, p393)

Cultivation of Nonviolence

I am an irrepressible optimist. My optimism rests on my belief in the infinite possibilities of the individual to develop nonviolence.

The more you develop it in your own being, the more infectious it becomes till it over-whelms your surroundings and by and by might over sweep the world. (H, 28-1-1939, p443)

I have known from early youth that nonviolence is not a cloistered virtue to be practiced by the individual for his peace and final salvation, but it is a rule of conduct for society if it is to live consistently with human dignity and make progress towards the attainment of peace for which it has been yearning for ages past. (GCG, pp42-44, pp170-1)

To practice nonviolence in mundane matters is to know its true value. It is to bring heaven upon earth. There is no such thing as the other world. All works are one. There is no 'here' and no 'there'. As Jeans has demonstrated, the whole universe including the most distant stars, invisible even through the most powerful telescope in the world, is compressed in an atom. I hold it, therefore, to be wrong to limit the use of nonviolence to cave-dwellers and for acquiring merit for a favoured position in the other world. All virtue ceases to have use if it serves no purpose in every walk of life. (H, 26-7-1942, p248)

Use on Mass Scale

Unfortunately for us, we are strangers to the nonviolence of the brave on a mass scale. Some even doubt the possibility of the exercise of nonviolence by groups, much less by masses of people. They restrict its exercise to exceptional individuals. Only, mankind can have no use of it if it is always reserved only for individuals. (H, 8-9-1946, p296)

Efficacy

I have been practicing with scientific precision nonviolence and its possibilities for an unbroken period of over fifty years. I have applied it in every walk of life, domestic, institutional, economic and political. I know of no single case in which it has failed. Where it has seemed sometimes to have failed, I have ascribed it to my imperfections.

I claim no perfection for myself. But I do claim to be a passionate seeker after Truth, which is but another name for God. In the course of that search, the discovery of nonviolence came to me. Its spread is my life mission. I have no interest in living except for the prosecution of that mission. (H, 6-7-1940, pp185-6) There is no hope for the aching world except through the narrow and straight path of nonviolence. Millions like me may fail to prove the truth in their own lives, that would be their failure, never of the eternal law. (H, 29-6-1947, p209)

The Nonviolent Society

I hold that nonviolence is not merely a personal virtue. It is also a social virtue to be cultivated like the other virtues. Surely society is largely regulated by the expression of nonviolence in its mutual dealings. What I ask for is an extension of it on a larger, national and international scale. (H, 7-1-1939, p417)

All society is held together by nonviolence, even as the earth is held in her position by gravitation. But when the law of gravitation was discovered, the discovery yielded results of which our ancestors had no knowledge. Even so, when society is deliberately constructed in accordance with the law of nonviolence, its structure will be different in material particulars from what it is today. But I cannot say in advance what the government based on nonviolence will be like. What is happening today is disregard of the law of nonviolence and enthronement of violence as if it were an eternal law. (H, 11-12-1939, p8)

Society based on nonviolence can only consist of groups settled in villages in which voluntary cooperation is the condition of dignified and peaceful existence. (H, 13-1-1940, pp410-11)

The Government

The Government cannot succeed in becoming entirely nonviolent, because it represents all the people. I do not today conceive of such a golden age. But I do believe in the possibility of a predominantly nonviolent society. And I am working for it. (H, 9-3-1940, p31)

There remains the question as to whether in an ideal society, there should be any or no government. I do not think we need worry ourselves about this at the moment. If we continue to work for such a society, it will slowly come into being to an extent, such that the people can benefit by it. Euclid's line is one without breadth, but no one has so far been able to draw it and never will.

All the same, it is only by keeping the ideal line in mind that we have made progress in geometry. What is true here is true of every ideal.

Anarchy

It must be remembered that nowhere in the world does a State without government exist. If at all it could ever come into being, it would be in India; for, ours is the only country where the attempt has, at any rate, been made. We have not yet been able to show that bravery to the degree which is necessary and for the attainment of which there is only one way. Those who have faith in the latter have to demonstrate it. In order to do so, the fear of death has to be completely shed, just as we have shed the fear of prisons. (H, 15-9-1946, p309)

Democracy and Nonviolence

Science of war leads one to dictatorship pure and simple. Science of nonviolence can alone lead one to pure democracy. (H, 15-10-1938, p290)

Democracy and violence can ill go together. The State that are today nominally democratic have either to become frankly totalitarian, or if they are to become truly democratic, they must become courageously nonviolent. (H, 12-11-1938, p328)

Holding the view that, without the recognition of nonviolence on a national scale, there is no such thing as a constitutional or democratic government, I devote my energy to the propagation of nonviolence as the law of our life, individual, social, political, national and international.

I fancy that I have seen the light, though dimly. I write cautiously for I do not profess to know the whole of the Law. If I know the success of my experiments, I know also my failures. But the successes are enough to fill me with undying hope. I have often said that if one takes care of the means, the end will take care of itself. Nonviolence is the means, the end for everyone is complete independence. There will be an international League only when all the nations, big or small, composing it are fully independent. The nature of that independence will correspond to the extent of nonviolence assimilated by the nations concerned. One thing is certain. In a society based on nonviolence, the smallest nation will feel as tall as the tallest. The idea of superiority and inferiority will be wholly obliterated.

...The conclusion is irresistible that for one like me, wedded to nonviolence, constitutional or democratic government is a distant dream so long as nonviolence is not recognized as a living force, an inviolable creed, not a mere policy. While I prate about universal nonviolence, my experiment is confined to India. If it succeeds, the world will accept it without effort. There is however a bit BUT. The pause does not worry me. My faith is brightest in the midst of impenetrable darkness. (H, 11-12-1939, p8)

Use of Power

By its very nature, nonviolence cannot 'seize' power, nor can that be its goal. But nonviolence can do more; it can effectively control and guide power without capturing the machinery of government. That is its beauty. There is an exception, of course. If the nonviolent noncooperation of the people is so complete that the administration ceases to function or if the administration crumbles under the impact of a foreign invasion and a vacuum results, the people's representatives will then step in and fill it. Theoretically that is possible.

But the use of power need not necessarily be violent. A father wields power over his children; he may even punish but not by inflicting violence. The most effective exercise of power is that which irks least. Power rightly exercised must sit light as a flower; no one should feel the weight of it.

The people accepted the authority of the Congress willingly. I was on more than one occasion invested with the absolute power of dictatorship. But everybody knew that my power rested on their willing acceptance. They could set me aside at any time and I would have stepped aside without a murmur. Prophets and supermen are born only once in an age. But if even a single individual realizes the ideal of ahimsa in its fullness, he covers and redeems the whole society. Once Jesus had blazed the trail, his twelve disciples could carry on his mission without his presence.

It needed the perseverance and genius of so many generations of scientists to discover the laws of electricity, but today everybody, even children use electric power in their daily life. Similarly, it will not always need a perfect being to administer an ideal State once it has come into being. What is needed is a thorough social awakening to begin with. The rest will follow. To take an instance nearer home, I have presented to the working class the truth that true capital is not silver or gold, but the labour of their hands and feet and their intelligence. Once labour develops that awareness, it would not need my presence to enable it to make use of the power that it will release. (TNH, pp91-93)

Ahimsa or the Way of Nonviolence

Nonviolence is the greatest force at the disposal of mankind. It is mightier than the mightiest weapon of destruction devised by the ingenuity of man. Destruction is not the law of the humans. Man lives freely by his readiness to die, if need be, at the hands of his brother, never by killing him. Every murder or other injury, no matter for what cause, committed or inflicted on another is a crime against humanity. (MM,49)

The first condition of nonviolence is justice all round in every department of life. Perhaps, it is too much to expect of human nature. I do not, however, think so. No one should dogmatize about the capacity of human nature for degradation or exaltation. (MT, V, 344)

Just as one must learn the art of killing in the training for violence, so one must learn the art of dying in the training for nonviolence. Violence does not mean emancipation from fear, but discovering the means of combating the cause of fear. Nonviolence, on the other hand, has no cause for fear. The votary of nonviolence has to cultivate the capacity for sacrifice of the highest type in order to be free from fear. He recks not if he should lose his land, his wealth, his life.

He who has not overcome all fear cannot practice ahimsa to perfection. The votary of ahimsa has only one fear, that is of God. He who seeks refuge in God ought to have a glimpse of the Atma that transcends the body; and the moment one has a glimpse of the imperishable Atma one sheds the love of the perishable body. Training in nonviolence is thus diametrically opposed to training in violence. Violence is needed for the protection of things external, nonviolence is needed for the protection of the Atma, for the protection of one's honour. (SB, 16)

It is nonviolence if we merely love those that love us. It is nonviolence only when we love those that hate us. I know how difficult it is to follow this grand law of love. But are not all great and good things difficult to do ? Love of the hater is the most difficult of all. But by the grace of God even this most difficult thing becomes, easy to accomplish if we want to do it. (SB, 18)

I have found that life persists in the midst of destruction and therefore there must be a higher law than that of destruction. Only under that law would a well-ordered society be intelligible and life worth living. And if that is the law of life, we have to work it out in daily life. Whenever there are jars, wherever you are confronted with an opponent conquer him with love. In this crude manner I have worked it out in my life. That does not mean that all my difficulties are solved. Only I have found that this law of love has answered as the law of destruction has never done. It is not that I am incapable of anger, for instance, but I succeed on almost all occasions to keep my feelings under control. Whatever may be the result, there is always in me conscious struggle for following the law of nonviolence deliberately and ceaselessly. Such a struggle leaves one stronger for it. The more I work at this law, the more I feel the delight in my life, the delight in the scheme of' the universe. It gives me a peace and a meaning of the mysteries of nature that I have no power to describe. (SB, 25)

I saw that nations like individuals could only be made through the agony of the Cross and in no other way. Joy comes not out of infliction of pain on others but out of pain voluntarily borne by oneself. (SB, 23)

If we turn our eyes to the time of which history has any record down to our own time, we shall find that man has been steadily progressing towards ahimsa. Our remote ancestors were cannibals. Then came a time when they were fed up with cannibalism and they began to live on chase. Next came a stage when man was ashamed of leading the life of a wandering hunter. He therefore took to agriculture and depended principally on mother earth for his food. Thus from being a nomad he settled down to civilized stable life, founded villages and towns, and from member of a family he became member of a community and a nation. All these are signs of progressive ahimsa and diminishing himsa. Had it been otherwise the human species should have been extinct by now, even as many of the lower species have disappeared. Prophets and avatars have also taught the lesson of ahimsa more or less. Not one of them has professed to teach himsa. And how should it be otherwise ? Himsa does not need to be taught. Man as animal is violent, but as Spirit is nonviolent. The moment he awakes to the Spirit within, he cannot remain violent. Either he progresses towards ahimsa or rushes to his doom. That is why the prophets and avatars have taught the lesson of truth, harmony, brotherhood, justice, etc. all attributes of ahimsa. (SB, 23)

I claim that even now, though the social structure is not based on a conscious acceptance of nonviolence, all the world over mankind lives and men retain their possessions on the sufferance of one another. If they had not done so, only the fewest and the most ferocious would have survived. But such is not the case. Families are bound together by ties of love, and so are groups in the so-called civilized society called nations. Only they do not recognize the supremacy of the law of nonviolence. It follows, therefore, that they have not investigated its vast possibilities. Hitherto, Out of sheer inertia, shall I say, we have taken it for granted that complete nonviolence is possible only for the few who take the vow of non-possession and the allied abstinences. Whilst it is true that the otaries alone can carry on research work and declare from time to time the new possibilities of the great eternal law governing man, if it is a law, it must hold good for all.

The many failures we see are not of the law but of the followers, many of Whom do not even know that they are under the law willy-nilly. When a mother dies for her child she unknowingly obeys the law. I have been pleading for the past fifty years for a conscious acceptance of the law and its zealous practice even in the face of failures. Fifty years' work has shown marvellous results and strengthened my faith. I do claim that by constant practice we shall come to a state of things when lawful possession will commend universal and voluntary respect. No doubt such possession will not be tainted. It will not be an insolent demonstration of the inequalities that surround us everywhere. Nor need the problem of unjust and unlawful possession appeal the votary of nonviolence. He has at his disposal the nonviolent weapon of Satyagraha and noncooperation which hitherto has been found to be a complete substitute of violence whenever it has been applied honestly in sufficient measure. I have never claimed to present the complete science of nonviolence. It does not lend itself to such treatment. So far as I know, no single physical science does, not even the very exact science of mathematics. I am but a seeker. (SB, 24-25)

In the application of Satyagraha, I discovered in the earliest stages that pursuit of truth did not admit of violence being inflicted on one's opponent but that he must be weaned from error by patience and sympathy. For, what appears to be truth to the one may appear to be error to another. And patience means self-suffering. So the doctrine came to mean vindication of truth, not by infliction of suffering on the opponent, but on one's self. (SB, 17-18)

In this age of wonders no one will say that a thing or idea is worthless because it is new. To say it is impossible because it is difficult, is again not in consonance with the spirit of the age. Things undreamt of are daily being seen, the impossible is ever becoming possible. We are constantly being astonished these days at the amazing discoveries in the field of violence. But I maintain that far more undreamt of and seemingly impossible discoveries will be made in the field of nonviolence. (SB, 31-32)

Man and his deed are two distinct things. It is quite proper to resist and attack a system, but to resist and attack its author is tantamount to resisting and attacking oneself. For we are all tarred with the same brush, and are children of one and the same Creator, and as such the divine powers within us are infinite. To slight a single human being is to slight those divine powers, and thus to harm not only that being but with him the whole world. (SB, 7-28)

Nonviolence is a universal principle and its operation is not limited by a hostile environment. Indeed, its efficacy can be tested only when it acts in the midst of and in spite of opposition. Our nonviolence would be a hollow thing and nothing worth, if it depended for its success on the goodwill of the authorities. (SB, 33)

The only condition of a successful use of this force is a recognition of the existence of the soul as apart from the body and its permanent nature. And this recognition must amount to a living faith and not mere intellectual grasp. (SB, 32)

Some friends have told me that truth and nonviolence have no place in politics and worldly affairs. I do not agree. I have no use for them as a means of individual salvation. Their introduction and application in everyday life has been my experiment all along. (SB, 33)

No man could be actively nonviolent and not rise against social injustice no matter where it occurred. (SB, 33)

Passive resistance is a method of securing rights by personal suffering; it is the reverse of resistance by arms. When I refuse to do a thing that is repugnant to my conscience, I use soul-force. For instance, the government of the day has passed a law which is applicable to me. I d° not like it. If by using violence I force the government to repeal the law, I am employing what may be termed body-force. If I do not obey the law and accept the penalty for its breach, I use soul-force. It involves sacrifice of self. Everybody admits that sacrifice of self is infinitely superior to sacrifice of others. Moreover, if this kind of force is used in a cause that is unjust, only the person using it suffers. He does not make others suffer for his mistakes. Men have before now done many things which were subsequently found to have been wrong. No man can claim that he is absolutely in the right or that a particular thing is wrong because he thinks so, but it is wrong for him so long as that is his deliberate judgements. It is therefore meet that he should not do that which he knows to be wrong, and suffer the consequence whatever it may be. This is the key to the use of soul-force. (SM 34)

A votary of ahimsa cannot subscribe to the utilitarian formula (of the greatest good of the greatest number). He will strive for the greatest good of all and die in the attempt to realize the ideal. He will therefore be willing to die, so that the others may live. He will serve himself with the rest, by himself dying. The greatest good of all inevitably includes the good of the greatest number, and, therefore, he and the utilitarian will converge in many points in their career but there does come a time when they must part company, and even work in opposite directions. The utilitarian to be logical will never sacrifice himself. The absolutist will even sacrifice himself. (SB, 38-39) You might of course say that there can be no nonviolent rebellion and there has been none known to history. Well, it is my ambition to provide an instance, and it is my dream that my country may win its freedom through nonviolence. And, I would like to repeat to the world times without number, that I will not purchase my country's freedom at the cost of nonviolence. My marriage to nonviolence is such an absolute thing that I would rather commit suicide than be deflected from my position. I have not mentioned truth in this connection, simply because truth cannot be expressed except by nonviolence. (SB, 142-43)

The accumulated experience of the past thirty years, the first eight of which were in South Africa, fills me with the greatest hope that in the adoption of nonviolence lies the future of India and the world. It is the most harmless and yet equally effective way of dealing with the political and economic wrongs of the downtrodden portion of humanity. I have known from early youth that nonviolence is not a cloistered virtue to be practiced by the individual for the peace and final salvation, but it is a rule of conduct for society if it is to live consistently with human dignity and make progress towards the attainment of peace for which it has been yearning for ages past. (SB, 145)

Up to the year 1906, I simply relied on appeal to reason. I was a very industrious reformer. I was a good draftsman, as I always had a close grip of facts which in its turn was the necessary result of my meticulous regard for truth. But I found that reason failed to produce an impression when the critical moment arrived in South Africa. My people were excited; even a worm will and does sometimes turn-and there was talk of wreaking vengeance. I had then to choose between allying myself to violence or finding out some other method of meeting the crisis and stopping the rot and it came to me that we should refuse to obey legislation that was degrading and let them put us in jail if they liked. Thus came into being the moral equivalent of war. I was then a loyalist, because I implicitly believed that the sum total of the activities of the British Empire was good for India and for humanity. Arriving in England soon after the outbreak of the war I plunged into it and later when I was forced to go to India as a result of the pleurisy that I had developed, I led a recruiting campaign at the risk of my life, and to the horror of some of my friends. The disillusionment came in 1919 after the passage of the Black Rowlatt Act (Act depriving Indian of some fundamental civil liberties.) and the refusal of the government to give the simple elementary redress of proved wrongs that we had asked for. And so, in 1920, I became a rebel. Since then the conviction has been growing upon me, that things of fundamental importance to the people are not secured by reason alone but have to be purchased with their suffering. Suffering is the law of human beings; war is the law of the jungle. But suffering is infinitely more powerful than the law of the jungle for converting the opponent and opening his ears, which are otherwise shut, to the voice of reason. Nobody has probably drawn up more petitions or espoused more forlorn causes than I and I have come to this fundamental conclusion that if you want something really important to be done you must not merely satisfy the reason, you must move the heart also. The appeal of reason is more to the head but the penetration of the heart comes from suffering. It opens up the inner understanding in man. Suffering is the badge of the human race, not the sword. (SB, 146-47)

Nonviolence is a power which can be wielded equally by all-children, young men and women or grown up people-provided they have a living faith in the God of Love and have therefore equal love for all mankind. When nonviolence is accepted as the law of life it must pervade the whole being and not be applied to isolated acts. (SB, 147)

If we are to be nonviolent, we must then not wish for anything on this earth which the meanest or the lowest of human beings cannot have. (SB, 16)

The principle of nonviolence necessitates complete abstention from exploitation in any form. (SB, 33)

My resistance to war does not carry me to the point of thwarting those who wish to take part in it. I reason with them. I put before them the better way and leave them to make the choice. (SB, 144)

I would say to my critics to enter with me into the sufferings, not only of the people of India but of those, whether engaged in the war or not, of the whole world. I cannot look at this butchery going on in the world with indifference. I have an unchangeable faith that it is beneath the dignity of man to resort to mutual slaughter. I have no doubt that there is a way out. (SB, 145) Perfect nonviolence is impossible so long as we exist physically, for we would want some space at least to occupy. Perfect nonviolence whilst you are inhabiting the body is only a theory like Euclid's point or straight line, but we have to endeavour every moment of our lives. (SB, 147)

Taking life may be a duty. We do destroy as much life as we think necessary for sustaining our body. Thus for food we take life, vegetable and other, and for health we destroy mosquitoes and the like by the use of disinfectants, etc., and we do not think that we are guilty of irreligion in doing so...for the benefit of the species, we kill carnivorous beasts.... Even man slaughter may be necessary in certain cases. Suppose a man runs amuck and goes furiously about, sword in hand, and killing anyone that comes in his way, and no one dares to capture him alive. Anyone who dispatches this lunatic will earn the gratitude of the community and be regarded as a benevolent man. (SB, 149)

I see that there is an instinctive horror of killing living beings under any circumstances whatever. For instance, an alternative has been suggested in the shape of confining even rabid dogs in a certain place and allowing them to die a slow death. Now my idea compassion makes this thing impossible for me. I cannot for a moment bear to see a dog, or for that matter any other living being, helplessly suffering the torture of a slow death. I do not kill a human being thus circumstanced because I have more hopeful remedies. I should kill a dog similarly situated because in its case I am without a remedy. Should my child be attacked with rabies and there was no helpful remedy to relieve his agony, I should consider it my duty to take his life. Fatalism has its limits. We leave things to fate after exhausting all the remedies. One of the remedies and the final one to relieve the agony of a tortured child is to take his life. (SB, 149)

In its positive form, ahimsa means the largest love, greatest charity. If I am a follower of ahimsa I must love my enemy. I must apply the same rules to the wrongdoer who is my enemy or a stranger to me, as I would to my wrongdoing father or son. This active ahimsa necessarily includes truth and fearlessness. As man cannot deceive the loved one, he does not fear or frighten him or her. Gift of life is the greatest of all gifts, a man who gives it in reality, disarms all hostility. He has paved the way for an honourable understanding. And none who is himself subject to fear can bestow that gift. He must therefore be himself fearless. A man cannot practice ahimsa and be a coward at the same time. The practice of ahimsa calls forth the greatest courage. (SB, 151)

Having flung aside the sword, there is nothing except the cup of love which I can offer to those who oppose me. It is by offering that cup that I expect to draw them close to me. I cannot think of permanent enmity between man and man, and believing as I do in the theory of rebirth, I live in the hope that if not in this birth, in some other birth, I shall be able to hug all humanity in friendly embrace. (SB, 151-52)

Love is the strongest force the world possesses and yet it is the humblest imaginable. (SB, 152)

The hardest heart and the grossest ignorance must disappear before the rising sun of suffering without anger and without malice. (SB, 152)

Nonviolence is not a resignation from all real fighting against wickedness; On the contrary, the nonviolence of my conception is a more active and real fight against wickedness than retaliation whose very nature is to increase wickedness. I contemplate a mental and therefore a moral opposition to immoralities. I seek entirely to blunt the edge of the tyrant's sword, not by putting up against it a sharper-edged weapon, but by disappointing his expectation that I would be offering physical, resistance. The resistance of the soul that I should offer would elude him. It would at first dazzle him and at last compel recognition from him, which recognition would not humiliate but would uplift him. It may be urged that this is an ideal state. And so it is. (SB, 152)

Ahimsa is a comprehensive principle. We are helpless mortals caught in the conflagration of himsa. The saying that life lives on life has a deep meaning in it. Man cannot for a moment live without consciously or unconsciously committing outward himsa. The very fact of his living eating, drinking and moving about-necessarily involves some himsa, destruction of life, be it ever so minute. A votary of ahimsa therefore remains true to his faith if the spring of all his actions is compassion, if he shuns to the best of his ability the destruction of the tiniest creature, tries to save it, and thus incessantly strives to be free from the deadly coil of himsa. He will be constantly growing in self-restraint and compassion, but he can never become entirely free from outward himsa. Then again, because underlying ahimsa is the unity of all life, the error of one cannot but affect all, and hence man cannot be wholly free from himsa. So long as he continues to be a social being, he cannot but participate in the himsa that the very existence involves. When two nations are fighting, the duty of a votary of ahimsa is to stop the war. He who is not equal to that duty, he who has no power of resisting war, he who is not qualified to resist war, may take part in war, and yet wholeheartedly try to free himself, his nation and the world from war. (AMG, 427-28)

I make no distinction, from the point of view of ahimsa between combatants and non-combatants. He who volunteers to serve a band of dacoits, by working as their carrier, or their watchman while they are about their business, or their nurse when they are wounded, is as much guilty of dacoity as the dacoits themselves. In the same way those who confine themselves to attending to the wounded in battle cannot be absolved from the guilt of war. (AMG, 428)

The question is subtle. It admits of differences of opinion, and therefore I have submitted my argument as clearly as possible to those who believe in ahimsa and who are making serious efforts to practice it in every walk of life. A devotee of Truth may not do anything in deference to convention. He must always hold himself open to correction, and whenever he discovers himself to be wrong he must confess it at all costs and atone for it. (AMG, 429)

Nonviolence to be a potent force must begin with the mind. Nonviolence of the mere body without the cooperation of the mind is nonviolence of the weak or the cowardly, and has therefore no potency. If we bear malice and hatred in our bosoms and pretend not to retaliate, it must recoil upon us and lead to our destruction. For abstention from mere bodily violence not to be injurious, it is at least necessary not to entertain hatred if we cannot generate active love. (SB, 154)

He is no follower of ahimsa who does not care a straw if he kills a man by inches by deceiving him in a trade or who would protect by force of arms a few cows and make away with the butcher or who, in order to do a supposed good to his country, does not mind killing of a few officials. All these are actuated by hatred, cowardice and fear. (SB, 155)

I object to violence because when it appears to do good, the good is only temporary; the evil it does is permanent. I do not believe that the killing of even every Englishman can do the slightest good to India. The millions will be just as badly off as they are today, if someone made it possible to kill off every Englishman tomorrow. The responsibility is more ours than that of the English for the present state of things. The English will be powerless to do evil if we will but do good. Hence my incessant emphasis on reform from within. (SB, 157)

History teaches one that those who have, no doubt with honest motives, ousted the greedy by using brute force against them, have in their turn become a prey to the disease of the conquered. (SB, 157)

From violence done to the foreign ruler, violence to our own people whom we may consider to be obstructing the country's progress is an easy natural step. Whatever may have been the result of violent activities in other countries and without reference to the philosophy of nonviolence, it does not require much intellectual effort to see that if we resort to violence for ridding society of many abuses which impede our progress, we shall add to our difficulties and postpone the day of freedom. The people unprepared for reforms because unconvinced of their necessity will be maddened with rage over their coercion, and will seek the assistance of the foreigner in order to retaliate. Has not this been happening before our eyes for the past many years of which we have still painfully vivid recollections? (SB, 159-60)

If I can have nothing to do with the organized violence of the government, I can have less to do with the unorganized violence of the people. I would prefer to be crushed between the two. (SB, 206)

I have been practicing with scientific precision nonviolence and its possibilities for an Unbroken period of over 50 years. I have applied it in every walk of life-domestic, institutional, economic and political. I know of no single case in which it has failed. Where it has seemed sometimes to have failed, I have ascribed it to my imperfections. I claim no perfection for myself. But I do claim to be a passionate seeker after Truth, which is but another name for God. In the course of that search the discovery of nonviolence came to me. Its spread is my life mission. I have no interest in living except for the prosecution of that mission. (MM, 42). It is to me a matter of perennial satisfaction that I retain generally the affection and trust of those whose principles and policies I oppose. The South Africans gave me personally their confidence and extended their friendship. In spite of my denunciation of British policy and system I enjoy the affection of thousands of Englishmen and women, and in spite of unqualified condemnation of modern materialistic civilization, the circle of European and American friends is ever widening. It is again a triumph of nonviolence. (MM, 3-4)

My experience, daily growing stronger and richer, tells me that there is no peace for individuals or for nations without practicing truth and nonviolence to the uttermost extent possible for man. The policy of retaliation has never succeeded. (MM, 44)

My love for nonviolence is superior to every other thing mundane or supramundane. It is equaled only by my love for truth which is to me synonymous with nonviolence through which and which alone I can see and reach Truth. My scheme of life, if it draws no distinction between different religionists in India, also draws none between different races. For me 'A man's a man for a' that'. (MM, 44)

I am but a weak aspirant, ever failing, ever trying. My failures make me more vigilant than before and intensify my faith. I can see with the eye of faith that the observance of the twin doctrine of truth and nonviolence has possibilities of which we have but very inadequate conception. (MM, 44)

I am an irrepressible optimist. My optimism rests on my belief in the infinite possibilities of the individual to develop a nonviolence. The more you develop it in your own being, the more infectious it becomes till it' overwhelms your surroundings and by and by might over sweep the world. (MM, 46)

In my opinion nonviolence is not passivity in any shape or form. Nonviolence, as I understand it, is the most active force in the world.... Nonviolence is the supreme law. During my half a century of experience I have not yet come across a situation when I had to say that I was helpless, that I had no remedy in terms of nonviolence. (MM, 46)

It is the acid test of nonviolence that in a nonviolent conflict there is no rancour left behind, and in the end the enemies are converted into friends. That was my experience in South Africa with General Smuts. He started with being my bitterest opponent and critic. Today he is my warmest friend. (MM, 46)

The strength to kill is not essential for self-defense; one ought to have the strength to die. When a man is fully ready to die, he will not even desire to offer violence. Indeed, I may put it down as a self-evident proposition that the desire to kill is in inverse proportion to the desire to die. And history is replete with instances of men who by dying with courage and compassion on their lips converted the hearts of their violent opponents. (MM, 48-49)

I am but a humble explorer of the science of nonviolence. Its hidden depths sometimes stagger me just as much as they stagger fellow-workers. (MM, 48)

It has become the fashion these days to say that society cannot be organized or run on nonviolent lines. I join issue on that point. In a family, when a father slaps his delinquent child, the latter does not think of retaliating. He obeys his father not because of the deterrent effect of the slap but because of the offended love which he senses behind it. That, in my opinion, is an epitome of the way in which society is or should be governed. What is true of the family must be true of society which is but a larger family. (MM, 50)

I do not want to live at the cost of the life even of a snake. I should let him bite me to death rather than kill him. But it is likely that if God puts me to that cruel test and permits a snake to assault me, I may not have the courage to die, but that the beast in me may assert itself and I may seek to kill the snake in defending this perishable body. I admit that my belief has not become so incarnate in me as to warrant my stating emphatically that I have shed all fear of snakes so as to befriend them as I would like to be able to. (MM, 52). I am not opposed to the progress of science as such. On the contrary, the scientific spirit of the West commands my admiration and if that admiration is qualified, it is because the scientist of the West takes no note of God's lower creation. I abhor vivisection with my whole soul. I detest the unpardonable slaughter of innocent life in the name of science and humanity so-called, and all the scientific discoveries stained with innocent blood I count as of no consequence. If the circulation of blood theory could not have been discovered without vivisection, the human kind could well have done without it. And I see the day clearly dawning when the honest scientist of the West will put limitations upon the present methods of pursuing knowledge. (MM, 54)

Nonviolence is not an easy thing to understand, still less to practice, weak as we are. We must all act prayerfully and humbly and continually asking God to open the eyes of our understanding being ever ready to act according to the light as we daily receive it. My task as a lover and promoter of peace, therefore, today consists in unflinching devotion to nonviolence in the prosecution of the campaign for regaining our liberty. And if India succeeds in so regaining it, it will be the greatest contribution to the world peace. (MM, 58)

Passive resistance is an all-sided sword; it can be used anyhow; it blesses him who uses it and him against whom it is used. Without drawing a drop of blood it produces far-reaching results. It never rusts and cannot be stolen. (MM, 63)

Disobedience to be civil must be sincere, respectful, restrained, never defiant, must be based upon some well-understood principle, must not be capricious and above all, must have no ill-will or hatred behind it. (MM, 64)

Jesus Christ, Daniel and Socrates represented the purest form of passive resistance or soul-force. All these teachers counted their bodies as nothing in comparison to their soul. Tolstoy was the best and brightest (modern) exponent of the doctrine. He not only expounded it, but lived according to it. In India, the doctrine was understood and commonly practiced long before it came into vogue in Europe. It is easy to see that soul-force is infinitely superior to body-force. If people in order to secure redress of wrongs resort to soul-force, much of the present suffering will be avoided. (MM,68)

Buddha fearlessly carried the war into the enemy's camp and brought down on its knees an arrogant priesthood. Christ drove out the money-changers from the temple of Jerusalem and drew down curses from Heaven upon the hypocrites and the Pharisees. Both were for intensely direct action. But even as Buddha and Christ chastised, they showed unmistakable gentleness and love behind every act of theirs. They would not raise a finger against their enemies, but would gladly surrender themselves rather than the truth for which they lived. Buddha would have died resisting the priesthood, if the majesty of his love had not proved to be equal to the task of bending the priesthood. Christ died on the cross with a crown of thorns on his head defying the might of a whole empire. And if I raise resistances of a nonviolent character, I simply and humbly follow in the footsteps of the great teachers. (MM, 68-69)

It is a law of Satyagraha that when a man has no weapon in his hands and when he cannot think of a way out, he should take the final step of giving up his body. (DM, 296)

Ahimsa is soul-force and the soul is imperishable, changeless and eternal. The atom bomb is the acme of physical force and, as such subject-to the law of dissipation, decay and death that governs the physical universe. Our scriptures bear witness that when soul-force is fully awakened in us, it becomes irresistible. But the test and condition of full awakening is that it must permeate every pore of our I being and emanate with every breath that we breathe.

But no institution can be made nonviolent by compulsion. Nonviolence and truth cannot be written into constitution. They have to be adopted of one's own free will. They must sit naturally upon us like next-to-skin garments or else they become a contradiction in terms. (MGP, II, 124-25)

Life is an aspiration. Its mission is to strive after perfection, which is self-realization. The ideal must not be lowered because of our weaknesses and imperfections.... One who hooks his fortunes to ahimsa, the law of love, daily lessens the circle of destruction, and to that extent promotes life and love; he who swears by himsa, the law of hate, daily widens the circle of destruction, and to that extent promotes death and hate. (MGP, II, 507)

In life, it is impossible to eschew violence completely. Now the question arises, where is one to draw the line ? The line cannot be the same for every one. For, although, essentially the principle is the same, yet everyone applies it in his or her own way. What is one man's food can be another's poison. Meat-eating is a sin for me. Yet, for another person, who has always lived on meat and never seen anything wrong in it, to give it up, simply in order to copy me, will be a sin.

If I wish to be an agriculturist and stay in a jungle, I will have to use the minimum unavoidable violence, in order to protect my fields. I will have to kill monkeys, birds and insects, which eat up my crops. If I do not wish to do so myself, I will have to engage someone to do it for me. There is not much difference between the two. To allow crops to be eaten up by animals, in the name of ahimsa, while there is a famine in the land, is certainly a sin. Evil and good are relative terms. What is good under certain conditions can become an evil or a sin, under a different set of conditions.

Man is not to drown himself in the well of the shastras, but he is to dive in their broad ocean and bring outpearls. At every step he has to use his discrimination as to what is ahimsa and what is himsa. In this, there is no room for shame or cowardice. The poet had said that the road leading up to God is for the brave, never for the cowardly. (MT, VII, 152-53)

To say or write a distasteful word is surely not violent especially when the speaker or writer believes it to be true. The essence of violence is that there must be a violent intention behind a thought, word, or act, *i.e.*, an intention to do harm to the opponent so-called. False notions of propriety or fear of wounding susceptibilities often deter people from saying what they mean and ultimately land them on the shores of hypocrisy. But if nonviolence of thought is to be evolved in individuals or societies or nations, truth has to be told, however harsh or unpopular it may appear to be for the moment. (SB, 150-51)

Never has anything been done on this earth without direct action. I reject the word 'passive resistance' because of its insufficiency and its being interpreted as a weapon of the weak. (SB, 153)

Nonviolence presupposes ability to strike. It is a conscious, deliberate restraint put upon one's desire for vengeance. But vengeance is any day superior to passive, effeminate and helpless submission. Forgiveness is higher still. Vengeance too is weakness. The desire for vengeance comes out of fear of harm, imaginary or real. A man who fears no one on earth would consider it troublesome even to summon up anger against one who is vainly trying to injure him. (SB, 153)

Nonviolence and cowardice go ill together. I can imagine a fully armed man to be at heart a coward. Possession of arms implies an element of fear, if not cowardice. But true nonviolence is an impossibility without the possession of unadulterated fearlessness. (SB, 154)

My creed of nonviolence is an extremely active force. It has no room for cowardice or even weakness. There is hope for a violent man to be some day nonviolent, but there is none for a coward. I have therefore said more than once in these pages that if we do not know how to defend ourselves, our women and our places of worship by the force of suffering, *i.e.*, nonviolence, we must, if we are men, be at least able to defend all these by fighting. (SB, 154)

The people of a village near Bettia told me that they had run away whilst the police were looting their houses and molesting their womenfolk. When they said that they had run away because I had told them to be nonviolent, I hung my head in shame. I assured them that such was not the meaning of my nonviolence. I expected them to intercept the mightiest power that might be in the act of harming those who were under their protection, and draw without retaliation all harm upon their own heads even to the point of death, but never to run away from the storm centre. It was manly enough to defend one's property, honour, or religion at the point of the sword. It was manlier and nobler to defend them without seeking to injure the wrongdoer. But it was unmanly, unnatural and dishonourable to forsake the post of duty and, in order to save one's skin, to leave property, honour or religion to the mercy of the wrongdoer. I could see my way of delivering ahimsa to those who knew how to die, not to those who were afraid of death. (SB, 155-56)

I would risk violence a thousand times than the emasculation of a whole race. (SB, 156)

My nonviolence does not admit of running away from danger and leaving dear ones unprotected. Between violence and cowardly flight, I can only prefer violence to cowardice. I can no more preach nonviolence to a coward than I can tempt a blind man to enjoy healthy scenes. Nonviolence is the summit of bravery. And in my own experience, I have had no difficulty in demonstrating to men trained in the school of violence the superiority of nonviolence. As a coward, which I was for years, I harboured violence. I began to prize nonviolence only when I began to shed cowardice. (MM, 47)

Nonviolence cannot be taught to a person who fears to die and has no power of resistance. A helpless mouse is not nonviolent because he is always eaten by pussy. He would gladly eat the murderess if he could, but he ever tries to flee from her. We do not call him a coward, because he is made by nature to behave no better than he does. But a man who, when faced by danger, behaves like a mouse, is rightly called a coward. He harbours violence and hatred in also heart and would kill his enemy if he could without hurting himself. He is a stranger to nonviolence. All sermonizing on it will be lost on him. Bravery is foreign to his nature. Before he can understand nonviolence he has to be taught to stand his ground and even suffer death, in the attempt to defend himself against the aggressor who bids fair to overwhelm him. To do otherwise would be to confirm his cowardice and take him farther away fro TM nonviolence. Whilst I may not actually help anyone to retaliate, I must not let a coward seek shelter behind nonviolence so-called. Not knowing the stuff of which nonviolence is made, many have honestly, believed that running away from danger every time was a virtue compared to offering resistance, especially when it was fraught with danger to one's life. As a teacher of nonviolence I must, so far as it is possible for me, guard against such an unmanly belief. (MM, 49)

No matter how weak a person is in body, if it is a shame to flee, he will stand his ground and die at his post. This would be nonviolence and bravery. No matter how weak he is, he will use what strength he has in inflicting injury on his opponent, and die in the attempt. This is bravery, but not nonviolence. If, when his duty is to face danger, he flees, it is cowardice. In the first case the man will have love or charity in him. In the second and third case, there would be a dislike or distrust and fear. (MM, 50)

Supposing I was a Negro, and my sister was ravished by a white or lynched by a whole community, what would be my duty? I ask myself. And the answer comes to me: I must not wish ill to these, but neither must I cooperate with them. It may be that ordinarily I depend on the lynching community for my livelihood. I refuse to cooperate with them, refuse even to touch the food that comes from them, and I refuse to cooperate with even my brother Negroes who tolerate the wrong. That is the self-immolation I mean. I have often in my life resorted to the plan. Of course, a mechanical act of starvation will mean nothing. One's faith must remain undimmed whilst life ebbs out, minute by minute. But I am every poor specimen of the practice of nonviolence, and my answer may not convince you. But I am striving very hard, and even if I do not succeed fully in this life, my faith will not diminish. (MT, IV, 61)

In this age of the rule of brute force, it is almost impossible for anyone to believe that anyone else could possibly reject the law of the final supremacy of brute force. And so I receive anonymous letters advising me that I must not interfere with the progress of the noncooperation movement even though popular violence may break out. Others come to me and, assuming that secretly I must be plotting violence, inquire when the happy moment for declaring open violence is to arrive. They assure me that the English will never yield to anything but violence, secret or open. Yet others, I am informed, believe that I am the most rascally person living in India because I never give out my real intention and that they have not a shadow of a doubt that I believe in violence just as much as most people do. Such being the hold that the doctrine of the sword has on the majority of mankind, and as success of noncooperation depends principally on absence of violence during its pendency, and as my views in this matter affect the conduct of a large number of people, I am anxious to state them as clearly as possible.

I do believe that, where there is only a choice between cowardice and violence, I would advise violence. Thus when my eldest son asked me what he should have done, had he been present when I was almost fatally assaulted in 1908, whether he should have run away and seen me killed or whether he should have used his physical force which he could and wanted to use, and defend me, I told him that it was his duty to defend me even by using violence. Hence it was that I took part in the Boer War, the so-called Zulu Rebellion and the late war. Hence also do I advocate training in arms for those who believe in the method of violence. I would rather have India resort to arms in order to defend her honour than that she should in a cowardly manner become or remain a helpless witness to her own dishonour.

But I believe that nonviolence is infinitely superior to violence, forgiveness is more manly than punishment. Forgiveness adorns a soldier. But abstinence is forgiveness only when there is the power to punish; it is meaningless when it pretends to proceed from a helpless creature. A mouse hardly forgives a cat when it allows itself to be turn to pieces by her. I, therefore, appreciate the sentiment of those who cry out for the condign punishment of General Dyer and his ilk. They would tear him to pieces if they could. But I do not believe India to be a helpless creature. Only I want to use India's and my strength for a better purpose.

Let me not be misunderstood. Strength does not come from physical capacity. It comes from an indomitable will. An average Zulu is anyway more than a match for an average Englishman in bodily capacity. But he flees from an English boy, because he fears the boy's revolver or those who will use it for him. He fears death and is nerveless in spite of his burly figure. We in India may in a moment realize that one hundred thousand Englishmen need not frighten three hundred million human beings. A definite forgiveness would, therefore, mean a definite recognition of our strength. With enlightened forgiveness must come a mighty wave of strength in us, which would make it impossible for a Dyer and a Frank Johnson to heap affront on India's devoted head. It matters little to me that for the moment I do not drive my point home. We feel too downtrodden not to be angry and revengeful. But I must not refrain from saying that India can gain more by waiving the right of punishment. We have better work to do, a better mission to deliver to the world.

I am not a visionary. I claim to be a practical idealist. Religion of nonviolence is not meant merely for the rishis and saints. It is meant for the common people as well. Nonviolence is the law of our species as violence is the law of the brute. The spirit, lies dormant in the brute, and he knows no law but that of physical might. The dignity of man requires obedience to a higher law, to the strength of the spirit.

I have ventured to place before India the ancient law of self-sacrifice. For Satyagraha and its offshoots, noncooperation and civil resistance, are nothing but new names for the law of suffering. The rishis, who discovered the law of nonviolence in the midst of violence, were greater geniuses than Newton. They were themselves greater warriors than Wellington. Having themselves known the use of arms, they realized their uselessness and taught a weary world that its salvation lay not through violence but through nonviolence.

Nonviolence in its dynamic condition means conscious suffering. It does not mean meek submission to the will of the evildoer, but it means putting of one's whole soul against the will of the tyrant. Working under this law of our being, it is possible for a single individual to defy the whole might of an unjust empire to save his honour, his religion, his soul, and lay the foundation for that empire's fall or its regeneration.

And so I am not pleading for India to practice nonviolence because it is weak. I want her to practice nonviolence being conscious of her strength and power. No training in arms is required for realization of her strength. We seem to need it, because we seem to think that we are but a lump of flesh. I want to recognize that she has a soul that cannot perish and that can rise triumphant above every physical weakness and defy the physical combination of a whole world.... If India takes up the doctrine of the sword, she may gain momentary victory. Then India will cease to be the pride of my heart. I am wedded to India because I owe my all to her. I believe absolutely that she has a mission for the world. She is not to copy Europe blindly. India's acceptance of the doctrine of the sword will be the hour of my trial. I hope I shall not be found wanting. My religion has no geographical limits. If I have a living Faith in it, it will transcend my love for India herself. My life is dedicated to the service of India through the religion of nonviolence which I believe to be the root of Hinduism. (MT, II, 5-8)

I must continue to argue till I convert opponents of I own defeat. For my mission is to convert every Indian, even Englishmen and finally the world, to nonviolence for regulating mutual relations whether political, economic, social or religious. If I am accused of being too ambitious, I should plead guilty. If I am told that my dream can never materialize, I would answer 'that is possible', and go my way. I am a seasoned soldier of nonviolence, and I have evidence enough to sustain my faith. Whether, therefore, I have one comrade or more or none, I must continue my experiment. (MT, V, 273)

It has been suggested by American friends that the atom bomb will bring in ahimsa, as nothing else can. It will, if it is meant that its destructive power will so disgust the world, that it will turn it away from violence for the time being. And this is very like a man glutting himself with the dainties to the point of nausea, and turning away from them only to return with redoubled zeal after the effect of nausea is well over. Precisely in the same manner will the world return to violence with renewed zeal, after the effect of disgust is worn out.

Often does good come out of evil. But that is God's, not man's plan. Man knows that only evil can come out of evil, as good out of good.....The moral to be legitimately drawn from the supreme tragedy of the atom bomb is that it will not be destroyed by counter violence. Mankind has to go out of violence only through nonviolence. Hatred can be overcome only by love. Counter hatred only increases the surface, as well as the depth of hatred.

I am aware that I am repeating what I have many times stated before and practiced to the best of my ability and capacity. What I first stated was itself nothing new. It was as old as the hills. Only I recited no copybook maxim but definitely announced what I believed in every fibre of my being. Sixty years of practice in various walks of life has only enriched the belief which the, experience of friends fortified. It is, however, the central truth by which one can stand alone without flinching. I believe in what Max Muller said years ago, namely, that truth needed to be repeated, as long as there were men who disbelieved it. (MT, VII, 171-73)

If India makes violence her creed, and I have survived, I would not care to live in India. She will cease to evoke any pride in me. My patriotism is subservient to my religion. I cling to India like a child to its mother's breast, because I feel that she gives me the spiritual nourishment I need. She has the environment that responds to my highest aspiration. When that faith is gone, I shall feel like an orphan without hope of ever finding a guardian. (MM, 133)

Nonviolence-The Intellectual Context

The ideas that shaped Gandhian nonviolence were drawn both from Western and Indian sources. The trial of Socrates as described in Plato's *Apology* had a profound impact on Gandhi. In 1908 he published a paraphrase of this work in English and Gujarati under the title *The Story of a Soldier of Truth.* Socrates was a model for all those who would resist nonviolently the violence of the state. The ethics of the Sermon on the Mount, as interpreted in Leo Tolstoy's *The Kingdom of God Is within You* (1893), had a lifelong influence on him. Another of Tolstoy's writings, *Letter to a Hindu* (1908), made Gandhi rethink the role of violence in Indian society. Tolstoy had argued that the British were able to hold India by violence because Indians themselves believed in violence as the basis of society. That is why they submitted themselves to their rajas and maharajas, and treated the untouchables with extreme cruelty. Under these circumstances, the complaints of Indians against colonial violence seemed to him to resemble the complaints of alcoholics against wine merchants. The removal of colonial violence would not solve India's problems with violence. They would be solved only if Indians made nonviolence the basis of a new India. Gandhi was so persuaded by the *Letter* that he translated and published it in both English and Gujarati.

Gandhi's study of Western jurisprudence made him a lifelong defender of the idea of the rule of law and the legitimacy of the limited, constitutional state. The fight against violence needed such a state as its ally. Here Gandhi departed from Tolstoy's radical pacifism that rejected the state as such.

John Ruskin's *Unto This Last* (1860) opened Gandhi's eyes to the hidden structures of violence in industrial capitalism. This work, too, Gandhi paraphrased and published in English and Gujarati (1908) under the title *Sarvodaya* (The welfare of all), a title that he later gave to his own economic philosophy.

Finally, there was the question of nationalism and how to free it from ethnic or religious or terrorist violence. Here he found help in the liberal nationalism of Giuseppe Mazzini, whose *An Essay on the Duties of Man,* published in 1892, became one of the recommended readings for all those who wanted to understand Gandhi's own fundamental work, *Hind Swaraj* (1909).

However, it was Indian philosophical thought that helped Gandhi to integrate the ideas he had absorbed from the West. Here three philosophical traditions were significant. The first was the pacifist tradition of Jainism, as interpreted by Rajchand—businessman, poet and mystic, and a personal friend. His advice was that a nonviolent way of life was possible only if one withdrew from politics and concentrated all one's energies on achieving inner harmony. Gandhi accepted the point about inner harmony but rejected the idea of withdrawing from politics. On the contrary, he sought to link the quest for inner harmony with that for outer harmony in society and polity.

The philosophy of yoga as expounded in the classic text, the *Yogasutra* of Patanjali, had also impressed Gandhi greatly. Like Jainism, it too believed in the incompatibility between maintaining inner harmony and engaging in active politics. However, it had recommended five moral virtues as being necessary for inner harmony. Nonviolence was one of them; the other four were truthfulness, abstention from theft, celibacy, and moderation in the use of material possessions. Gandhi gladly incorporated nonviolence into his ethical system—with one modification. He modified it from being a moral virtue into a civic virtue, thereby making it appropriate for political action.

But the philosophy that influenced him most was that of the *Bhagavad Gita.* He interpreted it as teaching the negative lesson of the futility of war. On the positive side, he interpreted it as teaching that the good life called for the disinterested service of one's fellow human beings, sustained by a deep love of God. Obstacles to the good life came from violence and the undisciplined state of the passions, notably anger, hatred, greed, and lust. Self-discipline therefore was the psychological key to nonviolence. The philosophical anthropology underlying Gandhi's theory of nonviolence is adapted from that underlying the *Bhagavad Gita.* Humans are composites of body and soul (atman). As such, body force and soul force were both seen as active in human affairs—the first as a fact and the second as a norm. The body was the source of violence and the passions; the soul was the source of sociability and of the knowledge of good and evil. It was because the spiritual soul was a constitutive element of human beings that nonviolence remained the norm of their behavior. A materialistic view of human life, in Gandhi's view, could not justify, much less sustain, a nonviolent way of life.

The philosophical anthropology of the *Bhagavad Gita* also gave Gandhi's nonviolence its ethical realism. Because humans are composite beings, perfect nonviolence was possible only in the atman's disembodied state, not in its embodied state. In its embodied state, the will to live always brought with it the will to use force in legitimate self-defense. In the embodied state, one must always abstain from culpable violence—that is, offensive violence used for illegitimate gains. Defensive violence used in legitimate self-defense is not judged culpable.

Gandhi and Nonviolence

Gandhi did not claim to be a prophet or even a philosopher. "There is no such thing as Gandhism," he warned, "and I do not want to leave any sect after me." There was only one Gandhian, he said, an imperfect one at that: himself. The real significance of the Indian freedom movement in Gandhi's eyes was that it was waged non-violently. He would have had no interest in it if the Indian National Congress had adopted Satyagraha and subscribed to nonviolence. He objected to violence not only because an unarmed people had little chance of success in an armed rebellion, but because he considered violence a clumsy weapon which created more problems than it solved, and left a trail of hatred and bitterness in which genuine reconciliation was almost impossible.

This emphasis on nonviolence jarred alike on Gandhi's British and Indian critics, though for different reasons. To the former, nonviolence was a camouflage; to the latter, it was sheer sentimentalism. To the British who tended to see the Indian struggle through the prism of European history, the professions of nonviolence rather than on the remarkably peaceful nature of Gandhi's campaigns. To the radical Indian politicians, who had browsed on the history of the French and Russian revolutions or the Italian and Irish nationalist struggles, it was patent that force would only yield to force, and that it was foolish to miss opportunities and sacrifice tactical gains for reasons more relevant to ethics than to politics.

Gandhi's total allegiance to nonviolence created a gulf between him and the educated elite in India which was temporarily bridged only during periods of intense political excitement. Even among his closest colleagues there were few who were prepared to follow his doctrine of nonviolence to its logical conclusion: the adoption of unilateral disarmament in a world armed to the teeth, the scrapping of the police and the armed forces, and the decentralization of administration to the point where the state would "wither away". Nehru, Patel and others on whom fell the task of organizing the administration of independent India did not question the superiority of the principle of nonviolence as enunciated by their leader, but they did not cope rider it practical politics. The Indian Constituent Assembly include a majority of members owing allegiance to Gandhi or at least holding him in high esteem, but the constitution which emerged from their labours in 1949 was based more on the Western parliamentary than on he Gandhian model. The development of the Indian economy during the last four decades cannot be said to have conformed to Gandhi's conception of "self-reliant village republics". On the other hand, it bears the marks of a conscious effort to launch an Indian industrial revolution.

Jawaharlal Nehru-Gandhi's "political heir"-was thoroughly imbued with the humane values inculcated by the Mahatma. But the man who spoke Gandhi's language, after his death, was Vinoba Bhave, the "Walking Saint", who kept out of politics and government, Bhave's Bhoodan (land gift) Movement was designed as much as a measure of land reform as that of a spiritual renewal. Though more than five million acres of land were distributed to the landless, the movement, despite its early promise, never really spiralled into a social revolution by consent. This was partly because Vinoba Bhave did not command Gandhi's extraordinary genius for organizing the masses for a national crusade, and partly because in independent India the tendency grew for the people to look up to the government rather than to rely on voluntary and cooperative effort for effecting reforms in society.

Soon after Gandhi's death in 1948, a delegate speaking at the United Nations predicted that "the greatest achievements of the Indian sage were yet to come" "Gandhi's times," said Vinoba Bhave, "were the first pale dawn of the sun of Satyagraha." Forty years after Gandhi's death, this optimism would seem to have been too high-pitched. The manner in which Gandhi's techniques have sometimes been invoked even in the land of his birth in recent years would appear to be a travesty of his principles. And the world has been in the grip of a series of crises in Korea, the Congo, the Vietnam, the Middle East, and South Africa with a never-ending trail of blood and bitterness. The shadow of a thermonuclear war with its incalculable hazards continues to hang over mankind. From this predicament, Gandhi's ideas and techniques may suggest a way out. Unfortunately, his motives and methods are often misunderstood, and not only by mobs in the street, Not long ago, Arthur Koestler described Gandhi's attitude as one "of passive submission to bayonetting and raping, to villages without sewage, septic childhood's and trachoma." Such a judgement is of course completely with the same tenacity with which he battled with the British Raj. He advocated nonviolence not because it offered an easy way out, but because he considered violence a crude and in the long run, an ineffective weapon. His rejection of violence stemmed from choice, not from necessity.

Horace Alexander, who knew Gandhi and saw him in action, graphically describes the attitude of the nonviolent resister to his opponent: "On your side you have all the mighty forces of the modern State, arms, money, a controlled press, and all the rest. On my side, I have nothing but my conviction of right and truth, the unquenchable spirit of man, who is prepared to die for his convictions than submit to your brute force. I have my comrades in armlessness. Here we stand; and here if need be, we fall." Far from being a craven retreat from difficulty and danger, nonviolent resistance demands courage of a high order, the courage to resist injustice without rancour, to unite the utmost firmness with the utmost gentleness, to invite suffering but not to inflict it, to die but not to kill.

Gandhi did not make the facile division of mankind into "good" and "bad". He was convinced that every human being-even the "enemy"-had a kernel of decency: there were only evil acts, no wholly evil men. His technique of Satyagraha was designed not to coerce the opponent, but to set into motion forces which could lead to his conversion. Relying as it did on persuasion and compromise, Gandhi's method was not always quick in producing results, but the results were likely to be the more durable for having been brought about peacefully. "It is my firm conviction," Gandhi affirmed, "that nothing enduring can be built upon violence. " The rate of social change through the nonviolent technique was not in fact likely to be much slower than that achieved by violent methods; it was definitely faster than that expected from the normal functioning of institutions which tended to fossilize and preserve the status quo.

Gandhi did not think it possible to bring about radical changes in the structure of society overnight. Nor did he succumb to the illusion that the road to a new order could be paved merely with pious wishes and fine words. It was not enough to blame the opponent or bewail the times in which one's lot was cast. However heavy the odds, it was the Satyagrahi's duty never to feel helpless. The least he could do was to make a beginning with himself. If he was crusading for a new deal for peasantry, he could go to a village and live there, If he wanted to bring peace to a disturbed district, he could walk through it, entering into the minds and hearts of those who were going through the ordeal, If an age-old evil like untouchability was to be fought, what could be a more effective symbol of defiance for a reformer than to adopt an untouchable child? If the object was to challenge foreign rule, why not act on the assumption that the country was already free, ignore the alien government and build alternative institutions to harness the spontaneous, constructive and cooperative effort of the people? If the goal was world peace, why not begin today by acting peacefully towards the immediate neighbour, going more than half way to understand and win him over?

Though he may have appeared a starry-eyed idealist to so me, Gandhi's attitude to social and political problems was severely practical. There was a deep mystical streak in him, but even his mysticism seemed to have little of the ethereal about it. He did not dream heavenly dreams nor see things unutterable in trance; when "the still small voice" spoke to him, it was often to tell how he could fight a social evil or heal a rift between two warring communities. Far from distracting him from his role in public affairs, Gandhi's religious quest gave him the stamina to play it more effectively. To him true religion was not merely the reading of scriptures, the dissection of ancient texts, or even the practice of cloistered virtue: it had to be lived in the challenging context of political and social life.

Gandhi used his nonviolent technique on behalf of his fellow-countrymen in South Africa and India, but he did not conceive it only as a weapon in the armoury of Indian nationalism. On the other hand, he fashioned it as an instrument for righting wrongs and resolving conflicts between opposing groups, races and nations. It is a strange paradox that though the stoutest and perhaps the most successful champion of the revolt against colonialism in our time, Gandhi was frees from the taint of narrow nationalism. As early as 1924, he had declared that "the better mind of the world desires today, not absolutely independent states, warring one against another, but a federation of independent, of friendly interdependent states".

Even before the First World War had revealed the disastrous results of the combination of industrialism and nationalism, he had become a convert to the idea that violence between nation-states must be completely abjured.

In 1931, during his visit to England, a cartoon in the Star depicted him in a loin cloth besides Mussolini, Hitler, de Valera and Stalin, who were clad in black, brown, green and red shirts respectively. The caption, "And he ain't wearing any blooming' shirt at all" was not only literally but figuratively true. For a man of nonviolence, who believed in the brotherhood of man, there was no superficial division of nations into good and bad, allies and adversaries. This did not, however, mean that Gandhi did not distinguish between the countries which inflicted and the countries which suffered violence. His own life had been one struggle against the forces of violence, and Satyagraha was designed at once to eschew violence and to fight injustice.

In the years immediately preceding the Second Word war, when the tide of Nazi and Fascist aggression was relentlessly rolling forward, Gandhi had reasserted his faith in nonviolence and commanded it to the smaller nation which were living in daily dread of being overwhelmed by superior force. Through the pages of his weekly paper the Harijan, he expounded the nonviolent approach to military aggression and political tyranny. He advised the weaker nations to defend themselves not by increasing their fighting potential, but by nonviolent resistance to the aggressor. When Czechoslovakia was black-mailed into submission in September 1938, Gandhi suggested to the unfortunate Czechs: "There is no bravery greater than a resolute refusal

To bend the knee to an earthly power, no matter how great, and that without bitterness of spirit, and in the fullness of faith that the spirit alone lives, nothing else does."

Seven years later when the first atomic bombs exploded over Hiroshima and Nagasaki, Gandhi's reaction was characteristic: "I did not move a muscle. On the contrary, I said to myself that unless now the adopts nonviolence, it will spell certain suicide for mankind." The irony of the very perfection of the weapons of war rendering them useless as arbiters between nations has become increasingly clear during the last forty years.

The atomic stockpiles which the major nuclear powers have already built up are capable of destroying civilization, as we know it several time over and peace has been precariously preserved by, what has been grimly termed, "the balance of atomic terror." The fact is that with the weapons of mass destruction, which are at hand now, to attack another nation is tantamount to attacking oneself. This is a bitter truth which old habits of thought have prevented from going home. "This splitting of the atoms has changed everything" bewailed Einstein, "save our modes of thinking and thus we drift towards unparalleled catastrophe."

Nonviolence, as Gandhi expounded it, has ceased to be a pious exhortation, and become a necessity. The advice he gave to the unfortunate Abyssinians and Czechs during the twilight years before the Second Word War, may have seemed utopian thirty years ago. Today, it sounds commonsense. Even some hardheaded military strategists such as Sir Stephen King-Hall have begun to see in Gandhi's method a possible alternative to suicidal violence. Gandhi would have been the first to deny that his method offered an instant or universal panacea for world peace. His method is capable of almost infinite evolution to suit new situations in a changing world. It is possible that "applied nonviolence" is at present at the same

Stage of development "as the invention of electricity was in the days of Edison and Marconi." The lives-and deaths-of Chief Lithuli and Dr. Martin Luther King have proved that there is nothing esoteric about nonviolence, limiting it to a particular country or a particular period.

Indeed Tagore, the great contemporary and friend of Gandhi, prophesies that the West would accept Gandhi before the East "for the West has gone through the cycle of dependence on force and material things of life and has become disillusioned. They want a return to the spirit. The East has not yet gone through materialism and hence has not become so disillusioned."

8

Gandhi and Status of Women

Women's Status at the Time

When Gandhiji assumed India's leadership the average life span of an Indian woman was only twenty seven years. Babies and the pregnant women ran a high risk of dying young. Child marriage was very common and widows were in very large number. Only 2% of the women had any kind of education and women did not have an identity of their own. In North India, they practiced the purdah (veil) system. Women could not go out of the house unless accompanied by men and the face covered with cloth. The fortunate ones who could go to school had to commute in covered carts (*tangas*).

It is in this context that we have to recognize the miracle of Gandhi's work. Gandhiji claimed that a woman is completely equal to a man and practiced it in strict sense. Thousands and millions of women, educated and illiterate, house wives and widows, students and elderly participated in the India's freedom movement because his influence. For Gandhiji, the freedom fight was not political alone; it was also an economic and social reform of a national proportion. After a couple of decades, this equality became very natural in India. After India's freedom (in1947) and adoption of constitution (1950), emphasized equality of women, when Hindu code was formulated, the population was not even impressed. They said-"Of course, it had to be done."

Woman and Progress

Gandhiji always advocated a complete reform which he called "*Sarvodaya*" meaning comprehensive progress. He believed that the difference between men and women was only physical and has expressed several times in his writings that in many matters especially those of tolerance, patience, and sacrifice the Indian woman is superior to the male. You will discover this when you read his articles from "Young India" and "Harijan". During the 40 years of his political career, he only found more reasons to deepen his faith in what he wrote. He never had a specific program for women, but women had a integral role to play in all his programs. I feel that this is one of the reasons why women participated in his programs so overwhelmingly.

Gandhiji declared that there is no school better than home and there is no teacher better than parents. He said men and women are equal, but not identical. "Intellectually, mentally, and spiritually, woman is equivalent to a male and she can participate in every activity."

Indian society is a male dominated one. Gandhiji has illustrated in his autobiography (*The stories of my experiments with truth*) how early in his marriage he too wanted to dominate his wife. He often said that paternal society is the root cause of inequality. In his book, there is a very touching chapter about when he asked his wife to clean a public toilet and the resulting conflict between him and his wife. He has written how ashamed he was of himself, and how he took care not to hurt her anymore for the rest of his life. Even though there was big gap between him and his wife intellectually, it did not affect their family life. He has said that Kasturba followed her husband more than was expected of her. Gandhiji followed *Bramacharya* (strict discipline of food, drinks, and of celibacy) from a very young age, but when his wife passed away, Gandhi grieved that without *Ba*, his life would have been meaningless. That was the bondage of his 62 years of marriage.

Woman and Social Service

Gandhiji struggled very hard to understand a woman's physical and mental pain. From a young age he introduced his wife and children to social sacrifice and service. He believed that service has to be performed for self-fulfillment, not for public consumption or exhibition. He believed that the publicity given to one's social service actually decrements the value of the service. He tried very hard to eliminate job indignity and bias based on caste system. He tried to do the work of a barber, *dhobi* (washer man), and janitor to understand them and demonstrate that the work one does has no impact on one's status in the society. For me, the fact that he contributed a great deal in raising his children is very modern concept. On one occasion the white midwife would not show up for his wife's delivery and Gandhiji himself delivered his child. He helped wife with feeding, bathing, and toiletries of the infant. In western countries these days men are encouraged to be with their wives during the delivery and the men are supposed to pitch in with diaper changing, etc. Gandhiji practiced this very modern concept 90 years ago in his own family.

Role of Women

"Womanhood is not restricted to the kitchen", he opined and felt that "Only when the woman is liberated from the slavery of the kitchen, that her true spirit may be discovered". It does not mean that women should not cook, but only that household responsibilities be shared among men, women and children. He wanted women to outgrow the traditional responsibilities and participate in the affairs of nation. He criticized Indian's passion for male progeny. He said that as long as we don't consider girls as natural as our boys our nation will be in a dark eclipse.

Child Widows

Gandhiji was especially considerate of the young widows. In the last 80 years, as a nation, if we have made any progress on the matter of child widows (girls used get married very early and after untimely deaths of their husbands, they were condemned to a life of great agony, shaving heads, living in isolation, and shunned by the society.) it is due to the reformers like Gandhiji and his contemporaries. Gandhiji once noted during his legendary travels across India that he never came across 13 year old who was not married. He declared the marriages in which the girls were not consulted were unholy. At that time in Madras presidency, the number of child widows were alarmingly large. He called upon the young to marry the widows and also to boycott child marriages. (It may be noted here that Gandhiji himself married when very young; he was thirteen.) The history of India knows of many such young men who married widows and went on to work as social reformers.

Temple Women and Prostitutes

Gandhiji was very disturbed by the plight of this low caste untouchable section of the society, namely the *Devadasis.* He was hurt by the miserable way the children of brothels were treated. He had made elaborate plans for their rehabilitation. He declared that protecting women's honour was important and as holy as protecting cows. His book "Women and Social Injustice" contains discussions of very deep thoughts and solutions on the topic. He felt that after India became free, the system of temple women and brothels must be abolished. Even though on paper we have abolished the system of Devadasis, rampant exploitation of women as sex servants has continued. There was no way Gandhiji could have predicted modern ways and means of prostitution (call girls, phone sex etc) but he certainly identified its social evil and tried to fight it.

Gandhiji's Contribution for Betterment of Women in India

As we look back at the Indian history and compare the conditions of women before Gandhi's rise, and now, the progress we have made is quite enormous. A whole generation of women leaders came up influenced by Gandhi's vision. If today in India so many women can go to work in offices, educational institutions, and factories without fear or hesitation, the roots for such system were laid 90 years ago by Gandhiji and his followers.

As mentioned earlier, Gandhiji formulated India's freedom struggle as a comprehensive plan for women's development. Even though a lot of inequalities remain in our society, there is a fundamental agreement that men and women are equal. As Indians, we can be very proud that the same cannot be claimed even by so called "advanced nations".

In Britain as well as in the U.S.A., women could not vote 75 years ago. But women's voting came very naturally to us from the beginning. About 100 years ago, the western woman could not own property, get a divorce or take the custody of her children. We just have to look at the life and struggles of Dr. Annie Besant to understand the status of western women during Gandhiji's time. The western women had to take to streets, overcome many stereotypes to establish themselves voting and other rights. But for us, political, economic and voting rights came so naturally through the constitution!

Legacy

Today, if Gandhi's agenda has fallen apart, it is due to Indian politics. The continued exploitation of women can be attributed to the degradation in moral values of the society, and utter poverty of our nation. We ignored the role of social service, job dignity, and self reliance. Once in a while we run into true volunteers (like Sushilamma-see visit to an *ashram*) who believe in Gandhiji's ideals and have implemented his programs. I hope that at least a few of the younger generation take up Gandhiji's unfinished manifesto and work to eliminate social barriers facing women.

Gandhi and Women

I am firmly of opinion that India's salvation depends on the sacrifice and enlightenment of her women. (SB, 239)

Ahimsa means infinite love, which again means infinite capacity for suffering. Who but woman, the mother of man, shows this capacity in the largest measure? She shows it as she carries the infant and feeds it during nine months and derives joy in the suffering involved. What can beat the suffering caused by the pangs of labour ? But she forgets them in the joy of creation. Who again suffers daily so that her babe may wax from day to day? Let her transfer that love to the whole of humanity, let her forget that she ever was or can be the object of man's lust. And she will occupy her proud position by the side of man as his mother, maker and silent leader. It is given to her to teach the art of peace to the warring world thirsting for that nectar. (SB, 241)

My own opinion is that, just as fundamentally man and woman are one, their problem must be one in essence. The soul in both is the same. The two live the same life, have the same feelings. Each is a complement of the other. The one cannot live without the other's active help.

But somehow or other man has dominated woman from ages past, and so woman has developed an inferiority complex. She has believe in the truth of man's interested teaching that she is inferior to him. But the seers among men have recognized her equal status. Nevertheless there is no doubt that at some point there is bifurcation. Whilst both are fundamentally one, it is also equally true that in the form there is a vital difference between the two. Hence the vocations of the two must also be different. The duty of motherhood, which the vast majority of women will always undertake, requires qualities which man need not possess. She is passive, he is active. She is essentially mistress of the house. He is the bread-winner. She is the keeper and distributor of the bread, She is the care-taker in every sense of the term. The art of bringing up tile infants of the race is her special and sole prerogative. Without her care the race must become extinct.

In my opinion it is degrading both for man and woman that woman should be called upon or induced to forsake the hearth and shoulder the rifle for the protection of that hearth. It is a reversion to barbarity and the beginning of the end. In trying to ride the horse that man rides, she brings herself and him down. The sin will be on man's head for tempting or compelling his companion to desert her special calling. There is as much bravery in keeping one's home in good order and condition as there is in defending it against attack from without. (SB, 239-40)

If I were born a woman, I would rise in rebellion against any pretension on the part of man that woman is born to be his plaything. I have mentally become a woman in order to steal into her heart. I could not steal into my wife's heart until I decided to treat her differently than I used to do, and so I restored to her all her rights by dispossessing myself of all my so-called rights as her husband. (MM, 111)

Of all the evils for which man has made himself responsible, none is so degrading, so shocking or so brutal as his abuse of the better half of humanity to me, the female sex, not the weaker sex. It is the nobler of the two, for it is even today the embodiment of sacrifice, silent suffering, humility, faith and knowledge. (MM, 111-12)

Woman must cease to consider herself the object of man's lust. The remedy is more in her hands than man's. (MM, 111)

Chastity is not a hot-house growth. It cannot be protected by the surrounding wall of the purdah. It must grow from within, and to be worth anything it must be capable of withstanding every unsought temptation. (SB, 248)

And why is there all this morbid anxiety about female purity ? Have women any say in the matter of male purity ? We hear nothing of women's anxiety about men's chastity. Why should men arrogate to themselves the right to regulate female purity? It cannot be superimposed from without. It is a matter of evolution from within and therefore of individual self-effort. (SB, 248)

Women, I hold, is the personification of self-sacrifice, but unfortunately today she does not realize what a tremendous advantage she has over man. As Tolstoy used to say, they are labouring under the hypnotic influence of man. If they would realize the strength of nonviolence they would not consent to be called the weaker sex. (MM,112)

To call woman the weaker sex is a libel; it is man's injustice to women. If by strength is meant brute strength, then, indeed, is woman less brute than man. If by strength is meant moral power, then woman is immeasurably man's superior. Has she nor greater intuition, is she not more self-sacrificing, has she not greater powers of endurance, has she not greater courage? Without her man could not be. If nonviolence is the law of our being, the future is with woman.... Who can make a more effective appeal to the heart than woman? (MM, 112)

Women are special custodians of all that is pure old religious in life. Conservative by nature, if they are slow to shed superstitious habits, they are also slow to give up all that is pure and noble in life. (MM, 112)

I believe in the proper education of women. But I do believe that woman will not make her contribution to the world by mimicking or running a race with men. She can run the race, but she will not rise to the great heights she is capable of by mimicking man. She has to be the complement of man. (MM, 113)

Woman is tile companion of man gifted with equal mental capacities. She has the right to participate in the minutest detail of the activities of man, and she has the same right of freedom and liberty as he. She is entitled to a supreme place in her own sphere of activity as man is in his. This ought to be the natural condition of things, and not a result only of learning to read and write. By sheer force of a vicious custom, even the most ignorant and wordless men have been enjoying a superiority over women which they do not deserve and ought not to have. (WSI, 4-5)

If only women will forget that they belong to the weaker sex, I have no doubt that they can do infinitely more than men against war. Answer for yourselves what your great soldiers and generals would do, if their wives and daughter's and mothers refused to countenance their participation in militarism in any shape or form. (WSI,18)

A sister who is a good worker, and was anxious to remain celibate in order to serve better the country's cause, has recently married having met the mate of her dreams. But she imaginesthat in doing so she has done wrong and fallen from the high ideal which she had set before herself. I have tried to rid her mind of this delusion. It is no doubt an excellent thing for girls to remain unmarried for the sake of service, but the fact is that only one in a million is able to do so. Marriage is a natural thing in life and to consider it derogatory in any sense is wholly wrong. When one imagines any act a fall it is difficult, however hard one tries, to raise oneself. The ideal is to look upon marriage as a sacrament and therefore to lead a life of self-restraint in the married estate. Marriage in Hinduism is one of the four ashramas. In fact the other three are based on it.

The duty of the above mentioned and other sisters who think like her is, therefore, not to look down upon marriage but to give it its due place and make of it the sacrament it is. If they exercise the necessary self-restraint, they will find growing within themselves a greater strength for self-ice. She who wishes to serve will naturally choose a partner in life who is of the same mind, and their joint service will be the country's gain. (SB, 246)

Marriage confirms the right of union between two partners to the exclusion of all the others when in their joint confers no right upon one partner to demand obedience of the other to one's wish for union. What should be done when one partner to demand obedience of the other to one's wish for union. What should be done when one partner on moral or other grounds cannot conform to the wishes of the other is a separate question. Personally if divorce was the only alternative, I should not hesitate to accept it, rather than interrupt my moral progress assuming that I wan t to restrain myself on purely moral grounds. (SB, 246-47)

It is a tragedy that generally speaking our girls are not taught the duties of motherhood. But if married life is a religious duty, motherhood must be too. To be a ideal mother is no easy task. The procreation of children has to be undertake a with a full sense of responsibility. The mother should know what is her duty, from the moment she conceives right up to the time the child is born. And she who gives intelligent, healthy and well brought up children to the country is surely rendering a service. When the latter grow up they too will be ready to serve. The truth of the matter is that those who are filled with a living spirit of service will always serve whatever their position in life. They will never adopt a way of life which will interfere with service. (WSI, 180)

Some people oppose a modification of laws relating to the right of a married woman to own property on the ground that economic independence of woman would lead to the spread of immortality among women and disruption of domestic life. What is your attitude on the question?'

I would answer the question by a counter question: Has not independence of man and his holding property led to the spread of immorality among men? If you answer 'yes' then let it be so also with women. And when women have rights of ownership and the rest like men, it will be found that the enjoyment of such fights is not responsible for their vices or their virtues. Morality Which depends upon the helplessness of a man or woman has not much to recommend it. Morality is rooted in the punt), of our hearts. (WSI, 184)

A young man has sent me a letter which can be given here only in substance. It is as under: 'I am a married man. I had gone out to a foreign corm-try. I had a friend whom both I and my parents implicitly trusted. During my absence he seduced my wife who has now conceived of him. My father now insists that the girl should resort to abortion; otherwise he says, the family would be disgraced. To me it seems that it would be wrong to do so. The poor woman is consumed with remorse. She cares neither to eat nor drink, but is always weeping. Will you kindly tell me as to what my duty is in the case?'

I have published this letter with great hesitation. A everybody knows such cases are by no means infrequent in society. A restrained public discussion of the question, therefore, does not seem to me to be out of place. It seems to me clear as daylight that abortion would be a crime. Countless husbands are guilty of the same lapse as this poor woman, but nobody ever questions them. Society not only excuses them but does not even censure them. Then, again, the woman cannot conceal her shame while man can successfully hide his sin.

The woman in question deserves to be pitied. It would be the sacred duty of the husband to bring up the baby with all the love and tenderness that he is capable of and to refuse to yield to the counsels of his father. Whether he should continue to live with his wife is a ticklish question. Circumstances may warrant separation from her. In that case he would be bound to provide for her maintenance and education and to help her to live a pure life. Nor should I see anything wrong in his accepting her repentance if it is sincere and genuine. Nay, further, I can imagine a situation when it would be the sacred duty of the husband, to take back an erring wife who has completely expiated for and redeemed her error. (WSI, 87)

Passive resistance is regarded as the weapon of the weak, but the resistance for which I had to coin a new name altogether is the weapon of the strongest. I had to coin a new word to signify what I meant. But its matchless beauty lies in the fact that, though it is the weapon of the strongest, it can be wielded by the weak in body, by the aged, and even by the children if they have stout hearts. And since resistance in Satyagraha is offered through self-suffering, it is a weapon pre-eminently open to women. We found last year that women in India, in many instances, surpassed their brothers in sufferings and the two played a noble part in the campaign. For the ideal of self-suffering became contagious and they embarked upon amazing acts of self-denial. Supposing that the women and the children of Europe became fired with the love of humanity, they would take the men by storm and reduce militarism to nothingness in an incredibly short time. The underlying idea is that women, children and others have the same soul, the same potentiality. The question is one of drawing out the limitless power of truth. (WSI, 187)

When a woman is assaulted, she may not stop to think in terms of' himsa or himsa. Her primary duty is self-protection. She is at liberty to employ every method or means that comes to her mind, in order to defend her honour. God has given her nails and teeth. She must use them with all her strength and, if need be, die the effort. The man or woman who has shed all fear of death will be able not only to protect himself or herself but others also through laying down Es or her life. In truth, we fear death most, and hence we ultimately submit to superior physical force. Some will bend the knee to the invader, some will resort to bribery, some will crawl on their bellies or submit to other forms of humiliation, and some women will even give their bodies rather than die. I have not written this in a carping spirit. I am only illustrating human nature. Whether we crawl on our bellies, or whether a woman yields to the lust of man is symbolic of that same love of life which makes us stoop to anything. Therefore, only he who loses his life shall save it. To enjoy life one should give up the lure of life. That should be part of our nature. (MT, VI, 78)

For me there can be no preparation for violence. All preparation must be for nonviolence if courage of the highest type is to be developed.... If there are women who when assailed by miscreants cannot resist themselves without arms, they do not need to be advised to carry arms. They evil! do so. There is something wrong in this constant inquiry as to whether to bear arms or not. People have to learn to be naturally independent. If they will remember the central teaching, namely, that the real, effective resistance lies in nonviolence, they will mould their conduct accordingly. And that is what the world has been doing, although unthinkingly. Since it has not the highest courage namely, courage' born of nonviolence, it arms itself even unto the atom bomb. Those who do not see in it the futility of' violence will naturally arm themselves to the best of' their ability. (MGP, I, 327)

It is for American women to show what power women can be in the world. But that can only be when you cease to be the toys of men's idle hours. You have got freedom. You can become a power for peace by refusing to be carried away by the flood-tide of the pseudo-science glorifying self-indulgence that is engulfing the West today and apply your minds instead to the science of nonviolence; for forgiveness is your nature. By aping men, you neither become men nor can you function as your real selves and develop your special talent that God has given you, God has vouchsafed to women the power of nonviolence more than to man. It is all the more effective because it is mute. Women are the natural messengers of the gospel of nonviolence if only they will realize their high estate. (MGP, II, 103)

But it is, my firm conviction that if the men and women of India cultivate in themselves the courage to face death bravely and nonviolently, they can laugh to scorn the power of armaments and realize the ideal of unadulterated independence in terms of the masses which would serve as an example to the world. In that women can take the lead for they are a personification of the power of self-suffering. (MGP, II, 104)

Woman's Status and Role in Society

Of all the evils for which man has made himself responsible, none is so degrading, so shocking or so brutal as his abuse of the better half of humanity to me, the female sex, not the weaker sex. It is the nobler of the two, for it is even today the embodiment of sacrifice, silent suffering, humility, faith and knowledge. (YI, 15-9-1921, p. 292)

Woman must cease to consider herself the object of man's lust. The remedy is more in her hands than man's. She must refuse to adorn herself for men, including her husband, if she will be an equal partner with man. I cannot imagine Sita even wasting a single moment on pleasing Rama by physical charms. (YI, 21-7-1921, p. 229)

If I was born a woman, I would rise in rebellion against any pretension on the part of man that woman is born to be his plaything. I have mentally become a woman in order to steal into her heart. I could not steal into my wife's heart until I decided to treat her differently than I used to do, and so I restored to her all her rights by dispossessing myself of all my so-called rights as her husband. And you see her today as simple as myself. You find no necklaces, no fineries on her. I want you to be like that. Refuse to be the slaves of your own whims and fancies, and the slaves of men. Refuse to decorate yourselves, and don't go in for scents and lavender waters; if you [woman] want to give out the proper scent, it must come out of your heart, and then you will captivate not man, but humanity. It is your birth-right. Man is born of woman, he is flesh of her flesh and bone of her bone. Come to your own and deliver your message again. (YI, 8-12-1927, p. 406)

Not Weaker Sex

To call woman the weaker sex is a libel; it is man's injustice to woman. If by strength is meant brute strength, then, indeed, is woman less brute than man. If by strength is meant moral power, then woman is immeasurably man's superior. Has she not greater intuition, is she not more self-sacrificing, has she not greater courage? Without her man could not be. If nonviolence is the law of our being, the future is with woman... Who can make a more effective appeal to he heart than woman? (YI, 10-4-1930, p. 121)

Had not man in his blind selfishness crushed woman's soul as he has done or had she not succumbed to 'the enjoyments' she would have given the world an exhibition of the infinite strength that is latent in her. The world shall see it in all its wonder and glory when woman has secured an equal opportunity for herself with man and fully developed her powers of mutual aid and combination. (YI, 7-5-1931, p. 96)

Woman, I hold, is the personification of self-sacrifice, but unfortunately today she does not realize what a tremendous advantage she has over man. As Tolstoy used to say, they are labouring under the hypnotic influence of man. If they would realize the strength of nonviolence they would not consent to be called the weaker sex. (YI, 14-1-1932, p. 19)

Perversion of Place

Woman is the companion of man, gifted with equal mental capacities. She has the right to participate in very minutest detail in the activities of man and she has an equal right of freedom and liberty with him. She is entitled to a supreme place in her own sphere of activity as man is in his. This ought to be the natural condition of things and not as a result only of learning to read and write. By sheer force of a vicious custom, even the most ignorant and worthless men have been enjoying a superiority over woman which they do not deserve and ought not to have. Many of our movements stop half way because of the condition of our women. (SW, p. 425)

Man the lawgiver will have to pay a dreadful penalty for the degradation he has imposed upon the so-called weaker sex. When woman, freed from man's snares, rises to the full height and rebels against man's legislation and institutions designed by him, her rebellion, no doubt nonviolent, will be none the less effective. (YI, 16-4-1925, p. 133)

Woman has circumvented man in a variety of ways in her unconsciously subtle ways, as man has vainly and equally unconsciously struggled to thwart woman in gaining ascendancy over him. The result is a stalemate. Thus viewed, it is a serious problem the enlightened daughters of Bharat Mata are called upon to solve. They may not ape the manner of the West, which may be suited to its environment. They must apply methods suited to the Indian genius and Indian environment. Theirs must be the strong, controlling, purifying, steadying hand, conserving what is best in our culture and unhesitatingly rejecting what is base and degrading. This is the work of Sitas, Draupadis, Savitris, and Damayantis, not of amazons and prudes. (YI, 17-10-1929, p. 340)

Man has regarded woman as his tool. She has learnt to be his tool, and in the end found it easy and pleasurable to be such because when one drags another in his fall the descent is easy. (H, 25-1-1936, p. 396)

I hold that the right education in this country is to teach woman the art of saying 'no' even to her husband, to teach her that it is no part of her duty to become a mere tool or a doll in her husband's hands. She has rights as well as duties. (H, 2-5-1936, p. 93)

Right Education

I believe in the proper education of woman. But I do believe that woman will not make her contribution to the world by mimicking or running a race with men. She can run the race, but she will not rise to the great heights she is capable of by mimicking man. She has to be the complement of man. (H, 27-2-1937, p. 19)

Self-protection

Those who see in Sita a willing slave under Rama do not realize the loftiness of either her independence or Rama's consideration for her in everything. Sita was no helpless, weak woman incapable of protecting herself or her honour. (H, 2-5-1936, p.93)

I have a fear that the modern girl loves to be Juliet to half a dozen Romeos. She loves adventure... The modern girl dresses not to protect herself from wind, rain and sun, but to attract attention. She improves upon nature by painting herself and looking extraordinary. The nonviolent way is not for such girls. (H, 31-12-1938, p. 409)

Woman may not look for protection to men. They must rely on their own strength and purity of character and on God as did Draupadi of old. (H, 15-9-1946, p. 312)

Rightful Place

Women are special custodians of all that is pure and religious in life. Conservative by nature, if they are slow to shed superstitious habits, they are also slow to give up all that is pure and noble in life. (H, 25-3-1933, p. 2)

I do not envisage the wife, as a rule, following an avocation independently of her husband. The care of the children, and the upkeep of the household are quite enough to fully engage all her energy. In a well-ordered society, the additional burden of maintaining the family ought not to fall on her. The man should look to the maintenance of the family, the woman to household management, the two thus supplementing and complementing each other's labours. Nor do I see in this any invasion of woman's rights or suppression of her freedom.... The epithets used in our literatures to describe a wife are Ardhangana, 'the better half' and sahadharmini, 'the helpmate'. The husband addressing the wife as devi or goddess does not show any disparagement. ... The woman who knows and fulfils her duty realizes her dignified status. She is the queen, not the slave, of the household over which she presides. (H, 12-10-1934, pp. 267-7)

But some how or other man has dominated woman from ages past, and so woman has developed an inferiority complex. She has believed in the truth of man's interested teaching that she is inferior to him. But the seers among men have recognized her equal status. Nevertheless there is no doubt that at some point there is bifurcation. Whilst both are fundamentally one, it is also equally true that in the form there is a vital difference between the two. Hence the vocations of the two must also be different. (H, 24-2-1940, p. 13)

Woman and Ahimsa

I do believe that it is woman's mission to exhibit ahimsa at its highest and best...For woman is more fitted than man to make explorations and take bolder action in ahimsa... For the courage of self-sacrifice woman is any-day superior to man, as I believe man is to woman for the courage of the brute. (H, 5-11-1938, p. 317)

My own opinion is that, just as fundamentally man and woman are one, their problem must be one in essence. The soul in both is the same. The two live the same life, have the same feelings. Each is a complement of the other. The one cannot live without the other's active help. (H, 24-2-1940, p. 13)

I have suggested...that woman is the incarnation of ahimsa. Ahimsa means infinite love, which again means infinite capacity for suffering. Who but woman, the mother of man, shows this capacity in the largest measure? She shows it as she carries the infant and feeds it during nine months and derives joy in the suffering involved. What can beat the suffering caused by the pangs of labour? But she forgets them in the joy of creation.

Who, again, suffers daily so that her babe may wax from day to day? Let her transfer that love to the whole of humanity, let her forget that she ever was or can be the object of man's lust. And she will occupy her proud position by the side of man as his mother, maker and silent leader. It is given to her to teach the art of peace to the warring world thirsting for that nectar. (ibid, pp. 13-14)

Special Mission

The duty of motherhood, which the vast majority of women will always undertake, requires qualities which man need not possess. She is passive, he is active. She is essentially mistress of the house. He is the bread-winner, she is the keeper and distributor of the bread. She is the care-taker in every sense of the term. The art of bringing up the infants of the race is her special and sole prerogative. Without her care the race must become extinct. In my opinion, it is degrading both for man and woman that woman should be called upon or induced to forsake hearth and shoulder the rifle for the protection of that hearth. It is a reversion to barbarity and the beginning of the end. In trying to ride the horse that man rides, she brings herself and him down.

The sin will be on man's head for tempting or compelling his companion to desert her special calling. There is as much bravery in keeping one's home in good order and condition as there is fin defending it against attack from without... My contribution to the great problem lies in my presenting for acceptance truth and ahimsa in every walk of life, whether for individuals or nations. I have hugged the hope that in this woman will be the unquestioned leader and, having thus found her place in human evolution, she will shed her inferiority complex.

If she is able to do this successfully, she must resolutely refuse to believe in the modern teaching that everything is determined and regulated by the sex impulse... (ibid, p. 13)

Woman is naturally more self-suffering. Nonviolence therefore comes more easily to her. (H, 5-5-1946, p. 118)

I expect love and toleration in a higher degree from women than from men. I wonder where they are drifting and what women will or can teach their children if their hearts are permeated with hate. (H, 18-5-1947, p. 155)

Equality of Sexes

I am uncompromising in the matter of women's rights. In my opinion, she should labour under no legal disability not suffered by men. I should treat the daughters and sons on a footing or perfect equality. (H, 17-10-1929, p. 340)

Equality of sexes does not mean equality of occupations. There may be no legal bar against a woman hunting or wielding a lance. But she instinctively recoils from a function that belongs to man, nature has created sexes as complements of each other. Their functions are defined as are their forms. (H, 2-12-1939, p. 359)

Legislation has been mostly the handiwork of men; and man has not always been fair and discriminate in performing that self–appointed task. The largest part of our effort in promoting the regeneration of women should be directed towards removing those blemishes which are represented in our Shastras as the necessary and ingrained characteristics of women. Who will attempt this and how? In my humble opinion, in order to make the attempt, we will have to produce women, pure, firm and self-controlled as Sita, Damayanti and Draupadi. If we do produce them, such modern sisters will receive the same homage from Hindu society as is being paid to their prototypes of yore. Their words will have the same authority as the Shastras. We will feel ashamed of the stray reflections on them in our Smritis, and will soon forget them. Such revolutions have occurred in Hinduism in the past, and will still take place in the future, leading to the stability of our faith. (SW, p.424)

I make no distinction between man and woman. Woman should feel just as independent as men. Bravery is not man's monopoly. (H, 5-1-1947, p. 478)

Today few women take part in politics and most of these do not do independent thinking. They are content to carry out their parents' or their husbands' behests. Realizing their dependence, they cry out for women's rights. Instead of doing this, however, women worker should enrol women as voters, impart or have import or have imparted to them practical education, teach them to think independently, release them from the chains of caste that bind them, so as to bring about a change in them which will compel men to realize woman's strength and capacity for sacrifice and give her places of honour. (H, 21-4-1946, p. 96)

There is no occasion for women to consider themselves subordinate or inferior to men. Languages proclaim that woman is half of man and, by parity of reasoning, man is half of woman. They are not two separate entities, but halves of one. The English language goes further and calls woman the better half of man. Therefore, I advise women to resort to civil rebellion against all undesirable and unworthy restraints. All restraints to be beneficial must be voluntary. There is no possibility of harm resulting from civil rebellion. It presupposes purity and reasoned resistance. (H, 23-3-1947, p. 80)

Man should learn to give place to woman and a country or community in which women are not honoured can not be considered as civilized. (YI, 25-11-1926, p. 415)

The Purdah

And why is there all this morbid anxiety about female purity? Have women any say in the matter of male purity? We hear nothing of women's anxiety about men's chastity. Why should men arrogate to themselves the right to regulate female purity? It cannot be superimposed from without. It is a matter of evolution from within and, therefore, of individual self-effort. (YI, 3-2-1927, p. 37). Chastity is not a hot-house growth. It cannot be protected by the surrounding wall of the purdah. It must grow from within and, to be worth anything, it must be capable of withstanding every unsought temptation. (H,23-5-1936, p. 117)

Dowry System

The system has to go. Marriage must cease to be a matter of arrangement made by parents for money. The system is intimately connected with caste. So long as the choice is restricted to a few hundred young men or young women of a particular caste, the system will persist no matter what is said against it. The girls or boys or their parents will have to break the bonds of caste if the evil is to be eradicated. All this means education of a character that will revolutionize the mentality of the youth of the nation. (YI, 21-6-1929, p.207)

Any young man who makes dowry a condition of marriage discredits his education and his country and dishonours womanhood. .....A strong public opinion should be created in condemnation of the degrading practice of dowry and young men who soil their fingers with such ill-gotten gold should be excommunicated from society. Parents of girls should cease to be dazzled by English degrees and should not hesitate to travel outside their little castes and provinces to secure true gallant young men for their daughters.

Widow Remarriage

Voluntary widowhood consciously adopted by woman who has felt the affection of a partner adds grace and dignity to life, sanctifies the home and uplifts religion itself. Widowhood imposed by religion or custom is an unbearable yoke and defiles the home by secret vice and degrades religion.

If we would be pure, if we would save Hinduism, we must rid ourselves of this poison of enforced widowhood. The reform must begin by those who have girl-widows taking courage in both their hands and seeing that the child-widows in their charge are duly and well married-not remarried. They were never really married. (YI, 5-8-1926, p. 276)

Divorce

Marriage confirms the right of union between two partners to the exclusion of all the others when, in their joint opinion, they consider such union to be desirable, but it confers no right upon one partner to demand obedience of the other to one's wish for union. What should be done when one partner on moral or other grounds cannot conform to the wishes of the other is a separate question. Personally, if divorce was the only alternative, I should not hesitate to accept it, rather than interrupt my moral progress, assuming that I want to restrain myself on purely moral grounds. (YI, 8-10-1925, p. 346)

Crimes Against Women

I have always held that it is physically impossible to violate a woman against her will. The outrage takes place only when she gives way to fear or does not realize her moral strength. If she cannot meet the assailant's physical might, her purity will give her the strength to die before he succeeds in violating her. Take the case of Sita. Physically she was a weakling before Ravana, but her purity was more than a match even for his giant might. He tried to win her with all kinds of allurements, but could not carnally touch her without her own physical strength or upon a weapon she possesses, she is sure to be discomfited whenever her strength is exhausted. (H, 1-9-1940, p. 266)

It is my firm conviction that a fearless woman, who knows that her purity is her best shield can never be dishonoured. However beastly the man, he will bow in shame before the flame of her dazzling purity. ......I therefore recommend women...to try to cultivate this courage. They will become wholly fearless if they can and cease to tremble as they do today at the thought of assaults.... Parents and husbands should instruct women in the art of becoming fearless. It can best be learnt from a living faith in God. Though He is invisible, He is one's unfailing protector. He who has this faith is the most fearless of all....When a woman is assaulted she may not stoop to think in terms of himsa or ahimsa. Her primary duty is self-protection. She is at liberty to employ every method or means that come to her mind in order to defend her honour. God has given her nails and teeth. She must use them with all her strength and, if need be, die in the effort. The man or woman who has shed all fear of death will be able not only to protect himself or herself but others also through laying down hi (or her) life. (H, 1-3-1942, p. 60)

In the society in the midst of which we are living, such outrages take place.... A nonviolent man or woman will and should die without retaliation, anger or malice, in self-defence or in defending the honour of his womenfolk. This is the highest form of bravery. (H, 15-9-1946, p. 312)

The art of dying bravely and with honour does not need any special training, save a living faith in God. (H, 5-10-1947, p. 334)

Prostitution

Prostitution is as sold as the world, but I wonder if it was ever a regular feature of town-life that is today. In any case, the time must come when humanity will rise against the curse and make prostitution a thing of the past, as it has got red of many evil customs, however time-honoured they might have been. (YI, 28-5-1925, p. 187)

The proper method of dealing with brothels is for the women to carry on a double propaganda, (a) amongst women who sell their honour for a livelihood, and (b) amongst men whom they must same into behaving better towards their sisters whom they ignorantly or insolently call the weaker sex. I remember years and years ago in the early nineties when the brave salvation Army people, at the risk of their own lives, used to carry on picketing at the corners of the notorious streets of Bombay which were filled with houses of ill-fame. There is no reason why some such thing should not be organized on a large scale. (H, 4-9-1937, p. 233)

"Prostitutes" is commonly supposed to apply to women of lewd character. But the men who indulge in vice are just as much, if not more, prostitutes than the women, who, in many instances, have to sell their bodies for the sake of earning a livelihood. The evil practice should be declared illegal. But the law can only help to a point. The evil exists clandestinely in every country in spite of the law. Vigorous public opinion can help the law as it also hinders. (H, 15-9-1946, p. 310)

The Ashram Vows

This is the maxim of life which I have accepted, namely, that no work done by any man, no matter how great he is, will really prosper unless he has religious backing. But what is religion?.... I for one would answer; not the religion which you will get after reading all the scriptures of the world; it is not really a grasp by the brain, but it is a heart grasp. It is a thing which is not alien to us but it is a thing which has to be evolved out of us. It is always within us; with some consciously so; with the other quite unconsciously. But it is [always] there; and whether we wake up this religious instinct in us through outside assistance or by inward growth, no matter how it is done, it has got to be done if we want to do any thing in the right manner and anything that is going to persist. Our scriptures have laid down certain rules as maxims of life and as axioms which we have to take for granted as self-demonstrated truths... believing in these implicitly for all these ling years and having actually endeavoured to reduce to practice these injunctions..., I have deemed it necessary to seek the association of those who think with me in founding this institution... the rules that have been drawn up and that have to be observed by every one who seeks to be a member of that Ashram [are as follows]:

The Vow of Truth

Not truth simply as we ordinarily understand it, not truth which merely answers the saying, 'Honesty is the best policy,' implying that, if it is not the best policy, we may depart from it. But here Truth as it is conceived means that we have to rule our life buy this flaw of Truth at any cost; and in order to satisfy the definition, I have drawn upon the celebrated illustration of the life of Prahlad. For the sake to Truth as he knew it, he was prepared to die without caring to return the blows that he had received from his father, or from those who were charged with his father's instructions. Not only that, he would not in any way even parry the blows; on the contrary, width a smile on his lips, he underwent the innumerable tortures to which he was subjected, with the result that at last Truth. That fact was there; but if he had died in the midst of tortures, he would still have adhered to Truth. That is the truth which I would like to follow ... in our Ashram we make it a rule that we must say 'No' when we mean 'No' regardless of consequences.

The Doctrine of Ahimsa

Literally speaking, ahimsa means 'non-killing'. But to me it has a world of meaning, and takes me into the realms much higher, infinitely higher.... Ahimsa really means that you may not offend anybody; you may not harbour an uncharitable thought, even in connection with one who may consider himself to be your enemy. For one who follows this doctrine there is no room for an enemy.... But there are people who consider themselves to be his enemies.... So it is held that we may not harbour an evil thought even in connection with such persons. If we return blow for blow, we depart from the doctrine of ahimsa. But when I say that we should not resent, I do not say that we should acquiesce; but by 'resenting' I mean wishing that some harm should be done to the enemy; or that he should be put out of the way, not even by any action of ours, but by the action of somebody else, or, say, buy divine agency. If we harbour even this thought, we depart from this doctrine of I ahimsa. Those who join the Ashram have literally to accept that meaning.

That does not mean that we practise that doctrine in its entirety. Far from it. It is an ideal which we have to reach, and it is an ideal to be reached even at this very moment, if we are capable of doing so. But is not a proposition in geometry; it is not even like solving difficult problems in higher mathematics-it is infinitely more difficult than solving those problems. Many of you have burnt the midnight oil in solving those problems. If you want to follow out this doctrine, you will have to do much more than burn the midnight oil. You will have to pass many a sleepless night, and go through many a mental torture and agony, before you can even be within measurable distance of this goal. It is the goal, it is the goal, and nothing less than that, which you and I have to reach if we want to understand what a religious life means.

.... A man who believed in the efficacy of this doctrine finds in the ultimate stage, when he is about to reach the goal, the whole world at his feet... if you express your love – ahimsa-in such a manner that it impresses it self indelibly upon your so-called enemy, he must return that love...... under this rule there is no room for organized assassinations, or for murders openly committed, or.... For any violence for the sake of your country or even for guarding the honour of precious ones that may be under your charge. After all, that would be a poor defence of their honour. This doctrine tells us that we may guard the honour of those under our charge by delivering ourselves into the hands of the man who would commit he sacrilege. And that requires far greater physical and mental courage than the delivering of blows. .... If you do not retaliate, but stand your ground between your charge and the opponent, simply receiving the blows without retaliating, what happens? I give you my promise that the whole of his violence will be expended on you, and your friend will not left unscathed. Under this plan of life there is no conception of patriotism which justifies such wars as you witness today in Europe.

The Vow of Celibacy

Those who want to perform national service, or to have a gleam of the real religious life, must lead a celibate life, whether married or unmarried. Marriage only brings a woman closer to man, and they become friends in a special sense, never to be parted either in this life or in the lives to come. But I do not think that, in our conception of marriage, our lusts should enter. Be that as it may, this is what is placed before those who come to the Ashram. I do not deal with that at any length.

The Vow of the Control of the Palate

A man who wants to control his animal passions easily does so if he controls his palate. I fear this is one of the most difficult vows to follow .... Unless we are prepared to rid ourselves of stimulating, heating, able to control the over-abundant, unnecessary, and exciting stimulation of the animal passions.... If we do not do that ...., we are likely to abuse the sacred trust of our bodies that has been given us, and to become less than animals and brutes, eating, drinking and indulging in passions which we share in common with the animals. But have you ever seen a horse or cow indulging in the abuse of the palate as we do? Do you suppose that it is a sign of civilization, a sign of real life, that we should multiply our eatables so far that we do not even know where we are; and seek dishes until, at last, we have become absolutely mad and run after the newspaper sheets which give us advertisements about these dishes?

The Vow of Non-Thieving

I suggest that we are thieves in a way. If I take anything that I do not need for my own immediate use and deep it, I thieve it from somebody else. It is the fundamental law of Nature, without exception, that Nature produces enough for our wants from day to day; and if only everybody took enough for himself and nothing more, there would be no pauperism in this world, there would be no man dying of starvation. I am no Socialist, and I do not want to dispossess those who have got possessions; but I do say that personally those of us who want to see light out of darkness have to follow this rule. I do not want to dispossess anybody; I should then be departing from the rule of nonviolence.

If somebody else possesses more than I do, let him. But so far as my own life has to be regulated, I dare not possess anything which I do not want. In India, we have got many millions of people who have to be satisfied with one meal a day, and that meal consisting of a chapatti containing no fat in it and a pinch of salt. You and I have no right to anything that we really have until these many million are clothed and fed. You and I, who ought to know better, must adjust our wants, and even undergo voluntary privation in order that they may be nursed, fed and clothed.

Women and India's Future

I am firmly of opinion that India's salvation depends on the sacrifice and enlightenment of her women.-H,27-6-36,i53. I had flattered myself that my contribution to the women's cause definitely began with the discovery of satyagraha. But the writer of the letter is of opinion that the fair sex requires treatment different from men. It is so, I do not think any man will find the correct solution. No matter how much he tries, he must fail because nature has made him different from woman. Only the toad under the harrow knows where it pinches him. Therefore ultimately woman will have to determine with authority what she needs. My own opinion is that, just as fundamentally man and woman are one, their problem must be one in essence. The soul in both is the same. The two live the same life, have the same feelings. Each is a complement of the other. The one cannot live without the other's active help.

But somehow or other man has dominated woman from ages past., and so woman has developed an inferiority complex. She has believed in the truth of man's interested teaching that she is inferior to him. But the seers among men have recognized her equal status. Nevertheless there is no doubt that at some point there is bifurcation. Whilst both are fundamentally one, it is also equally true that in the form there is a vital difference between the two. Hence the vocations of the two must also be different. The duty of motherhood, which the vast majority of women will always undertake, requires qualities which man need not possess. She is passive, he is active. She is essentially mistress of the house. He is the breadwinner. She is the keeper and distributor of the bread. She is the caretaker in every sense of the term. The art of bringing up the infants of the race is her special and sole prerogative. Without her care the race must become extinct.

In my opinion it is degrading both for man and woman that woman should be called upon or induced to forsake the hearth and shoulder the rifle for the protection of that hearth. It is a reversion to barbarity and the beginning of the end. In trying to ride the horse that man rides, she brings herself and him down. The sin will be on man's head for tempting or compelling his companion to desert her special calling. There is as much bravery in keeping one's home in good order and condition as there is in defending it against attack from without.

As I have watched millions of peasants in their natural surroundings and as I watch them daily in little Segaon, the natural division of spheres of work has forced itself on my attention. There are no women blacksmiths and carpenters. But men and women work on the fields, the heaviest work being done by the males. The women deep and manage the homes. They supplement the meagre resources of the family, but man remains the main breadwinner. The divisions of the spheres of work being recognized, the general qualities and culture required are practically the same for both the sexes.

My contribution to the great problem lies in my presenting for acceptance truth and ahimsa in every walk of life, whether for individuals or nations. I have hugged the hope that in this woman will be the unquestioned leader and, having thus found her place in human evolution, she will shed her inferiority complex. If she is able to do this successfully, she must resolutely refuse to believe in the modern teaching that everything is determined and regulated by the sex impulse. I fear I have put the proposition rather clumsily. But I hope my meaning is clear. I do not know that the millions of men who are taking an active part in the war are obsessed by the sex specter. Nor are the peasants working together in their fields worried or dominated by it. This is not to say or suggest that they are free from the instinct implanted in man and woman. But it most certainly does not dominate their lives as it seems to dominate the lives of those who are saturated with the modern sex literature. Neither man nor woman has time for such things when he or she is faced with the hard fact of living life in its grim reality.

I have suggested in these columns that woman is the incarnation of ahimsa. Ahimsa means infinite love, which again means infinite capacity for suffering. Who but woman, the mother of man, shows this capacity in the largest measure? She shows it as she carries the infant and feeds it during nine months and derives joy in the suffering involved. What can beat the suffering caused by the pangs of labour? But she forgets them in the joy of creation. Who again suffers daily so that her babe may wax from day to day? Let her transfer that love to the whole of humanity, let her forget that she ever was or can be the object of man's lust. And she will occupy her proud position by the side on man as his mother, maker and silent leader. It is given to her to teach the art of peace to the warring would thirsting for that nectar. She can become the leader in satyagraha which does not require the learning that books give but does require the stout heart that comes from suffering and faith.

My good nurse in the Sassoon Hospital, Poona, as I was lying on a sick bed years ago, told me the story of a woman who refused to take chloroform because she would not risk the life of the babe she was carrying. She had to undergo a painful operation. The only anesthetic she had was her love for the babe, to save whom no suffering was too great. Let not women, who can count many such heroines among them, ever despise their sex or deplore that they were not born men.

The contemplation of that heroine often makes me envy woman the status that is hers, if she only knew. There is as much reason for man to with that he was born a woman as for woman to do otherwise. But the wish is fruitless. Let us be happy in the state to which we are born and do the duty for which nature has destined us. –H, 24-2-40, 13.

The Problem

792. I passionately desire the utmost freedom for our women. I detest child marriages. I shudder to see a child widow, and shiver with rage when a husband just widowed contracts with brutal indifference another marriage. I deplore the criminal indifference of parents who deep their daughters utterly ignorant and illiterate and bring them up only for the purpose of marrying them off to some young man of means. Notwithstanding all this grief and rage, I realize the difficulty of the problem. Women must have votes and an equal legal status. But the problem does not end there. It only commences at the point where women begin to affect the political deliberations of the nation. –YI, 21-7-21, 229.

The Ideal of Marriage

The ideal that marriage aims at is that of spiritual union through the physical. The human love that it incarnates is intended to serve as a stepping stone to divine or universal love. S.F.G-18

The wife is not the husband's bond slave, but his companion and his helpmate, and an equal partner in all his joys and sorrows—as free as the husband to choose her own path—Auto, 38.

Child Marriage

What is kanaka in the case of little children? Has a father any rights of property over his children? He is their protector not owner. And he forfeits the privilege of protection when he abuses it by seeking to garter away the liberty of the ward. The least that a parent, who has so abused his trust as to give in marriage an infant to an old man in his dotage or to a boy hardly in his teens, can do, is to purge himself of his sin by remarrying his daughter when she becomes widowed. As I have said in a previous note, such marriages should be declared null and void from the beginning. –YI, 11-11-26, 388.

You must be able surely to control your lust to this extent, that you are not going to marry a girl that is under 16 years age. If I could do so I would lay down 20 as the minimum. Twenty years is early enough even in India. It is we who are responsible for the precocity of the girls, not even the Indian climate, because I know girls of the age of twenty who are pure and undefiled and able to stand the storm that may rage round. Let us not hug that precocity to ourselves. Some Brahman students tell me that they cannot follow this principle, that they cannot get Brahman girls sixteen years old, very few Brahmans keep their daughters unmarried till that age, the Brahman girls are married mostly before 10, 12 and 13 years. Then I say to the Brahman youth, "Cease to be a Brahman, if you cannot possibly control yourself. Choose a grown up girl of 16 who became a widow when she was a child. If you cannot get a Brahman widow who has reached that age, then go and take any girl you like. And I tell you that the God of the Hindus will pardon that boy who has preferred to marry out of his caste rather than ravish a girl of twelve. When your heart is not pure and you cannot master your passions, you cease to an educated man. You have called your institution a premier institution. I want you to leave up to the name of the premier institution which must produce boys who will occupy the front rank in character. And what is education without character and what is character without elementary personal purity? Brahmanism I adore. I have defended Varnashrama Dharma. But Brahmanism that can tolerate untouchability, virgin widowhood, spoliation of virgins, stinks in my nostrils. It is a parody of Brahmanism. There is no knowledge of Brahman therein. There is no true interpretation of the scriptures. It is undiluted animalism, Brahmanism is made of sterner stuff. –YI, 15-9-27, 314.

The Dowry System

The system has to go. Marriage must cease to be a matter of arrangement made by parents for money. The system is intimately connected with caste. So long as the choice is restricted to a few hundred-young men or young women of a particular caste, the system, will persist no matter what is said against it. The girls or boys or their parents will have to break the bonds of caste if the evil is to be eradicated. All this means education of a character that will revolutionize the mentality of the youth of the nation. –H, 23-5-36, 117.

There should be work done in the schools and colleges and amongst the parents of girls. The parents should so educate their daughters that they would refuse to marry a young man who wanted a price for marrying and would rather remain spinsters than be party to the degrading terms. The only honourable terms in marriage are mutual love and mutual consent. –YI, 27-12-28, 431.

Q. Namashudra girls are generally married at the age of 12 or 13; formerly the usual age was 8 or 9. The bridegroom has to pay a dowry of Rs. 150 for the bride. The average difference of age between the two is about 12 to 15 years. As a result of this the number of widows in namashudra society is rather large. Among one section of the caste, widow remarriage was prevalent. But in imitation of another section which was looked upon as superior, the former are giving up that practice. What is your advice regarding child marriage and widow remarriage?

A. Dealing with the question Gandhiji said that his opinion was definite. In the first instance there should be no possibility of child widows. He was averse to child marriages. It was an evil custom which unfortunately the namashudras had perhaps taken from the so-called higher castes.

Gandhiji was also against the system of dowry. It was nothing but the sale of girls. That there should be castes even amongst namashudras was deplorable and he would strongly advise them to abolish all caste-distinctions amongst themselves. And in this they should bear in mind the opinion the speaker had often expressed that all caste-distinctions should be abolished, and there should be only one caste, namely, bhangis and all Hindus should take pride in being called bhangis and nothing else. This applied to the namashudras as well.

When child marriages were abolished, naturally there would be few, if any, young widows. As a general rule he was for one man one wife for life, and one woman one husband for life. Custom had familiarized women in the so-called higher castes with enforced widowhood. Contrary was the rule with men. He called it a disgrace, but whilst society was in that pitiable condition, he advocated widow remarriage for all young widows. He believed in equality of the sexes and, therefore, he could only think of the same rights for women as men.-16-3-47, 67.

The Choice of Mates and Social Interference

In my opinion such marriages as are interdicted in a particular society cannot be recognized all at once or at the will of the individual. Nor has society or relatives of parties concerned any right to impose their will upon and forcibly curtail the liberty of action of the young people who may want to contract such marriages. In the instance cited by the correspondent both the parties had fully attained maturity. They could well think for themselves. No one had a right forcibly to prevent them from marrying each other if they wanted to. Society could at the most refuse to recognize the marriage, but it was the height of tyranny to drive them to suicide.

Marriage taboos are not universal and are largely based on social usage. The usage varies from province to province and as between different divisions. This does not mean that the youth may ride roughshod over all established social customs and inhibitions. Before they decide to do so, they must convert public opinion to their side. In the meantime, the individuals concerned ought patientlyto bide their time, or if they cannot do that calmly and quietly to face the consequences of social ostracism.

At the same time it is equally the duty of society not to take up a heartless, step-motherly attitude towards those who might disregard or break the established conventions. In the instance described by my correspondent the guilt of driving the young couple to suicide certainly rests on the shoulders of society if the version that is before me is correct. –H, 29-5-37. 125.

Q. You advocate inter-caste marriages. Do you also favour marriages between Indians professing different religions? Should they declare themselves as belonging to no denomination, or can they continue their old religious practices and yet intermarry? If so, what form should the marriage ceremony take? Is it to be a purely civil function or a religious function? Do you consider religion to be exclusively a personal matter?

A. Though Gandhiji admitted that he had not always held the view, he had come to the conclusion long ago that an inter-religious marriage was a welcome event whenever it took place. His stipulation was that such connection was not a product of lust. In his opinion it was no marriage. It was illicit intercourse. Marriage in his estimation was a sacred institution. Hence there must be mutual friendship, either party having equal respect for the religion of the other. There was no question in this of conversion. Hence the marriage ceremony would be performed by the priests belonging to either faith. This happy event could take place when the communities shed mutual enmity and had regard for the religions of the world. –H, 16-3-47, 63.

Q. You say that you are in favour of inter religious marriages, but at the same time you say that each arty should retain his or her own religion and, therefore, you said, you tolerated even civil marriages. Are there any instances of parties belonging to different religions keeping up their own religions to the end of their lives? And is not the institution of civil marriage a negation of religion and does it not tend towards laxity of religion?

A. Gandhiji said that the questions were appropriate. He had no instances in mind where the parties had clung to their respective faiths up to death, because these friends whom he knew had not yet died. He had, however, under his observation men and women professing different religions and each clinging to his or her own faith without abatement. But he would go so far as to say that they need not wait for the discovery of past instances. They should create new ones so that timid ones may shed their timidity.

As to civil marriages, he did not believe in them, but he welcomed the institution of civil marriage as a much needed reform for the sake of reform. –H, 16-3-47, 67.

Marriage and Love

A correspondent laid down the following conditions of marriage : (I) Mutual attraction or love; (2) Eugenic fitness; (3) Approval and consent of the respective families concerned; and consideration for the interest of the social order to which one belongs; (4) Spiritual development.

I accept generally the conditions for an ideal marriage enumerated by my correspondent. But I would change their order of importance and put 'love' last in the list. By giving it the first place, the other conditions are liable to be overshadowed by it altogether and rendered more or less nugatory. Therefore, spiritual development ought to e given the first place in the choice for marriage. Service should come next, family considerations and the interest of the social order should have the third place, and mutual attraction or 'love' the fourth and the last place. This means that 'love' alone, where the other three conditions are not fulfilled, should not be held as a valid reason for marriage. At the same time, marriage where there is no love should equally be ruled out even though all the other conditions are fully complied with. I should score out the condition of eugenic fitness, because the begetting of offspring being the central purpose of marriage, eugenic fitness cannot be treated as a 'condition'; it is the sine qua non of marriage. –H, 5-6-37, 131.

The Married Estate

A sister, who is a good worker, and was anxious to remain celibate in order to serve better the country's cause, has recently married having met the mate of her dreams. But she imagines that in doing so she has done wrong and fallen from the high ideal which she had set before herself. I have tried to rid her mind of this delusion. It is no doubt an excellent thing for girls to remain unmarried for the sake of service, but the fact is that only one in a million is able to do so. Marriage is a natural thing in life, and to consider it derogatory in any sense is wholly wrong. When one imagines any act a fall it is difficult, however hard one tries, to raise oneself. The ideal is to look upon marriage as a sacrament and therefore to lead a life of self-restraint in the married estate. Marriage in Hinduism is one of the four ashrams. In fact the other three are based on it.

The duty of the above-mentioned and other sisters who think like her is, therefore, not to look down upon marriage but to give it its due place and make of it the sacrament it is. If they exercise the necessary self-restraint, they will find growing within themselves a greater strength for service. She who wishes to serve will naturally choose a partner in life who is of the same mind, and their joint service will be the country's gain. –H, 22-3-42, 88.

Divorce

805. Marriage confirms the right of union between two partners to the exclusion of all the others when in their joint opinion they consider such union to be desirable, but it confers no right upon one partner to demand obedience of the other to one's wish for union. What should be done when one partner on moral or other grounds cannot conform to the wishes of the other is a separate question. Personally, if divorce was the only alternative, I should not hesitate to accept it, rather than interrupt my moral progress,- assuming that I want to restrain myself on purely moral grounds. –YI, 8-10-25, 346.

Widow Remarriage

The total of 1921 is a trifle higher than for the two (previous) decades They only demonstrate still further the enormity of the wrong done to the Hindu girl widows. We cry out for cow-protection in the name of religion, but we refuse protection to the girl widow. In the name of religion we force widowhood upon our three lakhs of girl widows who could not understand the import of the marriage ceremony. To force widowhood upon little girls is a brutal crime for which we Hindus are daily paying dearly. If our conscience was truly awakened there would be no marriage before 15, let alone widowhood, and we would declare that these three lakhs of girls were never married. Voluntary widowhood consciously adopted by a woman who has felt the affection of a partner adds grace and dignity to life, sanctifies the home and uplifts religions itself. Widowhood imposed by religion or custom is an unbearable yoke and defiles the home by secret vice and degrades religion.

If we would be pure, if we would save Hinduism, we must rid ourselves of this poison of enforced widowhood. The reform must begin by those who have girl widows taking courage in both their hands and seeing that the child widows in their charge are duly and well married –not remarried. They were never really married. –YI, 5-8-26, 276.

Widow-remarriage is no sin—if it be, it is as much a sin as the marriage of a widower is all widowhood is not holy. It is an adornment to her who can observe it. If this sister has the courage, then let her speak out her mind to her uncle and brothers and seek their help. It they cannot assist in the marriage, then the sister will have to quit their house and take refuge in some widow-remarriage institution. –(Translated from the Hindi Navajivan of 9-5-29.)

Some Brahman students told me that they cannot follow this principle, that they cannot get Brahman girls sixteen years old, very few Brahmans keep their daughters unmarried till that age, the Brahman girls are married mostly before 10, 12 and 13 years. Then I say to the Brahman youth, 'Cease to be Brahman if you cannot possibly control yourself. Choose a grown up girl of 16 who became a widow when she was a child. If you cannot get a Brahman widow who has reached that age, then go and take any girl you like. And I tell you that the God of the Hindus will pardon that boy who has preferred to marry out of his caste rather than ravish a girl of twelve.' –YI, 15-9-27, 314.

9

Gandhi's Philosophy

What is Gandhian philosophy? It is the religious and social ideas adopted and developed by Gandhi, first during his period in South Africa from 1893 to 1914, and later of course in India. These ideas have been further developed by later "Gandhians", most notably, in India, Vinoba Bhave and Jayaprakash Narayan. Outside of India some of the work of, for example, Martin Luther King Jr. can also be viewed in this light. Understanding the universe to be an organic whole, the philosophy exists on several planes- the spiritual or religious, moral, political, economic, social, individual and collective. The spiritual or religious element, and God, is at its core. Human nature is regarded as fundamentally virtuous. All individuals are believed to be capable of high moral development, and of reform.

The twin cardinal principles of Gandhi's thought are truth and nonviolence. It should be remembered that the English word "truth" is an imperfect translation of the Sanskrit, "satya", and "nonviolence", an even more imperfect translation of "ahimsa". Derived from "sat"-"that which exists"-"satya"contains a dimension of meaning not usually associated by English speakers with the word "truth". There are other variations, too, which we need not go into here. For Gandhi, truth is the relative truth of truthfulness in word and deed, and the absolute truth-the Ultimate Reality. This ultimate truth is God (as God is also Truth) and morality-the moral laws and code-its basis. Ahimsa, far from meaning mere peacefulness or the absence of overt violence, is understood by Gandhi to denote active love-the pole opposite of violence, or "himsa", in every sense. The ultimate station Gandhi assigns nonviolence stems from two main points. First, if according to the Divine Reality all life is one, then all violence committed towards another is violence towards oneself, towards the collective, whole self, and thus "self"-destructive and counter to the universal law of life, which is love. Second, Gandhi believed that ahimsa is the most powerful force in existence. Had himsabeen superior to ahimsa, humankind would long ago have succeeded in destroying itself. The human race certainly could not have progressed as far as it has, even if universal justice remains far off the horizon. From both viewpoints, nonviolence or love is regarded as the highest law of humankind.

Although there are elements of unity in Gandhi's thought, they are not reduced to a system. It is not a rigid, inflexible doctrine, but a set of beliefs and principles which are applied differently according to the historical and social setting. Therefore there can be no dogmatism, and inconsistency is not a sin. Interpretation of the principles underwent much evolution during Gandhi's lifetime, and as a result many inconsistencies can be found in his writings, to which he readily admitted. The reader of Gandhi's works published by Navajivan Trust will notice that many are prefaced with the following quotation from an April 1933 edition of "Harijan", one of Gandhi's journals. He states straightforwardly: "I would like to say to the diligent reader of my writings and to others who are interested in them that I am not at all concerned with appearing to be consistent. In my search after Truth I have discarded many ideas and learnt many news things.... What I am concerned with is my readiness to obey the call of Truth, my God, from moment to moment, and therefore, when anybody finds any inconsistency between any two writings of mine, if he still has any faith in my sanity, he would do well to choose the later of the two on the same subject."

That there are inconsistencies in Gandhi's writings accords with the fact that the ideas are not a system. In coming to grips with Gandhi's way of thinking it is most important to understand that the perception of truth undergoes an ongoing process of refinement which is evolutionary in nature.

In Gandhi's thought the emphasis is on idealism, but on practical idealism. It is rooted in the highest religious idealism, but is thoroughly practical. One label (and almost the only one) Gandhi was happy to have pinned on him was that of "practical idealist". The important principle of compromise is relevant here, as is the acknowledgement that perfect truth and perfect nonviolence can never be attained while the spirit is embodied.

As alluded to above, Gandhian philosophy is certainly considered by Gandhians as a universal and timeless philosophy, despite the fact that on the more superficial level it is set in the Indian social context. They hold that the ideals of truth and nonviolence, which underpin the whole philosophy, are relevant to all humankind. (Recently some have been suggesting that a distinction can be made between the core elements of Gandhi's thought and peripheral elements which, depending on the particular element under consideration, may or may not have timeless relevance.) Also, it can be universal despite being fundamentally religious, as its religious position stresses not so much the Hindu interpretation of reality as the beliefs which are common to all major religions, and that commonality itself. It holds all religions to be worthy of equal respect and in one sense to be equal. As all are creations of mortal and imperfect human beings, no single religion can embody or reveal the whole or absolute truth.

Gandhian philosophy is also compatible with the view that humankind is undergoing gradual moral evolution. While conflict is seen as inevitable, in fact not always undesirable, violence as the result of conflict is not regarded as inevitable. Simply put, human beings do have the capacity to resolve conflict nonviolently. This might be difficult, but it is not impossible. Liberation from a violent society is seen as requiring many decades or longer-but it is not an imposible ideal.

Importantly also, it is not an intellectual doctrine. Gandhi was not an intellectual. Rather, Gandhi's thought was conceived, to a great extent, out of action and as a guide to action, by a man of action. He hesitated to write about anything of which he did not have personal, first-hand experience. In the sense of it being a call to action, Gandhi's thought can also be seen as an ideology.

As a guide to action, Gandhian philosophy is a double-edged weapon. Its objective is to transform the individual and society simultaneously (rather than in sequence, as Marxism describes), in accordance with the principles of truth and nonviolence. The historic task before humankind is to progress towards the creation of a nonviolent political, economic and social order by nonviolent struggle. The social goal was described by Gandhi as Sarvodaya, a term he coined in paraphrasing John Ruskin's book Unto This Last, meaning the welfare of all without exception. Its political aspect was expressed by the late eminent Gandhian Dr R.R. Diwakar in the following words: "The good of each individual in society consists in his efforts to achieve the good of all."

As the foundation of the Gandhian or nonviolent social order is religious or spiritual, economic and political questions are seen from the moral or humanistic perspective. The welfare of human beings, not of systems or institutions, is the ultimate consideration. Materially, it centres on the following concepts and ideals:

- Political decentralisation, to prevent massive concentrations of political power in the hands of too few; rather, to distribute it in the hands of many. The Gandhian political order takes the form of a direct, participatory democracy, operating in a tier structure from the base village-level tier upward through the district and state levels to the national (and international) level.
- Economic decentralisation, to prevent massive concentrations of economic power in the hands of too few, and again, to distribute it in the hands of many. Therefore villages, which are anyway geographically decentralised, become the basic economic units. However, where unavoidable, certain industries may be organised on a more centralised basis, and their ownership and control come under the umbrella of the State.
- The minimisation of competition and exploitation in the economic sphere, and instead, the encouragement of cooperation.
- Production on the basis of need rather than greed, concentrating where India is concerned first on the eradication of poverty (and on the worst extreme of poverty).
- Recognition of the dignity of labour and the greater purity of rural life.
- The practice of extensive self-reliance by individuals, villages, regions and the nation.

- Absence of oppression on the basis of race, caste, class, language, gender or religion.
- A deep respect for mother nature, necessitating an economic system based upon the preservation rather than destruction of the natural environment.

Such concepts clearly represent pillars for a new social order. A theory closely linked to the concept of Sarvodaya, also developed by Gandhi, is that of Trusteeship. Its fundamental objective is to create nonviolent and non-exploitative property relationships. Gandhi believed that the concepts of possession and private property were sources of violence, and in contradiction with the Divine reality that all wealth belongs to all people. However, he recognised that the concept of ownership would not wither easily, nor would the wealthy be easily persuaded to share their wealth. Therefore a compromise was to encourage the wealthy to hold their wealth in trust, to use themselves only what was necessary and to allow the remainder to be utilised for the benefit of the whole society.

It is apparent that Gandhi's philosophy has much in common with several Western philosophies which uphold the ideal of a more just and equitable society. For example, the Gandhian social order has been described as "communism minus violence". (However, Marxists have traditionally rejected Gandhi because of what they regard as his "bourgeois" outlook. Gandhi rejected violent class conflict and the centralisation of political and economic power in the hands of the State as counterproductive to the development of a nonviolent society.) Nevertheless, Gandhian philosophy, particularly in the Sarvodaya ideal, does contain many socialist sentiments. In fact, such an entity as Gandhian Socialism emerged in theoretical literature during the 1970s and 1980s. Gandhi's thought has been likened also to Utopian Socialism and Philosophical Anarchism, and can be compared with strands of Maoist thought (though not a Western philosophy), and even Western liberal thought. However, Gandhi is incompatible with many aspects of Liberalism and is virtually entirely incompatible with the modern, intensely competitive, ecologically destructive and materialistic capitalism of the West.

As already observed, Gandhi's thought is equally a philosophy of self-transformation. The individual's task is to make a sincere attempt to live according to the principles of truth and nonviolence. Its fundamental tenets are therefore moral. They include-resisting injustice, developing a spirit of service, selflessness and sacrifice, emphasising one's responsibilities rather than rights, self-discipline, simplicity of life-style, and attempting to maintain truthful and nonviolent relations with others. It should be understood that by simplicity is meant voluntary simplicity, not poverty, which has no element of voluntarism in it. If there is one thing Gandhi does not stand for, it is poverty. A Gandhian should also avoid political office. He or she should remain aloof from formal party politics and equi-distant from all political groupings. But this is not to say, and in my view Gandhi does not require, that the individual should remain aloof from all politics. For often injustice cannot be resisted unless the political power holders and structures are engaged, nonviolently. What was the freedom struggle itself if not a political struggle, against the greatest concentration of political power the world had ever known, the British Empire? In my eyes, there is no particular virtue in attempting to avoid contact with politics. What must be avoided, however, is assumption of political power by a Gandhian (at least this is necessary in the short and medium terms in India), and cooperation with unvirtuous holders of political power on their terms.

The ultimate responsibility of a Gandhian is to resist clear injustice, untruth, in conjunction with others or alone. Resistance should be nonviolent if at all possible. But Gandhi did condone use of violent means in certain circumstances, in preference to submission which he regarded as cowardice and equivalent to cooperation with evil. In relation to the use of violence he stated categorically: "Where there is only a choice between cowardice and violence I would advise violence..." As surprising as it no doubt sounds, Gandhi disliked most not violence, but cowardice and apathy. The eminent peace researcher Johan Galtung has correctly observed that Gandhi preferred first, nonviolent resistance, second, violence in a just cause, and third, meaning least of all, apathy. In general, however, it is held that immoral means, such as violence, cannot produce moral ends, as means are themselves ends or ends in the making.

For the individual self-transformation is attempted with deliberateness rather than with haste. One should not seek to become a Mahatma overnight, because such attempts will surely fail, but to reform oneself over the whole of one's life, as far as one is capable. (Nor should there be any question of superficial imitation of Gandhi.) Gandhi viewed his own life as a process of development undertaken "one step at a time". He saw the need to continually "experiment with truth" (from which he derived the title of his autobiography) in whatever field, in order to come to see the truthful path. Though they were rooted in the highest idealism, the experiments were carried out on a very down-to-earth plane-India's moral, political and social needs as he saw them. Such an approach is available to all at all times. Gandhi believed his own moral and spiritual development to be far from complete at the time of his death. Despite the great heights he had attained, this was indeed true. He had not achieved perfection, as some of those who were close to him have testified.

The perception of what is the truthful path is largely a matter for the individual's reason and conscience, which therefore play key roles. The individual should subject each idea to the test of his or her own conscience and reason. Reason and rationality have enormous roles to play in the Gandhian way of thinking. This, I feel, is one of the major Western influences in Gandhi. If there is genuine, sincere disagreement, an idea can be discarded. However, once a principle is accepted a sincere attempt must be made to adhere to it. Ideally there should be harmony between thought, word and action. In this way the outer life becomes a true reflection of the inner, and a mental harmony is also achieved.

The remaining central concept in Gandhi's philosophy is Satyagraha. Defined most broadly (as Gandhi defined it), Satyagraha is itself a whole philosophy of nonviolence. Defined most narrowly, it is a technique or tool of nonviolent action. Because of the intention here to keep this discussion as simple as possible,Satyagraha will be described here in its latter guise. As a technique, Satyagraha was developed by Gandhi in South Africa to give the Indian population there a weapon with which to resist the injustices being perpetrated upon it by the colonial government. But Satyagraha can be practised in any cultural environment-provided the necessary ingredients are present, not least Satyagrahis (those capable of Satyagraha). A Satyagraha campaign is undertaken only after all other peaceful means have proven ineffective. At its heart is nonviolence. An attempt is made to convert, persuade or win over the opponent. It involves applying the forces of both reason and conscience simultaneously. While holding aloft the indisputable truth of his or her position, the Satyagrahi also engages in acts of voluntary self-suffering. Any violence inflicted by the opponent is accepted without retaliation. But precisely because there is no retaliation (which can make the opponent feel his violence is justified), the opponent can only become morally bankrupt if violence continues to be inflicted indefinitely.

Several methods can be applied in a Satyagraha campaign, primarily noncooperation and fasting. The action is undertaken in the belief in the underlying goodness of the opponent, and in his or her ability to acknowledge the injustice of the action and to cease the injustice, or at least to compromise. Satyagrahain this sense is highly creative. It creates no enemies, hatred or lasting bitterness, but ultimately only mutual regard. After a successful campaign there is not the least hint of gloating, nor is there any desire to embarrass the opponent. The former opponent becomes a friend. There are no losers, only winners. A truthful Satyagraha campaign, though it demands courage, self-discipline and humility on the part of the Satyagrahi, brings to bear tremendous moral pressure on the opponent and can bring about remarkable transformations.

Two factors are absolutely crucial to understand. There can be no Satyagraha in a cause which is not indisputably just and truthful. Nor can there be any element of violence or bitterness in a Satyagraha campaign-it must be conducted in a spirit of genuine nonviolence. Any campaign which is insincere in its spirit of nonviolence, or is not undertaken in a clearly just cause is not Satyagraha as Gandhi meant it.

To sum up, Gandhian philosophy is not only simultaneously political, moral and religious, it is also traditional and modern, simple and complex. It embodies numerous Western influences to which Gandhi was exposed, but being rooted in ancient Indian culture and harnessing eternal and universal moral and religious principles, there is much in it that is not at all new. This is why Gandhi could say: "I have nothing new to teach the world. Truth and nonviolence are as old as the hills." Gandhi is concerned even more with the spirit than with the form. If the spirit is consistent with truth and nonviolence, the truthful and nonviolent form will automatically re sult. Despite its anti-Westernism, many hold its outlook to be ultra-modern, in fact ahead of its time-even far ahead. Perhaps the philosophy is best seen as a harmonious blend of the traditional and modern. The multifaceted nature of Gandhi's thought also can easily lead to the view that it is extremely complex. Perhaps in one sense it is. One could easily write volumes in describing it! Yet Gandhi described much of his thought as mere commonsense. Dr Diwakar sums up Gandhi's thought in a few words: "The four words, truth, nonviolence, Sarvodaya and Satyagraha and their significance constitute Gandhi and his teaching." These are indeed the four pillars of Gandhian thought.

Gandhi's Vision and Values

As India prepares for the third millennium and celebrates 62 years of independence from the British *raj,* its much neglected Gandhian economic thought and praxis demand an exhaustive re-examination. *Swaraj* as Gandhi repeatedly clarified, however, is not only political. 'Real home-rule *[swaraj],*' as Gandhi asserted 'is self-rule or self-control.' Therefore, Indians acting in the pursuit of true *swaraj* will have to cultivate and nurture their spiritual selves in a self-disciplined manner. It is only with this Gandhian understanding of *swaraj* that the real dangers of division and dependency — arising from communal forces, corrupt local and national leaders, international financial institutions, and multinational corporations — can be resolutely confronted. In fact, the main and practical contention of this work is that the six ethical and moral principles — *swadeshi, aparigraha,* bread labour, trusteeship, non-exploitation, and equality-together with the concept of *swaraj* have contemporary relevance and need uncompromising integration into Indian planning.

As a point of departure, I have examined the implications of my suggestion only in relation to the agricultural sector. The Gandhian vision which I have portrayed is a means to rejuvenate the entire nation and all its other important sectors. Therefore, programs for social change and planning exercises in agriculture, on macro-or micro-levels, must be grounded in these moral values.

An awareness of Gandhi's philosophy in national planning and transformation of an agricultural society has not been totally absent in India during the post-independence years. As I have demonstrated-especially through exploration of current experiments and writings of Indian economists and planners-the contrary holds true. In fact, it is the volunteer-based, non-governmental organizations (NGOs), for the most part, which are assiduously working in a variety of areas to steer the people towards implementing, albeit selective aspects, Gandhi's *Constructive Programme* on a micro-level basis. Therefore, in different pockets of the vast nation people, particularly the poor and marginalized, are not only accepting Gandhian methods in their lives and economic activities, but gradually converting government officials and agencies to follow their lead. This, though an important and significant step, is clearly insufficient when the dimensions of the crisis are considered.

The inadequacy of the response is located in serious and distressing trends towards massive industrialization and mindless consumerism, in urban areas and towns, resulting in high unemployment and diversion of scarce resources. Together with these tendencies there is the more harmful disregard of moral and ethical principles. Here Gandhi's vision encounters its toughest challenge. Since its central tenets are based on voluntary effort and individual/community reflection and action it may appear that Gandhi's adherents cannot do much to remedy matters. This clearly is not so.

The adoption of *satyagraha* ('The way to it *[swaraj]* is through *satyagraha')* and nonviolent noncooperation will oblige the elected political representatives to honestly execute the wishes of the poor and oppressed millions in the rural areas and effectively stop those programs which are not in the interests of the entire polity. In situations where the representatives do not act according to the wishes of the people, Gandhi said 'we can protest and teach people to resist and make it clear to the Government that it cannot look us in this manner.' The path-breaking work undertaken in Ahmedabad, Ralegan Siddhi, and Seed provides substantial, though differing, examples by which Gandhi's vision for social change can certainly be set in motion in the India of the twenty-first century.

In addition, the gap between awareness and action on a mass scale in India can be bridged by the people directly addressing the important question of who benefits from individual/collective apathy and action. As a valid basis for social change in the interests of the entire community there is enough to be learnt from the selfless dedication of Ela Bhatt, Baburao Hazare, and the villagers of Seed.

What is crucial to recognize, as Gandhi repeatedly asserted in *Hind Swaraj,* is that adoption of either modernity or tradition has to enhance both the spiritual and the material well-being of the individual and society. Gandhi's philosophy and experiments in agriculture cannot be construed simply as a return to tradition, which they are in a very crude sense. Gandhi's vision for free India, even the struggle for independence, explicitly depended on whether it brought 'bread to the mouths of the people... for the poor bread is their God.' In fact, if India could adopt Gandhi's six moral principles and as a result only bring bread to all of its disempowered multitudes, then that in itself is true *swaraj.* That the present course of planning, as my critique of India's various Five Year Plans indicates, has enslaved and oppressed millions of poor Indians, especially in the agrarian sector, is a truism. A fundamental moral change has to be effected.

What India needs in its agricultural sector, as Gandhi envisaged in his *Constructive Programme,* are millions of *lok sevaks* selflessly devoting themselves, together with the village community, to the singular tasks of tapping the vast reservoir of human power to raise crops which will primarily feed the peasant, his/her family, and the village. In time this will make them self-sufficient and provide gainful employment to all. As a consequence, cultivators and peasants will be motivated to increase selectively the productivity of impoverished soils through adoption of scientific methods, and ensuring that critical agricultural output keeps ahead of population increase. Once this balance is achieved, then local self-help work projects will feed, clothe, and educate every child, woman and man. Simultaneously, local initiatives can foster the production of goods in cottage industries for primary consumption based on the principles of need and consequently exchange. In such a positive and caring environment resolution of disputes through harmonious reconciliation of competing interests and appeals to the rich and elite to respond to their *dharma* is possible. These steps will recreate the fervor, which once ignited the nation, for authentic *swaraj*.

The skills and resources for these enterprises exist. Baburao Hazare's inspiring example in the village of Ralegan Siddhi to truthfully take on this responsibility and carry it on in a nonviolent manner is an eloquent testimony to what can be achieved through collective human grit and pragmatism. That simple experiment needs to be repeated in whatever relevant and applicable form, given India's diversity, in the millions of Indian villages. What is certainly lacking is the political will and integrity on the part of India's elected leaders and the necessary enduring faith so pivotal for such an undertaking. This is why the crisis affecting India in its agricultural sector, and for that matter in other areas of its economy, is not entirely structural. The problem is at its core a crisis in human values. From Gandhi's early efforts in Phoenix to those at Sevagram, he diligently inculcated in his followers certain universal principles. He repeated the same experiments, namely, of creating community-oriented work projects, ensuring that the fundamental needs of the poorest were firmly kept in sight, and providing basic human necessities.

If India can revert to rechanneling its massive human resources towards these endeavours through a commitment to the Gandhian path it can resolve its crisis. Today in some communities in developed countries there are susmined and solid agricultural programs for use of organic methods; a decreasing dependence on governments for initiatives; decentralization as a basis for local government; cooperatives for mutual sharing of all kinds of resources; and a deep consciousness that the environment is a finite and fragile entity. It may well be that Gandhian ideas find a fertile soil in societies which see the bane of affluence and taste the bitter fruits of inhuman and excessive industrialization.

Whatever the reasons for India's earlier lack of political initiative in adopting Gandhi's ideas and experiments in restructuring Indian agriculture, the choice today is between death and life for the millions of poor people who are caught in this human tragedy. If the examples of SEWA, Ralegan Siddhi, and the village of Seed are any indication of what is happening at the grassroots of Indian society, it is plain that ultimately the poor women, children, and men of this nation can return to the Gandhian message of self-reliance. By forming local, self-governing, and democratic political organizations it is possible to nonviolently resist oppression and exploitation both by the state and market forces. Radically restructuring the usage of the environment is not an empty slogan. Self-imposed curbs on one's wants and production for one's needs can be achieved by discipline and selflessness. Devoting oneself first to cultivate the land for basic nutrition and only secondarily for exchange value is a must. Realization that self-help and bread labour are useful methods to frontally attack the vicious circle of poverty is imperative. Creation of democratic cooperatives for managing and allocating human and non-human resources in the spirit of trusteeship is requisite. All these steps, as I have practically demonstrated, are achievable. They, however, need to be slowly undertaken with utter dedication to empower individuals and communities, through adherence to the spiritual principles of truth and nonviolence, to live ethically and in harmony with themselves and nature. The key to making Gandhi's vision a reality and practising his values is to persistently subvert selfish worldly pursuits with ethical livelihood. This is the immediate struggle every Indian, on an individual and collective basis, has to non-violently and passionately wage.

10

Trusteeship

Gandhian Trusteeship as an" Instrument of Human Dignity"

Gandhi's economic ideas were part of his general crusade against poverty and, exploitation against socioeconomic injustice, and deteriorating moral standards. Gandhi was an economist of the masses. His approach was rooted in human dignity. His economic philosophy is a result of innumerable experiments which he conducted in the course of his life. His pragmatic approach gave a new direction to the existing socioeconomic problems in the process of protecting human dignity. The fluid international conditions fraught with ideological tensions in the economic domain demanded a fresh approach to economic philosophy, with emphasis on the ideals of human rights like democracy, economic freedom, and social justice. Gandhism as a socio-economic philosophy suits not only to accomplish the higher ideals of democratic freedom and socialism but it was also thoroughly developed to meet the challenge of national and international forces of communism and capitalism.

The core of Gandhian economic thought is the protection of the dignity of human person and not mere material prosperity. He aimed at the development, upliftment, and enrichment of human life rather than a higher standard of living with scant respect for human and social values. The fundamental ethical values dominated his economic ideas. He wanted to liberate the modern economic philosophy from the quagmire of materialism and bring it to a higher spiritual plane. Human actions were motivated by social objectives of the protection of human rights.

Gandhi's efforts towards "spiritualizing economics" are truly reflected in his concept of trusteeship. He based his doctrine of trusteeship on the first sloka of Isopanisad, according to which one is asked to dedicate everything to God and then use it only to the required extent. The principal condition laid down in it is that one must not covet what belongs to others. In other words, in the first instance, everything must be surrendered to God and then out of it one may use only that which is necessary for the service of God's creation, according to one's strict needs. This makes it clear beyond doubt that it is not in industrial and business sectors only that the doctrine of trusteeship is to be made applicable. The spirit of this doctrine is detachment and service. Unless these two virtues are inculcated, it is impossible to obey the command "covet not anybody's riches." Therefore Gandhi's idea of trusteeship arose from his faith in the law of non-possession. It was founded on his religious belief that everything belonged to God and was from God. Therefore the bounties of the world were for His people, as a whole, not for any particular individual. When an individual had more than his respective portion, he became a trustee of that portion for God's people. God who is all-powerful has no need to store. He creates things afresh everyday. Therefore man should also live his life from day to day without trying to store things for future. If this principle was imbibed by people in general, it would have become legalised and trusteeship would have become a legalised institution. Gandhi wished it became a gift from India to the world (*Harijan,* 23 February 1947).

Basically Gandhi suggested this doctrine as an answer to the economic inequalities of ownership and income-a kind of nonviolent way of resolving all social and economic conflicts which grew out of inequalities and privileges of the present social order. Gandhi never ceased to believe in trusteeship in theory from the beginning or, at any 'rate, towards the later part of life, though the method was proving ineffective. He believed in the indispensability of nonviolence, non-cooperation and Satyagraha in converting the privileged classes into trustees. He even advocated violence as a last resort to dispossess property-owners of their wealth.

Therefore man's dignity, and not his material prosperity, is the centre of Gandhian economics. Gandhian economics aims at a distribution of material prosperity keeping only human dignity in view. Thus it is dominated more by moral values than by economic ideas. According to Gandhi, trusteeship is the only ground on which he can work out an ideal combination of economics and morals. In concrete form, the trusteeship formula reads as follows:

- Trusteeship provides a means of transforming the present capitalist order of society into an egalitarian one. It gives no quarter to capitalism, but gives the present owning class a chance to reform itself. It is based on the faith that human nature is never beyond redemption.
- It does not recognise any right of private ownership of property except so far as it may be permitted by society for its own welfare.
- It does not exclude legislation of the ownership and use of wealth.
- Thus under state regulated trusteeship, an individual will not be free to hold or use his wealth for selfish satisfaction in disregard to the interests of society.
- Just as it is proposed to give a decent minimum living wage, a limit should be fixed for the maximum income that would be allowed to any person in society. The difference between such minimum and maximum incomes should be reasonable and equitable and variable from time to time, so much so that the tenancy would be towards the obliteration of the difference.
- Under the Gandhian economic order, the character of production will be determined by social necessity and not by personal greed.

The theory of trusteeship applies equally to both tangible and intangible property, "such as the muscular energy of the labourers and the talents of a Helen Keller" (K.G. Mashurwala, *Gandhi and Marx*, Navajivan Trust, Ahmedabad, 1951, p. 79). According to Gandhi, all property belongs to God and in his concept of trusteeship the trustees have no right to destroy that property deliberately and wantonly. Besides, trusteeship aims at the rising of the morale of the people by giving them a sense of security in the hands of the trustees. The trustees, in their turn, are beholden to creating an urge among the masses for a higher standard of life. As man advances from a narrow sphere of personal satisfaction to the nobler concept of the welfare of all, he marches closer towards self-realization. The whole idea of possessing wealth only to guard it from being misused and to distribute it equitably aims at protecting human dignity. If it is possessed for any other objective, it is objectionable on moral grounds. Gandhi enjoins this moral obligation on the part of the trustees as he is fully aware of the ills of capitalism which widen the gap between the rich and the poor.

The Gandhian theory of trusteeship departs significantly from Marxian economic philosophy too. If Marxism is the child of the Industrial Revolution, Gandhian theory can be understood only in the context of certain basic spiritual values of the Indian tradition. Marxian socialism aims at the destruction of the class called capitalists, whereas the Gandhian approach is not to destroy the institution, but to reform it. Gandhian socialism, being ethical, is different from Marxia'" socialism. Man, to him, is an ethical being first and a social being later.

The most significant difference between Marxian socialism and Gandhian socialism lies in the method they recommend to achieve it. Whereas Marxian socialism harps on violence, Gandhian socialism aims at a change of heart on the part of the rich. There is no place for violence, but only trust. The common man trusts his trustee and the latter plays the role of a custodian. Thus Gandhian socialism radically departs from both capitalism and socialism; it is trusteeship socialism. Though this kind of socialism is difficult to achieve, Gandhi advocated it as he believed in the basic strength of the goodness of man and the value of morals. All other "isms" address the problem superficially, whereas trusteeship strikes it at the root.

Gandhi wanted Zamindars to act as trustees of their lands and allow them to be used by tenants. This idea was based mainly upon the fact that India is an agricultural country where more than 80 percent of the population lives in villages. By providing them trust land, Gandhi was solving one of the major economic problems of an independent India to be. In the socialist collective agricultural system, we find the same idea implemented. The success of this system in certain countries shows that the concept is not impracticable at all. The failure of this system is often attributed to the will of the people. But a more sound reason seems to be the force that was being applied while putting this system into practice.

At the centre of this concept is the urge to protect human dignity. They are, broadly speaking, the demands or desires of the modem man. The revolutions that are raised from time to time in different countries are motivated by the same objectives of human dignity, justice, and equity. It is very clear that the idea is relevant today as it aims at the social, economic, and political changes in the world. One of the first steps to achieve this human dignity, justice, and equity is to eliminate the ever-present troublesome element of class struggle in the society. Though the Gandhian concept of trusteeship does not seek to destroy any particular class, it provides us with an idea of how to narrow the class gap. The practice of all the democratic nations has been to reduce the gap between the rich and the poor to a minimum. In India we find this motive behind our cooperative policies, the community development projects, and the taxation policy that heavily taxes the upper class and gives some relief to the lower strata of society. We find the manifestations of the Gandhian concept of trusteeship in these policies.

Gandhian Trusteeship in Theory and Practice

Mahatma Gandhi held that all human beings are implicitly responsible to God, the Family of Man and to themselves for their use and treatment of all goods, gifts and talents that fall within their domain. This is so because Nature and Man are alike upheld, suffused and regenerated by the Divine. There is a luminous spark of divine intelligence in the motion of the atom and in the eyes of every man and woman on earth. We incarnate our divinity when we deliberately and joyously nurture our abilities and assets for the sake of the larger good. In this sense, the finest exemplars of trusteeship are those who treat all possessions as though they were sacred or deeply precious beyond any worldly scale of valuation. Thus, it is only through daily moral choice and the meritorious use of resources that we sustain our inherited or acquired entitlements. For this reason, the very idea of ownership is misleading and, at root, a form of violence. It implies rights and privileges over Man and Nature that go beyond the bounds of human need–although not necessarily beyond the limits of human law and social custom. It obscures the generous bounty of Nature, which provides enough for all if each holds in trust only what he needs, without excess or exploitation.

Gandhi sensed that all our resources and possessions, at any level, are not merely fragments of the Divine but are also inherently mortal and mutable. The Divine in its active aspect is ceaselessly creative and ever fluid in form. By analogy, human needs and material circumstances alter even while cultural patterns and social customs purport to maintain temporal continuity through established traditions. Ownership, from this standpoint, is truly a costly and illusory attempt to ensure permanency and succession. It gives birth to unwarranted attachments and insupportable expectations. The selfish grasping for possessions of any kind not only violates the deeper purposes of our human odyssey but eventually breeds possessiveness and greed, exploitation and revenge. This appalling moral malaise leads to inordinate self-assertion and self-projection which can only yield distrust, sorrow and "loss of all". But when we attain the sacred mental posture of the trustee who regards all possessions as held in trust for the good of all, we can progressively approach the high spiritual state of mental renunciation. We can, in the Upanishadic phrase, "renounce and enjoy". It is only when we voluntarily relinquish our unnatural claims and consecrate ourselves to a higher purpose that we can freely enjoy what we have. Thus, self-satisfaction is a natural outcome of a generous perspective and a greater purity of heart. It is truly a function of the harmonious cultivation of our spiritual, mental and material resources. In Gandhian terms, guilt-free enjoyment is inseparable from ethical probity. The real issue, then, is not how much or how little we possess in the way of property or talent, but the reasons and motives behind their allocations and uses.

Gandhi approached the concept of trusteeship at four different levels. First of all, trusteeship, as the sole universalizable means of continuously redistributing wealth, could be seen as a corollary of the principle of nonviolence and simultaneously assure the generation and intelligent use of wealth. No other theory is compatible with nonviolence. In the nonviolent method the wrongdoer compasses his own end, if he does not undo the wrong. For, either through Nonviolent Noncooperation he is made to see his error, or he finds himself completely isolated.

Even if wealth could be coercively redistributed, the resulting greed and inexperience on the part of many and the resentment on the part of the dispossessed would lead to economic instability and rapid decline. More likely than not, it would lead to class war, anomic violence and widespread self-alienation. Trusteeship, however, encourages owners to see themselves as vigilant trustees of their accumulated wealth for the larger community without threatening them.

Secondly, Gandhi's practical psychological intuition allowed him to see that fear would prevent other means of economic distribution from succeeding in the long run. A fundamental change in the concepts of activity and courage is needed to overcome passivity and cowardice. Courage must be detached from violence, and creativity must be dislodged from the self-protective formulations of entrenched 6lites. This involves rooting new notions of noetic activity which are creative, playful and tolerant, and new notions of moral courage which are heroic, magnanimous and civil, in a search for universal self-transcendence. An individual must feel, both abstractly and concretely, a secure sense of joyous eros in fellowship, and a positive sense of solidarity with hapless human beings everywhere. He must feel at one with the victims of incomplete revolutions, with the understandably impatient and occasionally mistaken pioneers of great revolutions, and even more with those willing to defy every presumptuous criterion and form of authority which trespasses upon individuality.

The fearful man tyrannizes others: forced redistribution would bring fearful responses from owners, who would see their lives and futures threatened, and fearful masses would deal with excess wealth incompetently. For Gandhi, the ever-present possibility of social change must be approached from a position of truth and courage, whereas fear is weakness which leads to violence. Strength should not be mistaken for the modalities of violence, which are instruments of fear and always lead to varying degrees of self-destruction. Since strength rests on human dignity and respect, workers must approach exploitative capitalists from a position of self-respect based on the capital of labour, for "labour is as much capital as metal". To abolish fear and even failure itself requires a fundamental change in the social structure. The feasibility of this social transformation does not lie in denying the judgements of others, but rather in regarding them as partially relevant though in no sense compelling. Individuals can commit themselves to increasing their own capacity for self-transcendence of external criteria of differentiation, and thereby attain liberation from the self-perpetuating iniquities and horrors of the System.

Therefore, workers, instead of regarding themselves as enemies of the rich, or regarding the rich as their natural enemies, should hold their labour in trust for those who are in need of it. This they can do only when, instead of feeling so utterly helpless as they do, they realize their importance in human economy and shed their fear or distrust of the rich. Fear and distrust are twin sisters born of weakness. When labour realizes its strength it won't need to use any force against moneyed people. It will simply command their attention and respect.

Gandhi discerned the critical role acceptability plays in legitimating a social order, and distinguished between a people's tacit acceptance and active dislike of an economic regime. So long as any society finds its socioeconomic system acceptable, that system will stand even if a militant minority detests it. But should a significant number of individuals find it unacceptable, it is shaken to its foundations, regardless of the complacency of privileged élites.

Thirdly, Gandhi contended that the idea of trusteeship could be put into practice non-violently, because it could be instituted by degrees. When asked if such 'trustees'–individuals who possessed wealth and yet saw themselves as stewards for society–could be found in India in his day, he rejected the question as strictly irrelevant to the theory, which can only be evaluated by extensive testing over time.

At this point I may be asked as to how many trustees of this type one can really find. As a matter of fact, such a question should not arise at all. It is not directly related to our theory. There may be just one such trustee or there may be none at all. Why should we worry about it? We should have faith that we can, without violence or with so little violence that it can hardly be called violence, create such a feeling among the rich. We should act in that faith. That is sufficient for us. We should demonstrate through our endeavour that we can end economic disparity with the help of nonviolence. Only those who have no faith in nonviolence can ask how many trustees of this kind can be found.

Gandhi knew that he sought the widespread realization of a forgotten ideal, but he repudiated the conventional notion that an experiment is unworthy to be tried simply because it stems from an exacting ideal. Even if one argued that trusteeship was doomed to failure, it ran no greater risk than the conventional social proposals of the day. Committed to principles but flexible in policies, Gandhi saw no reason to neglect ideals and to institute social reforms from a defeatist standpoint. Such an approach only guaranteed that structural faults would be built into the new social order. Rather, he emphasized, it is better to move towards the ideal and make appropriate adjustments necessitated by the specific failures encountered in attempting to reach it. In doing so, principles would remain uncompromised and the possibility of improvement would always remain, whereas in a system which assumes cupidity and corruption in human nature, nothing encourages their eradication.

Gandhi not only had faith that it was possible for human beings to become trustees of their resources for the sake of all, but also that many in fact were already and had always been trustees. They are the preservers of culture and tradition, who show their ethical stance through countless daily acts of graciousness and concern for others. To treat man as man requires not so much the acceptance of the equal potentialities of all men, let alone the infinite potentialities of all men, but rather the acceptance of the unknown potentialities of all human beings. Given scarce resources and the limits of productivity and of taxable income, there are definitely limits to what the State can do, but is there any reason why voluntary associations should not be entrusted with the task of extending the avenues of opportunity available to the disinherited? The socialist could argue that by an indefinite extension of opportunities (not always requiring State action) and by changing not only the structure but the entire ethos and moral tone of society, new social values could slowly emerge and usher in an era in which men show mutual respect which is not based on skills and promotions, rank and status. The minimal goal of basic economic equity is easily stated, yet it is the fundamental first stage for the uplift of the whole. Everybody should be able to get sufficient work to make the two ends meet. And, this ideal can be universally realized only if the means of production of elementary necessaries of life remain under the control of the masses. These should be freely available to all as God's air and water are, or ought to be; they should not be made a vehicle of traffic for the exploitation of others. Their monopolization by any country, nation or groups of persons would be unjust. The neglect of this simple principle is the cause of the destitution that we witness today, not only in this unhappy land, but other parts of the world, too.

The principle of trusteeship in its application to the equitable distribution of wealth, as well as to the nonviolent socialist reformation it underpins, is practicable because it does not require everyone to undertake it all at once. Unlike most socialists who reason that they must seize the power of the State before instituting effective reforms, Gandhi held that enlightened individuals could initiate the process of divesting themselves of what is unnecessary while becoming true trustees of their own possessions.

It is perfectly possible for an individual to adopt this way of life without having to wait for others to do so. And if an individual can observe a certain rule of conduct, it follows that a group of individuals can do likewise. It is necessary for me to emphasize the fact that no one need wait for anyone else in order to adopt a right course. Men generally hesitate to make a beginning, if they feel that the objective cannot be had in its entirety. Such an attitude of mind is in reality a bar to progress.

Once the barrier in consciousness is broken, the principle of trusteeship can be made to work by letting go of the demand for a mechanically equal distribution, something Gandhi doubted could ever be realized. Instead, he held to the revolutionary ideal of *equitable* distribution, which would not only be possible but necessary in the nonviolent socialist State. Should attempts to encourage the abandonment of exploitation through misappropriation of the means of production fail, trusteeship could be made to work through nonviolent noncooperation, wherein workers realize the capital worth and collective strenght of their labour. Should it succeed, ideas which arise out of narrow acquisitive thinking would vanish because they were rooted in unacceptable and illusory assumptions. If the trusteeship idea catches, philanthropy, as we know it, will disappear.... A trustee has no heir but the public.

Gradually, statutory trusteeship could be introduced in which the duties of the trustee and the public could be formalized. The trustee may serve so long as the people find his services beneficial. He may even designate his successor, but the people must confirm it. Should the State become involved, the trustee's power of appointment and the State's power of review will strike a balance in which the welfare of the people will be safeguarded.

Fourthly and finally, Gandhi believed that social conditions were ripe for imaginative applications of the principle of trusteeship. The collapse of Western imperialsim, the spiritual and social poverty of fascism and totalitarianism, the psychological failure of capitalism, the moral bankruptcy of state socialism and the ideological inflexibility of communism all indicate an ineluctable if gradual movement towards a reconstitution of the social order which will compel some form of redistribution.

The limits to growth make themselves felt through the undermining of social virtues like trust and truthfulness, restraint and mutual acceptance, as well as a sense of fraternal obligation, all of which are essential to individual initiative in a contractual economic system. If such virtues are treated as public goods necessary to universal welfare, then unrestricted individualism faces noticeable limits, lest the social justification and viability of the whole system be destroyed. C.B. MacPherson went so far as to predict that the time will come when it will no longer be feasible to put acquisition ahead of spiritual values, and that national power will become a function not of market power but of moral stature. Although we have to confront scarcity, the emphasis on Hobbesian self-preservation alone is adequate.

The rich should ponder well as to what is their duty today. They who employ mercenaries to guard their wealth may find those very guardians turning on them. The moneyed classes have got to learn how to fight either with arms or with the weapons of nonviolence.... I see coming the day of the rule of the poor, whether that rule be through force of arms or of nonviolence.

Even though the war against poverty will take a long time to win, it is necessary for the State to adopt various measures to reduce the sharp economic inequalities that undermine the working of mass democracy, and to strengthen the organizing power of peasants, artisans, and industrial and clerical workers. In addition to fiscal and monetary measures to reduce income ceilings, it would be desirable to assist wealthy landlords and industrialists in parting with portions of their wealth, property and earnings as public contributions towards specific local schemes and plans. The more the redistributive process can be extended beyond legal compulsion and political action, the more democracy is strengthened at the social level. The more the State can bring together representatives of richer and poorer groups, stronger and weaker sections of society, in planning local programs, the better it will be for all.

At this point the socialist's faith as well as his integrity are tested, and so are his ultimate premises. Does he believe in perfectibility or in original sin? If, like Condorcet, he believes that the historical process and the progress of humanity involve an increasing equality among nations, equality within nations and the perfectibility of man, how much emphasis does it put on human growth and perfectibility rather than on inherent flaws and weaknesses? If committed socialists are not imbued with atavistic or original sin, if they hold to a truly open view of human nature, then they could adopt a different parapolitical standpoint. They could say that it is because they believe in the unknown possibilities of every human being that they are concerned to extend the idea of human excellence to a point where external social distinctions do not matter, but where trusteeship is honoured wherever it is witnessed in human beings.

Owing to his unshakeable conviction that violence can never produce permanent results, only Gandhi's modesty prevented him from asserting that his ethical solution would come to be seen as the only feasible alternative to wholesale misery and destruction, if not now, then in the foreseeable future. He deliberately avoided elaborating a complete system of statutory or voluntary trusteeship out of the conviction that structural and organizational details necessarily varied with the social and political context and with the personnel, whilst the essential core of the ideal was universally applicable. Thus he could gain a serious hearing from those who would be most affected by the implementation of his proposals without threatening them.

I am not ashamed to own that many capitalists are friendly towards me and do not fear me. They know that I desire to end capitalism almost, if not quite, as much as the most advanced Socialist or even Communist. But our methods differ, our languages differ. My theory of 'trusteeship' is no make-shift, certainly no camouflage. I am confident that it will survive all theories.

The Gospel of Trusteeship

Economic equality is the master key to nonviolent independence. Working for economic equality means abolishing the eternal conflict between capital and labour. It means the levelling down of the few rich in whose hands is concentrated the bulk of the nation's wealth on the one hand, and the levelling up of the semi-starved naked millions on the other. A nonviolent system of government is clearly an impossibility, so long as the wide gulf between the rich and the hungry millions persists. The contrast between the palaces of New Delhi and the miserable hovels of the poor, labouring class nearby cannot last one day in a free India in which the poor will enjoy the same power as the richest in the land.

A violent and bloody revolution is a certainty one day unless there is a voluntary abdication of riches and the power that riches give and sharing them for the common good. (CP, pp. 20-21)

I adhere to my doctrine of trusteeship in spite of the ridicule that has been poured upon it. It is true that it is difficult to reach. So is nonviolence. But we made up our minds in 1920 to negotiate that steep ascent. We have found it worth the effort. (ibid, p. 21)

Nonviolent Way

By the nonviolent method, we seek not to destroy the capitalist, we seek to destroy capitalism. We invite the capitalist to regard himself as a trustee for those on whom he depends for the making, the retention and the increase of his capital. Nor need the worker wait for his conversion. If capital is power, so is work. Either is dependent on the other. Immediately the worker realizes his strength, he is din a position to become a co-sharer with the capitalist instead of remaining his slave. If he aims at becoming the sole owner, he will most likely be killing the goose that lays the golden eggs. Not need I be afraid of some one else taking my place when I have non-co-operated. For I expect to influence my co-workers so as not to help the wrongdoing of my employer. This kind of education of the mass of workers is no doubt a slow process, but as it is also the surest, it is necessarily the quickest. It can be easily demonstrated in the end of the worker and as no human being is so bad as to be beyond redemption, no human being is so perfect as to warrant his destroying him whom he wrongly considers to be wholly evil. (YI, 26-3-1931, p. 49)

Community Welfare

I am inviting those people who consider themselves as owners today to act as trustees, i.e., owners, not in their own right, but owners in the right of those whom they have exploited. (YI, 26-11-1931, p. 369)

It has become the fashion these days to say that society cannot be organized or run on nonviolent lines. I join issue on that point. In a family, when the father slaps his delinquent child, the latter does not think of retaliating. He obeys his father not because of the deterrent effect of the slap but because of the offended love which he senses behind it. That, in my opinion, is an epitome of the way in which society is or should be governed. What is true of the family must be true of society which is but a larger family. (H, 3-12-1938, p. 358)

Supposing I have come by a fair amount of wealth—either by way of legacy, or by means of trade and industry—I must know that all that wealth does not belong to me; what belongs to me is the right to an honourable livelihood, no better than that enjoyed by millions of others. The rest of my wealth belongs to the community and must be used for the welfare of the community. I enunciated this theory when the socialist theory was placed before the country in respect to the possessions held by zamindars and ruling chiefs. They would do away with these privileged classes. I want them to outgrow their greed and sense of possession, and to come down in spite of their wealth to the level of those who earn their bread by labour. The labourer has to realize that the wealthy man is less owner of his wealth than the labourer is owner of his own, viz., the power to work.

In Practice

The question how many can be real trustees according to this definition is beside the point. If the theory is true, it is immaterial whether many live up to it or only one man lives up to it. The question is of conviction. If you accept the principle of ahimsa, you have to strive to live up to it, no matter whether you succeed or fail. There is nothing in this theory which can be said to be beyond the grasp of intellect, though you may say it is difficult of practice. (H, 3-6-1939, p. 145)

I am not ashamed to own that many capitalists are friendly towards me and do not fear me. They know that I desire to end capitalism, almost, if not quite, as much as the most advanced Socialist or even Communist. But our methods differ, our languages differ.

No Make-shift

My theory of 'trusteeship' is no make-shift, certainly no camouflage. I am confident that it will survive all other theories. It has the sanction of philosophy and religion behind it. That possessors of wealth have not acted up to the theory does not prove its falsity; it proves the weakness of the wealthy. No other theory is compatible with nonviolence. In the nonviolent method wrongdoer compasses his own end, if he does not undo the wrong. For, either through nonviolent noncooperation he is made to see the error, or he finds himself completely isolated. (H, 16-12-1939, p. 376)

Acquisition of Wealth

Those who own money now, are asked to behave like trustees holding their riches on behalf of the poor. You may say that trusteeship is a legal fiction. But if people meditate over it constantly and try to act up to it, then life on earth would be governed far more by love than it is at present. Absolute trusteeship is an abstraction like Euclid's definition of a point, and is equally unattainable. But if we strive for it, we shall be able to go further in realizing state of equality on earth than by any other method.

It is my conviction that it is possible to acquire riches without consciously doing wrong. For example I may light on a gold mine in my one acre of land. But I accept the proposition that it is better not to desire wealth than to acquire it, and become its trustee. I gave up my own long ago, which should be proof enough of what I would like others to do. But what am I to advise those who are already wealthy or who would not shed the desire for wealth? I can only say to them that they should use their wealth for service.

It is true that generally the rich spend more on themselves than they need. But this can be avoided. Jamnalalji spent far less on himself than men of his own economic status and even than many middle-class men. I have come across innumerable rich persons who are stingy on themselves. For some it is a part of their nature to spend next to nothing on themselves, and they do not think that they acquire merit in so doing. The same applies to the sons of the wealthy. Personally, I do not believe in inherited riches. The well-to-do should educate and bring up their children so that they may learn how to be independent. The tragedy is that they do not do so. Their children do get some education, they even recite verses in praise of poverty, but they have no compunction about helping themselves to parental wealth. That being so, I exercise my common sense and advise what is practicable. Those of us, however, who consider it a duty to adopt poverty and believe in and desire economic equality may not be jealous of the rich, but should exhibit real happiness in our poverty which others may emulate. The sad fact is that those who are thus happy are few and far between. (H, 8-3-1942, p. 67)

A trustee has no heir but the public. In a State built on the basis of nonviolence, the commission of trustees will be regulated. Princes and zamindars will be on a par with the other men of wealth. (H, 12-4-1942, p. 116)

The Choice

As for the present owners of wealth, they will have to make their choice between class war and voluntarily converting themselves into trustees of their wealth. They will be allowed to retain the stewardship of their possessions and to use their talent, to increase the wealth, not for their own sakes, but for the sake of the nation and, therefore, without exploitation. The State will regulate the rate of commission, which they will get commensurate with the service rendered, and its value to society. Their children will inherit the stewardship only if they prove their fitness for it.

Supposing India becomes a free country tomorrow, all the capitalists will have an opportunity of becoming statutory trustees. But such a statute will not be imposed from above. It will have to come from below. When the people understand the implications of trusteeship and the atmosphere is ripe for it, the people themselves, beginning with gram panchayats, will begin to introduce such statutes. Such a thing coming from below is easy to swallow. Coming from above it is liable to prove a dead weight. (H, 31-3-1946, pp. 63-64)

Zamindars, Kisans

I am quite prepared to say for the sake of argument that the Zamindars are guilty of many crimes and of omissions and commissions. But that is no reason for the peasant and the labourer who are the salt of the earth to copy crime. If salt loses its savour, wherewith can it be salted?... To the landlords I say that, if what is said against you is true, I will warn you that your days are numbered.

You can no longer continue as lords and masters. You have a bright future if you become trustees of the poor Kisans. I have in mind not trustees in name but in reality. Such trustees will take nothing for themselves that their labour and care do not entitle them to. They then will find that no law will be able to reach them. The Kisans will be their friends. (H, 4-5-1947, p. 134)

If the Zamindars really become the trustees of their Zamindari for the sake of the ryots, there never could be an unholy league [between the two]. There is the difficult Zamindari question awaiting solution.... What one would love to see is proper, impartial and satisfactory understanding between the Zamindars, big and small, the ryots and the Governments, so that when the law is passed, it may not be a dead letter nor need force be used against the Zamindars or the ryots. Would that all changes, some of which must be radical, take place throughout India without bloodshed and without force! (H, 21-9-1947, p. 332)

Practical Trusteeship Formula

Trusteeship provides a means of transforming the present capitalist order of society into an egalitarian one. It gives no quarter to capitalism, but gives the present owning class a chance of reforming itself. It is based on the faith that human nature is never beyond redemption. It does not recognize any right of private ownership of property except so far as it may be permitted by society for its own welfare. It does not exclude legislative regulation of the ownership and use of wealth.

Thus under State-regulated trusteeship, an individual will not be free to hold or use his wealth for selfish satisfaction or in disregard of the interests of society. Just as it is proposed to fix a decent minimum living wage, even so a limit should be fixed for the maximum income that would be allowed to any person in society. The difference between such minimum and maximum incomes should be reasonable and equitable and variable from time to time so much so that the tendency would be towards obliteration of the difference.

Under the Gandhian economic order the character of production will be determined by social necessity and not by personal whim or greed. (H, 25-10-1952, p. 301; the document, it is believed, was drafted by Prof. M. L. Dantwala)

Gandhi's Philosophy on Trusteeship

Economic equality is the master key to nonviolent independence. Working for economic equality means abolishing the eternal conflict between capital and labour. It means the leveling down of the few rich in whose hands is concentrated the bulk of the nation's wealth on the one hand, and the leveling up of the semi-starved naked millions on the other. A nonviolent system of government is clearly an impossibility, so long as the wide gulf between the rich and the hungry millions persists. The contrast between the palaces of New Delhi and the miserable hovels of the poor, labouring class nearby cannot last one day in a free India in which the poor will enjoy the same power as the richest in the land.

A violent and bloody revolution is a certainty one day unless there is a voluntary abdication of riches and the power that riches give and sharing them for the common good. I adhere to my doctrine of trusteeship in spite of the ridicule that has been poured upon it. It is true that it is difficult to reach. So is nonviolence. But we made up our minds in 1920 to negotiate that steep ascent. We have found it worth the effort.

Nonviolent Way

By the nonviolent method, we seek not to destroy the capitalist, we seek to destroy capitalism. We invite the capitalist to regard himself as a trustee for those on whom he depends for the making, the retention and the increase of his capital. Nor need the worker wait for his conversion. If capital is power, so is work. Either is dependent on the other. Immediately the worker realizes his strength, he is din a position to become a co-sharer with the capitalist instead of remaining his slave. If he aims at becoming the sole owner, he will most likely be killing the goose that lays the golden eggs.

Not need I be afraid of some one else taking my place when I have non-co-operated. For I expect to influence my co-workers so as not to help the wrong-doing of my employer. This kind of education of the mass of workers is no doubt a slow process, but as it is also the surest, it is necessarily the quickest. It can be easily demonstrated in the end of the worker and as no human being is so bad as to be beyond redemption, no human being is so perfect as to warrant his destroying him whom he wrongly considers to be wholly evil.

Community Welfare

I am inviting those people who consider themselves as owners today to act as trustees, i.e., owners, not in their own right, but owners in the right of those whom they have exploited. It has become the fashion these days to say that society cannot be organized or run on nonviolent lines. I join issue on that point. In a family, when the father slaps his delinquent child, the latter does not think of retaliating. He obeys his father not because of the deterrent effect of the slap but because of the offended love which he senses behind it. That, in my opinion, is an epitome of the way in which society is or should be governed. What is true of the family must be true of society which is but a larger family.

Supposing I have come by a fair amount of wealth—either by way of legacy, or by means of trade and industry—I must know that all that wealth does not belong to me; what belongs to me is the right to an honourable livelihood, no better than that enjoyed by millions of others. The rest of my wealth belongs to the community and must be used for the welfare of the community. I enunciated this theory when the socialist theory was placed before the country in respect to the possessions held by zamindars and ruling chiefs. They would do away with these privileged classes. I want them to outgrow their greed and sense of possession, and to come down in spite of their wealth to the level of those who earn their bread by labour. The labourer has to realize that the wealthy man is less owner of his wealth than the labourer is owner of his own, viz., the power to work.

In Practice

The question how many can be real trustees according to this definition is beside the point. If the theory is true, it is immaterial whether many live up to it or only one man lives up to it. The question is of conviction. If you accept the principle of ahimsa, you have to strive to live up to it, no matter whether you succeed or fail. There is nothing in this theory which can be said to be beyond the grasp of intellect, though you may say it is difficult of practice. (H, 3-6-1939, p. 145) I am not ashamed to own that many capitalists are friendly towards me and do not fear me. They know that I desire to end capitalism, almost, if not quite, as much as the most advanced Socialist or even Communist. But our methods differ, our languages differ.

No Make-shift

My theory of 'trusteeship' is no make-shift, certainly no camouflage. I am confident that it will survive all other theories. It has the sanction of philosophy and religion behind it. That possessors of wealth have not acted up to the theory does not prove its falsity; it proves the weakness of the wealthy. No other theory is compatible with nonviolence. In the nonviolent method wrong-doer compasses his own end, if he does not undo the wrong. For, either through nonviolent noncooperation he is made to see the error, or he finds himself completely isolated.

Acquisition of Health

Those who own money now, are asked to behave like trustees holding their riches on behalf of the poor. You may say that trusteeship is a legal fiction. But if people meditate over it constantly and try to act up to it, then life on earth would be governed far more by love than it is at present. Absolute trusteeship is an abstraction like Euclid's definition of a point, and is equally unattainable. But if we strive for it, we shall be able to go further in realizing state of equality on earth than by any other method.

It is my conviction that it is possible to acquire riches without consciously doing wrong. For example I may light on a gold mine in my one acre of land. But I accept the proposition that it is better not to desire wealth than to acquire it, and become its trustee. I gave up my own long ago, which should be proof enough of what I would like others to do. But what am I to advise those who are already wealthy or who would not shed the desire for wealth? I can only say to them that they should use their wealth for service.

It is true that generally the rich spend more on themselves than they need. But this can be avoided. Jamnalalji spent far less on himself than men of his own economic status and even than many middle-class men. I have come across innumerable rich persons who are stingy on themselves. For some it is a part of their nature to spend next to nothing on themselves, and they do not think that they acquire merit in so doing.

The same applies to the sons of the wealthy. Personally, I do not believe in inherited riches. The well-to-do should educate and bring up their children so that they may learn how to be independent. The tragedy is that they do not do so. Their children do get some education, they even recite verses in praise of poverty, but they have no compunction about helping themselves to parental wealth. That being so, I exercise my common sense and advise what is practicable.

Those of us, however, who consider it a duty to adopt poverty and believe in and desire economic equality may not be jealous of the rich, but should exhibit real happiness in our poverty which others may emulate. The sad fact is that those who are thus happy are few and far between. A trustee has no heir but the public. In a State built on the basis of nonviolence, the commission of trustees will be regulated. Princes and zamindars will be on a par with the other men of wealth.

The Choice

As for the present owners of wealth, they will have to make their choice between class war and voluntarily converting themselves into trustees of their wealth. They will be allowed to retain the stewardship of their possessions and to use their talent, to increase the wealth, not for their own sakes, but for the sake of the nation and, therefore, without exploitation. The State will regulate the rate of commission, which they will get commensurate with the service rendered, and its value to society. Their children will inherit the stewardship only if they prove their fitness for it.

Supposing India becomes a free country tomorrow, all the capitalists will have an opportunity of becoming statutory trustees. But such a statute will not be imposed from above. It will have to come from below. When the people understand the implications of trusteeship and the atmosphere is ripe for it, the people themselves, beginning with gram panchayats, will begin to introduce such statutes. Such a thing coming from below is easy to swallow. Coming from above it is liable to prove a dead weight.

Zamindars,Kisans

I am quite prepared to say for the sake of argument that the Zamindars are guilty of many crimes and of omissions and commissions. But that is no reason for the peasant and the labourer who are the salt of the earth to copy crime. If salt loses its savour, wherewith can it be salted?...

To the landlords I say that, if what is said against you is true, I will warn you that your days are numbered. You can no longer continue as lords and masters. You have a bright future if you become trustees of the poor Kisans. I have in mind not trustees in name but in reality. Such trustees will take nothing for themselves that their labour and care do not entitle them to. They then will find that no law will be able to reach them. The Kisans will be their friends. (H, 4-5-1947, p. 134)

If the Zamindars really become the trustees of their Zamindari for the sake of the ryots, there never could be an unholy league [between the two]. There is the difficult Zamindari question awaiting solution.... What one would love to see is proper, impartial and satisfactory understanding between the Zamindars, big and small, the ryots and the Governments, so that when the law is passed, it may not be a dead letter nor need force be used against the Zamindars or the ryots. Would that all changes, some of which must be radical, take place throughout India without bloodshed and without force!

Trusteeship (Gandhism)

Trusteeship is a socioeconomic philosophy that was propounded by Mahatma Gandhi. Putting it in Gandhiji's words "Supposing I have come by a fair amount of wealth -- either by way of legacy, or by means of trade and industry – I must know that all that wealth does not belong to me; what belongs to me is the right to an honourable livelihood, no better than that enjoyed by millions of others. The rest of my wealth belongs to the community and must be used for the welfare of the community." Gandhiji along with his followers, after their release from the prison formulated a "simple" and a "practical" formula where Trusteeship was explained.

It had the following 6 points, which were later published in the newspaper 'Harijan'.

"1) Trusteeship provides a means of transforming the present capitalist order of society into an egalitarian one. It gives no quarter to capitalism, but gives the present owning class a chance of reforming itself. It is based on the faith that human nature is never beyond redemption.

2) It does not recognize any right of private ownership of property except so far as it may be permitted by society for its own welfare.

3) It does not exclude legislative regulation of the ownership and use of wealth.

4) Thus under State-regulated trusteeship, an individual will not be free to hold or use his wealth for selfish satisfaction or in disregard of the interests of society.

5) Just as it is proposed to fix a decent minimum living wage, even so a limit should be fixed for the maxmum income that

would be allowed to any person in society. The difference between such minimum and maximum incomes should be reasonable and equitable and variable from time to time so much so that the tendency would be towards obliteration of the difference.

6) Under the Gandhian economic order the character of production will be determined by social necessity and not by personal whim or greed." – *Harijan, 25-10-1952*

Influences

The founder of the Tata group, JRD Tata was influenced by Gandhi's idea of trusteeship. He developed his personal and professional life based on this idea.

Corps and Trusteeship: A Gandhian Perspective

Obviously, corps and the world economy they have largely shaped have changed tremendously since Mohandas Gandhi was killed in 1948. Nevertheless, much is the same except in degree. Gandhi's comprehensive vision has relevance for corps today. Much of the following is culled from R. B. Upadyaya's 1976 book, Social Responsibility of Business and the Trusteeship Theory of Mahatma Gandhi.

Gandhi had some things to say about corporate power, and had much to say about how to respond to that and other power. He strongly supported the right to private property, "subject, *of course*, to the fact that it does not come into conflict with social interest." [emphasis added] Private property was seen as necessary for people's livelihoods, which were to be locally based as much as possible. But there was no question that the bundle of rights that made property "private" should not extend to the point where they would damage community interest. Under trusteeship "no unrestricted and irresponsible ownership can be permitted."

Recognizing that the accumulation of large amounts of capital by "big business" could confer great power on certain individuals, Gandhi's view was that "these may be subject to special limitation and regulation, to cooperative ownership or 'diversified' public ownership under the control and management of the community, so that they do not unduly increase the power of an individual or a group of individuals or the State itself to the detriment of individual freedom and social interest."" The trusteeship theory considers hard work and intelligence as virtues to be materially rewarded. Accordingly, "the social structure should afford adequate opportunities to all to use their labour and intelligence to the fullest extent possible and to enrich themselves, of course, always with fair means." And recognizing that society in large part enables individuals to legitimately accumulate wealth, Gandhi believed the well-off have a moral obligation to give back to society. But that wealth must have been accumulated fairly and honestly; the trusteeship concept leaves no room for "ill-gotten wealth acquired from exploitation of others." Land, of direct and immediate importance to many more people in early 20th Century India than it is for us today, had a special place in the trusteeship theory. It was considered to belong to society, "available for equal distribution among its cultivators". This implies "reasonable" limits upon individual land ownership.

While social norms and established institutions are essential for a society's stability, the social system "should not allow concentration of power in the hands of a few." People do harm to each other not so much because of their inherent nature, but mainly due to the nature of the corps that control so much of our lives. Thus, power should be decentralized among many institutions. It should primarily rest at the local level, radiating outward from there, rather than the reverse. If necessary, the entire social order should be changed to make this happen.

Knowing that many people were unaware of alternatives, Gandhi actually preferred violent resistance to oppression rather than passive acceptance of it. But he basically believed that change should not be accomplished by violence. Even where violence is successful in eliminating one form of oppression, it invariably substitutes another. Rather, societal change begins with a change of heart in each one of us as we open ourselves to our connections with others and actively search for truth. From there, the basis of change moves to dialogue that seeks change of heart in others by persuasion, and that keeps us open to the further changes that may (some say *do*) result from true dialogue.

In dealing with oppressive structures, such dialogue is often very difficult to achieve. It may be necessary to use "pressure and force of circumstances" to remove structural obstacles, or to bring people in positions of power to see the need for dialogue. Elections, in a society in which meaningful voting is possible, are the next appropriate means for bringing about necessary change. Only after those means have been tried and found insufficient should direct, nonviolent pressure campaigns be instituted. And even when such campaigns are undertaken, their purpose should remain the same: to remove obstacles to true dialogue, that is, dialogue among equals in power.

Pinpointing a crucial difference between such pressure tactics and violence, Gandhi once said, "Love compels, it does not coerce." Societal pressures based upon love may pressure people into making decisions they would not otherwise make, or leave them no room to act in certain oppressive ways, but that is an acceptable alternative to allowing oppressive conditions that allow other people few or no choices, and that constitute violence against the human spirit. For instance, legislation is appropriate to prevent excessive accumulation of land or wealth, as such accumulation "has its origin in the exploitation and oppression of the people."

Gandhi believed that greater corporate control meant greater likelihood of exploitation. While recognizing the value of some large-scale industry, he said it should be limited, with most people self-employed in small farms, trade, cottage industries, etc. He said large corps that do exist should be run on trusteeship principles "as socioeconomic institutions", that is, they should serve societal interests first and foremost.

Getting back to individual change of heart, Gandhi believed that most large corps could not exist if people would do away with their "superfluous desires". However, today's sophisticated and pervasive advertising industry had not been appreciably developed in Gandhi's time, and one can only wonder what his response would be now. He might well make it the focus of a major campaign.

11

Dandi March

Introduction

One of the momentous events in the history of Indian struggle for independence was the Dandi Salt March, launched under the unparalleled leadership of M K Gandhi. With this historic event, The Civil Disobedience Movement was formally introduced on a nation-wide basis. Within the context of the Indian freedom struggle, the Dandi Salt March holds a place of paramount importance. The entire nation coalesced under the call of a single man, internalizing the cherished doctrines of ahimsa or non violence, and satyagraha or passive resistance. With an awakened political consciousness, all segments of the Indian community plunged into a battle, which till date is an instance of the indefatigable power of civilian resistance.

Circumstances Leading to the Dandi March

The political and social milieu of India was in turmoil following the formation of the Simon Commission for drawing up a constitution for India and the subsequent rejection of the Nehru Report. Gandhi requested the Viceroy, Lord Irwin, to mellow his stance in dealing with the constitutional crisis. On March 2nd 1930, Gandhi wrote a letter to the Viceroy wherein he highlighted an 11 point Charter of Demands. This included a considerable reduction in the Pound-Sterling-Rupee exchange rate, curtailing of military budget, a fifty percent reduction in land revenue, preservation of indigenous textile machinery, abolition of Salt Tax and releasing political prisoners. The British government did not react favorably to any of the propositions made by the Congress. The political segment of the country took no time to realize that the British government would not relent to any kind of persuasions. Anti British sentiments flared up as never before and the launch of a civil disobedience movement became inevitable. On February 15th, the Congress Working committee gave the authority to Gandhi and his followers to initiate the civil disobedience. The first step in this direction was the Dandi March.

Violation of British laws constituted an integral part of civil disobedience. The British salt tax law captured the attention of Gandhi and soon became the center of his anti British agendas. According to the British salt tax law, the sale or manufacture of salt by any other source barring the British government would be adjudged as a criminal offence, liable for punishment by law. Salt was extremely essential for the people of India, particularly for its temperate climate. The low-lying coastal regions of the country had extensive reserves of the mineral that were easily available to the laborers. The new salt tax law, however, impelled them to purchase the mineral that could be collected free of cost. In Gandhi's words; "There is no article like salt, outside water, by taxing which the sate can reach even the starving millions, the sick, the maimed and the utterly helpless. The tax constitutes, therefore, the most in human poll tax, the ingenuity of man can devise." Moreover, the issue of salt cut across class, caste, regional and ethnic distinctions and Gandhi could unite the entire country bound by a single cause. This oppressive salt tax law thus became the pivot around which the program of civil disobedience was designed. The British salt tax law provided the apt background against which a massive satyagraha struggle could be launched, throughout the country.

The Commencement of the Dandi March

When the Viceroy turned a deaf ear to the pleas of Gandhi, a disheartened Mahatma said; "On bended knees I asked for bread and I have received stone instead". In the letter to Lord Irwin, Gandhi had mentioned; "If my letter makes no appeal to your heart, on the eleventh day of his month I shall proceed with such co-workers of the Ashram as I can take, to disregard the provision of the Salt Laws." To give effect to this promise made by Gandhi in his letter to Lord Irwin, on the historic day of March 12th, he embarked on his Dandi March. Gandhi's entourage consisted of seventy nine members of his Sabarmati Ashram, who were well trained in the principles of satyagraha. As part of the preparation of this massive satyagraha campaign, Gandhi addressed a mass meeting on 10th March attended by the inmates of the Sabarmati ashram. At the prayer meeting on 11th March at Sabarmati Ashram, Gandhi invoked the inner strength of the satyagrahis and resolved to continue their non violent means of passive resistance until swaraj could be achieved in India. Finally, on 12th March at 6.30 a.m., Gandhi set out on his two hundred miles long journey, from Sabarmati Ashram to Dandi in the company of his few chosen followers. In this journey to Dandi, Gandhi's trail increased in size as thousands of inspired followers joined him in his march.

On 13th March Gandhi delivered a speech at Bareja, where he invited the villagers among whom there was a considerable number of Christians and Muslims, to join hands in supporting the cause of India's freedom. In his 14th March speech at Vasana, Gandhi asked the amassed audience whether they would believe him, if he made a prediction that a day would dawn when the British would apologize to the Indians. Gandhi addressed to the people of Dabhan on March 15th. In this speech he appealed to the people that if they have the armor of inner strength, they should boycott Government jobs, endorse Khadi, reject foreign made goods and abandon alcohol. Armed with an innate commitment to the eternal spirit of truth and self righteousness, they should join the army of salt satyagrahis.

On 17th March Gandhi delivered a speech at Anand, wherein he urged the students to withdraw from their academic pursuits, until the salt satyagraha campaign achieved its goal. On 23rd March, he challenged the British government's capability to arrest him although he had embarked on a mission to disobey British laws. In the speech delivered on 25th March, Gandhi declared that he had decided to stay at the residence of a Muslim friend, from where he would undertake his satyagraha struggle. In his way Gandhi sought to garner the support of the Muslim community as well in his satyagraha campaign against the unjust British salt tax law. On 26th March, 28th March and 29th March, Gandhi delivered speeches at Ankleshwar, the bank of River Keem and Bhatgam respectively. In Bhatgam, Gandhi condemned indulgence and extravagance and said that there is no place for these in a satyagraha campaign. Addressing the cloth merchants of Bombay who attended his speech at Sandihiyer on March 30th, Gandhi said that the involvement of the merchant class in the satyagraha struggle signifies their commitment to the cause of Indian's struggle for freedom.

On April 5th, Gandhi addressed the associated press at Dandi. He appreciated the government for resorting to absolute non interference, while he was on his march to Dandi. With the blessings of God, he communicated his noble intention to initiate civil disobedience in the company of his followers on 6th April. Since the incident of Jallianwallah Bagh massacre, 6th April had come to symbolize a day of self abasement and purging of the soul. The day, declared Gandhi would begin with fasting and prayer. On 6th March, Gandhi, on the Dandi beach, breached the British salt laws. He picked up a fistful of salt and mud and manufactured salt by boiling it in sea water. He urged his followers to violate the British Salt Tax law by manufacturing salt all along the sea coast. It was decided that the crusade against the salt tax would be carried on till April 13th that mark the National Week.

The Impact of Dandi March

The immediate repercussion of the Dandi march was the arrest of Nehru and several other delegates of the Congress. On 5th May, midnight, Gandhi was arrested from Karadi. The wider impact of Dandi march on all sections of the society was simply insurmountable. The entire nation joined forces with Mahatma Gandhi. Salt was being made and bought illegally throughout the country. Gandhi's popularity reached an all time high, with several new followers joining the troop of his satyagrahis. The Dandi episode unfolded a new chapter in the history of Indian nationalism. The large scale participation of the masses in India's struggle for freedom commenced with the Dandi march.

The event of Dandi March assumed a much wider significance as it not only remained a landmark incident in India's pre independence history, but took a symbolic significance that eternally appealed to the political and social scenario of the world. Dandi March has come to epitomize the inherent potential of any form of passive civilian resistance. It affirmed the halo of Gandhi as the Mahatma, for he proved to the world that the victory of a guide is in practicing what he preaches. His ideologies of satyagraha and ahimsa found physical manifestation in his simple gesture of picking up a stick and walking a distance of two hundred miles, as an expression of his denial and violation of British laws.

History of Dandi March

The march on foot undertaken by Gandhi and seventy-eight Congress volunteers was the most significant event in the history of the breach of salt law in our country. It was commenced in accordance with a fixed schedule to be carried on by them during the long journey ending at Dandi. Undoubtedly, it was a disciplined band of nonviolent satyagrahis who were to present a new model of Satyagraha which later on converted into a bigger movement at all-India level. On 12 March 1930 at 6-10 A.M. Gandhi came out of his room, calm and composed, accompanied by Prabhashankar Patani, Mahadev Desai and Pyarelal, his secretary. He offered prayers, looked at his watch and exactly at 6.30 A.M. commenced his march with seventy-eight volunteers.

With his usual gentle smile, betokening his unifying faith in the justice of the cause he was pursuing and in the success of the great campaign he had embarked upon, he headed the procession with quick and unfaltering steps. 'Like the historic march of Ram Chandra to Lanka, the march of Dandi would be memorable' exclaimed Motilal Nehru in a message. P.C. Ray called it the 'exodus of Israelites under Moses? Jawaharlal Nehru called Gandhi, '.... the pilgrim on his quest of truth, quiet, peaceful, determined and fearless who would continue that quiet pilgrimage regardless of consequences.' The satyagrahis were to face a fatiguing journey through heat and dust of the Kheda villages. Thousands of men, women and children accompanied the marching column for a few miles and thousands lined the route and showered flowers, coins, currency notes and kum kum at the satyagrahis.

Following the commencement of his epic Dandi March, a tremendous wave of enthusiasm swept over the entire country. The historic day was celebrated all over India. Calcutta woke that morning amidst sounds of conch shells and shouts of 'Gandhiji ki Jai'. At a conference of the Congress leaders of Bengal a decision was taken to appoint immediately an ad hoc council to be called the Bengal Civil Disobedience Council, with the object of carrying out the programme outlined by Gandhiji. J. M. Sen Gupta appealed to all men and women of the province to enrol themselves as volunteers for the Civil Disobedience Movement. He said, 'Bengal is on trial. She had always been in the vanguard of the country's battle for freedom and cannot lag behind. Let us plunge head-long in the fight and regain the rights which are ours.'

In Bombay, a public meeting was held under the presidentship of K. F. Nariman. He exhorted the audience to get ready for the fight. The 'War Council' of the Bombay Provincial Congress Committee announced a lit of 'iron-sides' to join the first detachment of volunteers from the town. In Madras, at a public meeting at Tilak Ghat, prayers were offered for the success of Civil Disobedience campaign by the Madras District Congress Committee, Andhra Congress Committee, the Triplicate Congress Sabha and the political section of the Youth League. The meeting reiterated India's resolve to achieve Swaraj by nonviolent means under Gandhi's leadership by following his path.'

In Lahore, a band of Congress volunteers paraded the streets and raised shouts of 'Mahatma Gandhi Ki Jai'. In a mammoth meeting of the citizens of the town, held under the auspices of the City Congress Committee, Maulana Abdul Qadir, in opening the proceedings, said, 'The 12th of March would be a red letter day and it would figure in letters of gold in the future history of India'. He hoped that the people of India, from that day onward would give practical demonstration of their determination to win freedom. He believed that as soon as the people of the Punjab would receive the news of Gandhi's arrest, they would suspend their business and work out the plan of the movement.

In Peshawar, the 'Satyagraha Day' was observed by taking out a procession and holding a public meeting. Resolutions reiterating the pledge of independence and wishing Godspeed to the soldiers of freedom and congratulating Vallabhbhai Patel on his imprisonment were unanimously passed. Besides, a large number of volunteers were enlisted for the Satyagraha. Civil Disobedience Day was celebrated in Delhi in a meeting attended by about 10,000 persons, including a large number of ladies. Devdas Gandhi gave the detailed history of the salt tax and called it the most 'barbarous' tax which effected the poor classes, and pleaded for its abolition immediately. He also exhorted the people to observe complete but peaceful hartal if Mahatma Gandhi was arrested.

Allahabad, the nerve centre of U. P. politics, witnessed scenes of enthusiasm in connection with the celebration of the commencement of the Satyagraha campaign. Jawaharlal Nehru hoisted the national flag over the building occupied by the offices of the A.I.C.C., the City Congress Committee and the All-India Spinners' Association, U.P. branch. A large gathering participated in the ceremony. While addressing the audience, Nehru said that the pledge of Satyagraha laid stress on nonviolence which was the very basis of the Civil Disobedience campaign. He warned that only those who were convinced of the efficacy of that method either as a creed or as a policy in the present circumstances of the country, should take the pledge. He opined that nonviolence was not a convenient shelter either for cowards or for those who wanted to prepare for violence. He asked the non-believers in nonviolence to withdraw from the movement to give others a chance. In Ahmedabad, a meeting of the Youth League was held in which a resolution was passed empowering the secretaries to enlist volunteers for Civil Disobedience Movement. About twenty-five names were enlisted on the spot including two secretaries and Miss Mridula Ambalal, daughter of a local mill-magnate. The 'Dandi March Day' was observed in Nagpur by hoisting the national flag. A procession passed through the main bazaars of the town, and, thereafter, a public meeting was also held. Gandhi's letter to the Viceroy was read out and explained to the audience. An appeal for the enlistment of volunteers was also made. While exhorting the people to give the moment their whole-hearted support M. V. Abhyankar said, 'I shall perish in the struggle for Independence or live to enjoy freedom after its achievement? 14

Similar celebrations were held all over the country and considerable enthusiasm was aroused with people for participating in the Civil disobedience Movement. For the first time, a new spirit for Swaraj-full and complete-was found bubbling everywhere. The Viceroy informed the Secretary of State on 13 March 1930, 'Most of my thought at the moment is concentrated upon Gandhi. I wish I felt sure what the right way to deal with him is.' The same day Gandhi and his satyagrahis reached a small village, Aslali, where they were received well by the villagers. Gandhi emphasised the importance of salt and criticised the salt tax levied by the government. He stated, 'The poor destitute villagers do not have the strength to get this tax repealed. We want to develop this strength... We should make a resolve that we shall prepare salt, eat it, sell if to the people and, while doing so, court imprisonment, if necessary. If, out of Gujarat's Population of 90 lakhs, we leave out women and children, and the remaining 30 lakhs et ready to violate the salt tax, the Government does not have enough accommodation in jails to house so many people.'

Next day, Gandhi, who was apprehensive of his arrest, informed Jawaharlal Nehru, 'The news given to me of my impending arrest was said to be absolutely authentic. But we have reached the second stage. We take the third tonight' The second halt of the Dandi marchers was at Bareja, a village with a Population of 2,500. He emphasised the importance of Khadi, its production and use by the villagers. 'Khadi is the foundation of our freedom struggle.... I request you to renounce luxuries and buy Khadi from this heap before you.

'We have come forward to win our freedom from this tyrannical and oppressive Government. If we cannot put our own house in order in an organized manner, how shall we run the country's Government? I ask you, therefore, to learn order and organization.... This struggle against the Government on which we have embarked is not going to reach its conclusion with five, or twenty-five, or even millions of men getting killed. We have to look after other things also simultaneously.' 18 As Gandhi entered the Kheda district, memories-some sweet, some bitter-filled his mind. It was while working in this district that he became one with the lives of people. He had seen nearly all the villages of the district and had covered many of them on foot. He stated, 'I have come to Navagam in the middle of a battle... The Government found some pretext or other to arrest Vallabhbhai... Pressure was brought to hear on the Magistrate some how to serve a notice on Sardar and he was arrested. What could a poor Magistrate do where the entire atmosphere is vitiated?

When some headmen and matadars of Kheda district submitted their resignations as a protest against the oppressive policy of the government, Gandhi advised them, 'Remember that in the resignations, you have handed in I see God's hand. The Kheda District has made an auspicious beginning.' At Vasana, where the villagers had gathered to accord reception to the marchers and listen to their leader, Gandhi explained that abolition of the salt-tax or remission of some taxes would not mean Swaraj for them. Winning of Swaraj was not going to be so easy as they might think. It was only a way to it and by following it they would reach the goal of freedom. He had a word of praise for the headmen of Navagam, Vavdi, Agam, Mahelaj and other villages who had tendered their resignations. 'Why should they stick to Headmanship for the mere five rupees a month that the government pays them? If the Collector summons a Headman, let him say, 'Give us back our Sardar. Grant us a remission in land revenue.' At Nadiad, a town with a population of thirty-one thousand, Gandhi reminded the people, 'Bound by the chains of slavery, we are being crushed at present and we want to shake them off.' He wished all government servants to give up their jobs. A government job gave them the power to tyrannize over others. Finally, be asked them to enlist themselves as volunteers. And as soon as he got behind the bars or as soon as the All-India Congress Committee gave a call, they should come forward to offer themselves for being jailed. 'Then alone shall I believe that Nadiad has made its contribution to our struggle'.

In a letter to Jayaprakash Narayan which Gandhi wrote from Anand on 17 March, he explained, 'No where else have I observed such zeal for sacrifice as has been displayed by the Ashram women. At present the women are to a great extent managing the internal affairs of the Ashram. The chance of acquiring such experience will never be repeated. I would therefore advise you to send Prabhavati there. After my arrest the Ashram women too will court imprisonment. I think Prabhavati should join them. She is worthy in every respect.'

At Anand, an educational centre of Patidars, Gandhi demanded, 'In your hands lies the honour of the Patidars of Charotar. You are like salt in the sea of Patidars. If the salt loses its savour, wherewith shall it be salted ? Salt is more sapid than either sugar or juggery. The latter may even cause jaundice, whereas a pinch of salt adds flavour to the meal. If Anand gives up its savour if courage and such other virtues which have been attributed to the Patidars are not displayed in Anand at this juncture, where else can one see them?.' The students' services to the national cause were also applauded. They were advised to suspend their studies for as long as this struggle continued. Formerly, Gandhi had asked his students to leave schools and to set up national schools.

But this time he asked them to leave schools and come out on the 'battle-field' and become 'mendicants' for the sake of the country. But he did not ask them to give up their studies for good, but only to give up book-learning so long as the struggle lasted. At Borsad, the reception of Gandhi and his satyagrahis was celebrated with the immediate announcement of the resignations of headmen, matadars and ravanias of twenty villages of the taluka. Over one hundred village officers of twenty-five villages submitted their resignations.

The government sources commented, 'Gandhi's attention is directed on two points *i.e.* resignations of patels and enrolling volunteers. Under his instructions local workers are trying to get more resignations under the threat of social boycott. They were warmly received by the village folk. They were keen to listen to Gandhi's discourse· He explained to them, 'Our patience has been severely tried. We must free ourselves from the yoke of this Government and we are prepared to undergo any hardships that we may have to suffer in order to secure Swaraj, it is our duty as well as our right to secure Swaraj.

'Today we are defying the salt law. Tomorrow we shall have to consign other laws to the wastepaper basket. Doing so we shall practise such severe noncooperation that finally it will not be possible for the administration to be carried on at all. Let the Government then, to carry on its rule, use guns against us, send us to prison, hang us. But how many can be given such punishment? Try and calculate how much time it will take a lakh of Britishers to hang thirty crores of persons.'

Gandhi once again exhorted the students to leave their institutions and join the struggle for independence. He desired that all students studying in the local high school and who were above the age of fifteen, and all teachers too, should enrol themselves. He pleaded that wherever revolutions had taken place, that is, in Japan, China, Egypt, Ireland and in England, students and teachers had played a prominent role. In Europe, war broke out on 4 August 1914, and when Gandhi reached England on the 6th of the same month, he found that students had left colleges and marched out with arms. Gandhi further explained that his prostrating himself on the ground for the sake of removing the hardships of crores of people was of no avail. He had spared no efforts in drafting appeals.

He became a revolutionary when politeness and persuasion proved infructious. He indeed found peace in describing himself as a revolutionary and appealed that in a revolution of that nature which was calm, peaceful and truthful, people should get themselves enrolled regardless of the religious faith to which they belonged. He was confident that if they enlisted themselves with sincerity and if they could keep up their courage, the salt tax would have been abolished, this administration would have come to an end and all the hardships enumerated in the letter to the Viceroy as well as those which had not been enumerated would have to cease. On 19 March, the party of satyagrahis reached Ras Taluka where Sardar Patel was arrested and sentenced to prison and in which he had carried on such a vigorous struggle in 1924 that the Government had finally to admit its 'error and mete out justice that should not have required a struggle. It is as if Sardar was sentenced to prison as a reward for having served you'.

During the short stay of Gandhi, some of the headmen and matadars had handed in their resignations. But Gandhi expressed unhappiness on the small number of resignations at Ras. In fact, the headman, talati and revania were the representatives of the government in the villages and it was through these persons that the latter carried on its administration. A village which was afraid of a handful of men and continued to act in a manner contrary to its own wishes, neither enhanced the prestige of the headman, the talati or the revania nor that of the villagers themselves. Sardar Patel had been making great effort to end this indignity. Gandhi praised the services rendered by Sardar Patel. He also apprised the villagers of his mission. He explained 'Sardar neither made speeches nor came here to foment trouble. Neither the Magistrate nor you had acted any sort of trouble. The task for which Sardar had approached you was not a secret to anyone. A satyagrahi has no secrets....... What secret can a satyagrahi like Sardar have?' He had come there to clear the way for Gandhi and he had not come there to convey the message regarding salt. Gandhi was at a loss to know about the offence committed by Sardar Patel and wondered that a man of his stature should have been awarded a sentence of three months' jail and labelled it a matter of shame to the Sardar and to the government. Gandhi wished that a person like Sardar Patel should be sentenced to a term of seven years' imprisonment or be exiled. 'It would not befit the Government to sentence me to three months' imprisonment. Exile for life or hanging would be a punishment fit for a person like me. I am guility of sedition. It is my dharma to commit sedition against the

Government. I am teaching this dharma to the people. A regime under which tyranny is being perpetrated, under which the rich and the poor are made to pay the same amount of tax on an item like salt under which exorbitant sums are being spent on watchmen, the police and the army under which the highest executive receives a salary which is five thousand times the income of the cultivator, under which an annual revenue of 25 crores of rupees is derived from narcotics and liquor, under which foreign cloth of the value of Rs. 60 cores is imported every year, and under which crores of persons continue to remain unemployed, it is one's dharma to rise against and destroy such a regime, to pray that fire may consume its policies.

Meanwhile, the A.I.C.C. held a meeting on the banks of the Sabarmati on 20 March. Besides the president Jawaharlal Nehru, it was attended by other prominent leaders like Maulana Azad, Sarojini Naidu, P. D. Tandon, Abbas Tyabji, Darbar Gopaldas, J. B. Kripalani, N.C. Kalelkar, Kasturba Gandhi, Ansuyabehn and Mrs. Ambalal.

Many members excused themselves from attendance on the plea that they were busy with preparations for Civil Disobedience Movement, in their own areas. The leaders met under a sense of 'heavy' responsibility and the result was foregone conclusion. By its principal resolution, the A.I.C.C. confirmed the Working Committee's resolution authorising Gandhi to launch Civil Disobedience Movement. It laid down the conditions under which the various provinces should start Satyagraha on a mass scale.

The Provincial Congress Committees were given wide discretion about the manner, the form and the place of Civil Disobedience. It was open to them, to prepare their provinces for any form of Satyagraha, best suited to them. But it was clearly laid down that the salt Satyagraha should be undertaken in every province when it was possible. Other forms of Satyagraha might be prepared for, but should be reserved for the second stage of the campaign. In case Gandhi was arrested, the Provincial Congress Committees should immediately determine to start Civil Disobedience, and if he was not arrested, they should await instructions which he might issue on reaching his destination. He would give the necessary signal and the Provincial Congress Committees would be informed immediately through the A.I.C.C. Office.

The Government of India felt much concern over the resolution of Congress. The Home Member suggested, 'it is essential that we should able to give timely warning owing to local Governments'. He also suggested that the correspondence of the members of the Working Committee; the correspondence of the head office of the Congress and of all provincial Congress offices and provincial Congress Presidents and of any particular individual whose correspondence in local government concerned might regard as likely to yield 'specially important' information, should be censured.

It was barely ten days ago that Gandhi had begun his historic march and the actual campaign was yet to be started. The whole country was already in a state of forewent for a parallel to which one might recollect the 'hottest days' of the Noncooperation Movement of 1920-22. People in the provinces were planning to start the movement, and in some cases preliminary steps had already been initiated. In Bengal, for instance, which had for the moment, lost both its outstanding leaders, a 'War Council' had been formed. In the United Provinces, the Provincial Congress Committee had started a Satyagraha committee consisting of prominent leaders, including the President of the Congress himself. Judging from the signs, the whole country appeared in the throes of an agitation of unprecedented magnitude.

The Civil Disobedience plans of Gandhi and the Congress leaders. As the march proceeded, so the pressure of publicity and social boycott was built up and resignations began to occur in large numbers. By 22 March, approximate number of resignations were four from Ahmedabad district: twenty-seven from Kaita (of whom sixteen were from Borsad taluka) seventeen from Broach, and two from Surat. But Surat soon became the most affected district by 5 April. One hundred and forty headmen had resigned and ten clays later, the figure had risen to two hundred and twenty seven. Gandhi warned them, 'It will be regarded as cowardice to hand in one's resignation and then to withdraw it. There is no compulsion to resign. It is advisable to give up the post of Headman, looking upon it as something base, dirty and filthy.'

The speech delivered by Gandhi at Broach on 26 March dealt with the communal question. He explained that he had never dreamt that he could win Swaraj merely through his effort or assisted only by the Hindus. He sought the assistance of Muslims,

Parsis, Christians, Sikhs, Jews and all other Indians. He needed the assistance even of Englishmen. 'But I know too that all this combined assistance is worthless if I have not one other assistance, that is, from God. All is vain without His help. And if he is With this struggle, no other' help is necessary.

In a letter to Jawaharlal Nehru on 31 March Gandhi expressed his optimism about he forthcoming movement. 'Things seem to be shaping very well indeed in Gujarat... I feel you are right in attention to the salt tax for the time being. What more we can or should do. Unless you hear from me to the contrary, please take 6th April as the date for simultaneous beginning.'

At Jambusar, Kamaladevi Chattopadhyaya arrived to see Gandhi to remove the general impression that had gone abroad that as he had not included women in his first batch of volunteers, they might not be taken up at all. Gandhiji told her, 'If impatient mothers will be a little patient they will find ample scope for their zeal and sacrifice in this national struggle for freedom'. She asked Gandhi what women with children should do. He said that he neither desired nor expected women to neglect their children. They might have to wait and bide their time, and thus be of use in some ways. Those women, however, who could make some satisfactory arrangements to have the children well looked after, should join the struggle.

At Surat where Gandhi and the satyagrahis reached on I April, they received a big welcome. He called the salt tax as beastly, inhuman and a Satanic Law. 'I have not heard of such justice anywhere in the world where it prevails... To bow to an empire which dispenses such justice is not dharma but adharma. A man who prays to God every morning at dawn cannot, must not, pray for the good of such an empire. On the contrary while praying or saying the namaaz he should ask God to encompass the destruction of such a Satanic empire, such an inhuman government. To do so is dharma.' In a message to the nation in the issue of Young India dated 3 April 1930, Gandhi exhorted the people 'Remember 5th April', and scart mass Civil Disobedience regarding the salt laws. He advised them to observe nonviolence in the fullest sense of the term. This was to be the spontaneous action. The workers were required to merely guide the masses in initial stages. Later, the masses would regulate the movement themselves.

The congress volunteers would render aid wherever needed. They, however, would be expected to be in the forefront. They were advised not to take sides in any communal quarrel. Wherever, there was a violent eruption, volunteers were expected to die in the attempt to quell violence. Those who were to be engaged in Civil Disobedience were occupy themselves and induce others to be engaged in some national service, such as Khadi work, liquor and opium picketing, foreign-cloth shops, village sanitation, assisting the families of civil resistance prisoners in a variety of ways. Gandhi also expected that if there was a real response about civil resistance regarding the salt tax, people should by proper organisation secure boycott of foreign cloth through Khadi and secure total prohibition. This would mean a saving of 91 crores per year, and supplementary work for the millions of unemployed. 'If we secure these things, we cannot be far from independence. And not one of these things is beyond our capacity.

Thus at each village, where the party stopped, Gandhi spoke briefly, telling the villagers that a great ordeal was at hand. He filled his political appeal with exhortation relevant to village life, such as Khadi, cow-protection, cleanliness and untouchability. His appeal was not for money but for change of attitudes: he called on village officials to resign their posts which buttressed the exploitive regime. As he journeyed, he continued to give press interviews and to write to Navajivan and Young India, spreading his massage of Swaraj and giving instructions for the conduct of the campaign during the days ahead. Out of twenty-five days, which the journey took, the party of satyagrahis had walked for twenty-two days, excluding three days of Gandhi's silence. On his way, Gandhi passed by forty villages and towns and everywhere he addressed the audience. The whole countryside was awake to the call of the Mahatma.

At least fifty thousand persons heard his stirring message to the nation: his speeches were generally impassioned and always brave and there was a tone of pathos which had gone home to the hearts of the listeners. Despite all the fatigue and other hardships of the journey, he never allowed himself any comfort that was denied to the last man of his 'army'.

The satyagrahis reached Dandi on 5 April. Sarojini Naidu had already arrived there to welcome them. When interviewed by special correspondent of The Bombay Chronicle, Gandhi said, '

Government, perhaps, deserves congratulations for their policy of non-interference which is not exactly in keeping with their proved capacity for provoking popular sentiment.'

Next day he was to break the salt tax law. If the Civil Disobedience Movement become widespread in the country and the government tolerated it, the salt law, Gandhi declared, might be taken as abolished. He indeed had no doubt in his mind that the salt tax stood abolished the very moment that the decision to break that salt laws was reached. 'If they arrest me or my companions tomorrow, I shall not be surprised. I shall certainly not be pained. It would be absurd to be pained if we get something that we have invited on ourselves.'

Gandhi advised the people to make salt freely in every home, as our ancestors used to, and sell it from place to place, and they should continue doing so wherever possible till the government yielded, so much so that the salt in government stocks would become superfluous. 'If the awakening of the people in the country is true and real, the salt law is as good as abolished'.

Gandhi highlighted the importance of Dandi and praised the efforts of the people of the taluka. He explained,' Dandi was chosen not by a man but by God. How otherwise could we have chosen for the battlefield of Satyagraha such an out-of-the-way place-a place where no food grains are to be had, where there is scarcity of water, where thousands can assemble only with difficulty, walking ten miles from the railway station, and where if you are travelling on foot, you have to negotiate creeks full of slush and mud? The truth is that in this struggle we have to put up with suffering. You have made the road from Navsari to Dandi famous throughout the world by arranging for free drinking-water at frequent intervals all along it... Dandi should be a sacred ground for us, where we should utter no untruth, commit so sin. Everyone coming here should come with this devout feeling in his heart.' 'If you have not yet gone out to remove salt, let the whole village get together and go. Hold the salt in your fist and think that you are carrying in your hand salt worth Rs. 6 Crores. Every year the Government has been taking away from us Rs. 6 Crores through its monopoly of salt.'

Gandhi and his volunteers broke the salt laws at 8-30 A.M. on 6 April 1930 by taking a lump of natural salt which was deposited in a small pit. Hundreds of persons witnessed this scene. Sarojini Naidu stood by Gandhiji's side, and, as the symbolic gesture was made, she cried, 'Hail Deliverer'.

Gandhi, while picking up a lump of salt in his hand, said, 'With this, I am shaking the foundation of the British Empire.' Not a single policeman or excise officer was present there. While talking to the representative of the free press, Gandhi said, 'Now that the technical or ceremonial breach of the Salt Law has been committed it is open to any one who would take the risk of prosecution' under the Salt Law to manufacture salt wherever he wishes and wherever it is convenient. My advice is that the workers should everywhere manufacture salt to make use of it and to instruct the villagers to do so.'

'Thus the war against the salt tax should be continued during the national week. Those who are not engaged in this sacred work should devote themselves to a vigorous propaganda for the boycott of foreign cloth and the use of Khadar. They should also endeavour to manufacture as much Khadar as possible.' After Gandhi had addressed the meeting on 6 April about two tolas of salt which was taken by him in the morning and also cleaned by him, was auctioned for Rs. 525/-to Seth Ranchhod Shodhan, a mill-owner of Ahmedabad.

Gandhi's march on foot, form village to village through Gujarat which was his home and where his influence was greatest, aroused considerable interest and excitement. It has in fact appealed to the imagination of multitudes of people who were emotionally swayed by the dramatic turn of events. Throughout the march, Gandhiji went on preaching his cult of truth and nonviolence to the multitudes that gathered from far and near and he did not hesitate to impose the strictest discipline on the satyagrahis that flocked to his banner. The salt became the symbol of India's will to freedom. The same day the salt laws were broken throughout India at least by five million people at over 5,000 meetings. The entire countryside became acutely conscious of the struggle for Swaraj which was intensifying. The Dandi march received worldwide publicity. Soon the Civil Disobedience Movement spread simultaneously in western, northern, central, eastern and southern regions of India.

Bibliography

Ahmad, Razi, *Indian Peasant Movement and Mahatma Gandhi*, Shabd Prakashan, Delhi, 1987.

Andrews, C. F.: *The Gandhian Thought: Social & Political Development*, Akashdeep Pub. House, Delhi, 1990.

Bari, S.A.: *Gandhi's Doctrine of Civil Resistance*, Kalamkar Prakashan, New Delhi, 1971.

Bhattacharya, Bhabani: *Mahatma Gandhi*, Arnold Heinemann Publishers (India), New Delhi, 1977.

Brown, Judith M.: *Gandhi and Civil Disobedience*, Cambridge University Press, London, 1977.

Clement, Catherine: *Gandhi: The Power Of Pacifism*, Harry N. Abrams, New York, 1996.

Cohn, Bernard S.: *The Changing Status of a Depressed Caste*, The University of Chicago Press, Chicago, 1955.

Dalton, Dennis: *Mahatma Gandhi: Nonviolent Power In Action*, Columbia University Press, New York, 1993.

Epstein, T. S.: *Economic Development and Social Change in South India*, Manchester University Press, Manchester, 1962.

Gandhi, M. K.: *For Workers Against Untouchability*, Navjivan Publishing House, Ahmedabad, 1954.

Ghosh, Tapan: *The Gandhi Murder Trial*, Asia Pub. House, New York, 1975.

Gorhe, Neelam: *Social Development and Dalit Women*, Gyan Pub. House, New Delhi, 1995.

Green, Martin: *The Challenge of the Mahatmas*, Basic Books, New York, 1978.

Hunt, James D.: *Gandhi in London*, Promilla & Co., New Delhi, 1978.

Jha, D. C.: *Mahatma Gandhi, the Congress, and the Partition of India*, Sanchar Pub. House, New Delhi, 1995.

Kamble, J. R.: *Rise and Awakening of Depressed Classes in India*, National Publishers, New Delhi, 1979.

Krishnaiah Chetty, V.B.: *Scheduled Castes and Development Programmes in India*, Vohra, Allahabad, 1991.

Lal, Shyam: *Caste and Political Mobilisation: The Bhangis*, Panchsheel Prakashan, Jaipur, 1981.

Mathur, D. B.: *Gandhi, Congress, and Apartheid*, Aalekh Publishers, Jaipur, 1986.

Maw, Martin: *Visions of India*, Vertag Perer Lang, London, 1990.

Nanda, B. R.: *Gandhi and His Critics*, Oxford UP, Delhi, 1985.

Nye, Robert: *Conflict Among Harijans*, Springer Publications, NY, 1973.

Parekh, Bhikhu: *Gandhi's Political Philosophy: A Critical Examination*, MacMillan, London, 1989.

Prasad, R.C.: *Preface to Ambedkarism*, Motilal Banarsidass, Delhi, 1993.

Rao, K. L. Seshagiri: *Mahatma Gandhi and Comparative Religion*, Motilal Banarsidass, New Delhi, 1978.

Richards, Glyn: *The Philosophy of Gandhi: A Study of his Basic Ideas*, Curzon Press, London, 1982.

Risley, Herbert: *The People of India*, Spink and Co., Calcutta, 1908.

Sankhdher, M. M.: *Gandhi, Gandhism and the Partition of India*, Deep & Deep Publications, New Delhi, 1982.

Shirer, William L.: *Gandhi, a Memoir*, Simon and Schuster, New York, 1979.

Singh, K. K.: *Patterns of Caste Tensions*, Asia Publishing House, Bombay, 1967.

Singh, Shankar Dayal: *Gandhi's First Step: Champaran Movement*, B.R. Pub. Corp., Delhi, 1994.

Uppal J. N.: *Gandhi, Ordained in South Africa*, Ministry of Information and Broadcasting, Govt. of India, New Delhi, 1995.

Woodcock, George: *Mohandas Gandhi*, Viking Press, New York, 1971.

Index

♦♦♦